THE
COMPLETE
FOOD
HANDBOOK

THE COMPLETE FOOD HANDBOOK

by

Rodger P. Doyle

and

James L. Redding

GROVE PRESS, INC

NEW YORK

For
Clara C. Redding
and
Doris Doyle

First Black Cat Edition 1977, Revised 1978, 1980 Edition 1979
First Printing 1980 Edition 1979
ISBN: 0-394-17398-8
Grove Press ISBN: 0-8021-4274-5
Library of Congress Catalog Card Number: 79-52123

Library of Congress Cataloging in Publication Data

Doyle, Rodger P.
  The complete food handbook.

  Bibliography: p. 347
  Includes index.
1. Food. 2. Nutrition. I. Redding, James L.,
joint author. II. Title.
TX353.D68 1979   641.1 79-52123
ISBN 0-394-17398-8

Manufactured in the United States of America

Distributed by Random House, Inc., New York

GROVE PRESS, INC., 196 West Houston Street, New York, N.Y. 10014

Acknowledgments

For their kindness in supplying invaluable information, we wish to thank: Denis P. Burkitt, M.D., Medical Research Council, London; Dr. W. O. Caster, School of Home Economics, University of Georgia, Athens, Ga.; Nancy B. Chrisman, Executive Director, Dairy Council of the Niagara Frontier, Buffalo, N.Y.; Jennifer Cross, author of *The Supermarket Trap;* J. H. Cummings, M.D., Medical Research Council, London; Michael F. Jacobson, Ph.D., Co-Director of the Center for Science in the Public Interest, Washington, D.C.; Dr. Constance Kies, Professor of Nutrition, University of Nebraska; R. G. McGovern, President, Pepperidge Farm, Inc.; Dr. Kurt Oster, Chief, Section of Cardiology, Park City Hospital, Bridgeport, Conn.; Dorothy M. Rathmann, Ph.D., of the Best Foods Research Center, Union, N.J.; John A. Rikert, Ph.D., Associate Scientific Director, The Fleischmann Laboratories, Stamford, Conn.; D.A.T. Southgate, M.D., Dana Nutritional Laboratories, Cambridge, England; Hugh Trowell, M.D.; and Jasper Guy Woodroof, Ph.D., Alumni Distinguished Professor Emeritus of Food Science, University of Georgia.

The comments and suggestions of Janet Barkas and Broady Richardson were most useful. Fred Derf was of great service in gathering food-product information.

For permission to adapt material from his article in the *Journal of Dental Research* (45:1556, 1966), we wish to thank Dr. R. M. Stephan. We also thank the *American Journal of Clinical Nutrition* for permission to use material from articles by R. A. Ahrens (27:414, 1974) and by E. R. Monsen and L. Adriaenssens (22:458, 1969). Our thanks also to the Macmillan Publishing Company for permission to quote from *Pharmacological Basis of Therapeutics,* 4th edition, L. S. Goodman and A. Gilman, editors.

We particularly wish to thank Paul Kopczynski for his excellent work in gathering and interpreting information on nutritive supplements. We are also very grateful to Beverly Paigen, Ph.D., Senior Research Scientist at Roswell Park Memorial Institute, Buffalo, N.Y., for her encouragement and enthusiasm.

C. K. Huang, Director of the Health Sciences Library, State University of New York at Buffalo, and the many members of the library staff, through their thoughtfulness and courtesy, greatly facilitated the research for this book.

Contents

Introduction

It is a notorious fact that advertising cannot be trusted. As skeptical consumers we should always act on this principle, but the skeptic's problem is in getting at the facts.

When it comes to food, our problem is compounded by an over-supply of information which is difficult to assess. Health-food writers tell us that brewer's yeast or sea salt is essential to health; the Food and Drug Administration assures us of the safety of food colors; a Nobel Prize-winner exhorts us to take vitamin C tablets; the Environmental Defense Fund warns that the most basic nutrient of all, water, may cause cancer.

In order to fill the need for an objective source of information about food, we have examined all the important products from supermarkets and health-food stores in the light of modern nutritional knowledge. For each type of product, we have evaluated the effect of food processing on nutritional value, the safety of additives, the possible danger of environmental contaminants, and, where pertinent, have dealt with the advertising claims and the health faddist claims.

The facts and conclusions presented in this volume were developed by thousands of nutritionists, chemists, biologists, biochemists, microbiologists, toxicologists, physicians, and food technologists as reported in scores of books and over a thousand articles in scientific journals. Where these experts disagree, we have attempted to present all sides so that the reader can make his own choice.

In total, over 200 types of food are evaluated. These products are grouped into eight chapters according to type: cereal products; fruits and vegetables; dairy products; meat, poultry, and fish; fats and oils; beverages; sweets; and a chapter devoted to "other foods," that is, those foods impossible to classify in the other categories. A separate chapter is devoted to nutritive supplements. The subject of fiber, which may prove to be the most important new development in nutrition, is also treated in a separate chapter.

Several appendixes contain additional information, including the important new *Dietary Goals for the U.S.* issued by the Senate Select Committee on Nutrition and Human Needs.

The book can be read as a narrative, in which case we recommend that you begin with Chapter I, "An Overview of the Food Industry," which deals with the broader issues common to most foods sold in America.

The book is also, and perhaps more importantly, designed to be used as a quick reference source to information on particular foods. For convenience in finding information quickly, the major references in the Index are given in boldface type.

If you are not familiar with bio-medical terms—such as *epidemiology, dental caries* and *carcinogen*—we suggest you start by taking a few minutes to read the Glossary on pages 347 to 353.

We hope that this book will help you to become a more efficient skeptic and that you will find it a useful tool for choosing better food at a better price.

Rodger P. Doyle   James L. Redding
Buffalo, New York   Boston, Mass.

CHAPTER I

An Overview
of the Food Industry

Protest against the quality of processed food is an American tradition.

As long ago as the 1880's, Dr. Harvey W. Wiley, the chief chemist of the United States Department of Agriculture, crusaded across the country against the overchemicalization of foodstuffs.

The publishing sensation of 1906 was Upton Sinclair's *The Jungle*, an expose of the meat industry. In 1933, one of the best sellers was *100,000,000 Guinea Pigs* by Arthur Kallet and Frederick J. Schlink, which exposed adulteration in foods and cosmetics. More recently, Ralph Nader and other consumer advocates such as James Turner, author of *The Chemical Feast*, have attacked such American institutions as breakfast cereals, baby foods and the government agencies that regulate the quality of these foods.

At the root of the controversy is a technology that divorces the final consumer from the production process. When most consumers baked their own bread, grew their own vegetables, drank milk from their own cows and ate chickens from their own backyards, there was little room for suspicion about the quality of food. The divorce of production from use has led to countless opportunities for adulteration, mispresentation and misunderstanding. Indeed, food products are

1

ideally suited for manipulation as the consumer has limited ability to evaluate such aspects as the effect of processing on nutritive value, the long term health effect of additives, and the veracity of advertising claims.

Technology has a habit of bringing mixed blessings, and food technology is no exception. Among the beneficial consequences has been the virtual elimination of scurvy, made possible, at least in part, by the year round availability of canned vegetables and fruits. Pasteurization, which is perhaps the greatest single achievement of food science, helped to lower the infant mortality rate and brought a cheap, safe source of nutrients within the means of most people.

Among the less beneficent innovations was the introduction of steel roller milling and the consequent abundance of white refined flour. Even more important in its long run health aspects were the series of technical innovations that made possible a large and cheap supply of white sugar. These ingredients, together with such products of the new technology as hydrogenated fat and chemical additives, are indispensable to most of the convenience foods and snack foods that have proliferated since World War II. These foods tend to be high in calories and low in vitamins, minerals and fiber. They are, in other words, the "empty calorie" foods.

The new technology has not only brought new types of foods and increased the supply of old foods, it has also brought a huge increase in the number of chemical compounds never before ingested by man. Thousands of new compounds—preservatives, emulsifiers, artificial colors, artificial flavors and such unintentional additives as pesticide residues—have been added to the food supply, mostly within the last two generations.

The effect of these new compounds on health is largely unknown. Many critics have claimed that they may cause cancer, birth defects and unwelcome mutations on a wide scale.

If all additives now in use are shown to have no direct toxic effect, they would still have an *indirect* adverse effect. Artificial color and artificial flavor, for example, are used to increase the consumer appeal of highly refined, diluted and nutritionally depleted foods. Such low quality foods would be virtually unsalable if it were not for these additives. Orange drink, for example, typically contains only 10 per cent orange juice. This highly diluted product, with virtually no flavor and pale color, would be a commercial flop without the addition of sugar, flavoring and orange coloring.

When additives are used in this way—to give the illusion that a junk food is better than it really is—the practice is deceptive. This type of nutritional deception was not so critical in the days when such products fell primarily into the category of snacks, for their lack of nutritive value was offset when consumed along with a balanced diet consisting mainly of natural foods. Today, however, with the proliferation of these low nutrition foods as both snacks and as components of regular meals, there is an increased possibility of nutritional deficiency.

In defending the use of additives, the food industry claims that they cut the cost of food because they are far cheaper than natural ingredients. The chemicalized foods, however, actually cost more than nutritionally equivalent natural products. Equivalency is the key concept. In orange drinks, for example, the diluted, colored and flavored product no doubt will cost less than real orange juice—perhaps selling for half the price—but it contains only one-tenth the juice. Thus the chemicalized drink actually costs five times as much as real juice per ounce of real ingredients.

The true cost, however, is not to the pocketbook but to health. Virtually all experts agree that changes in the American diet during this century are related to widespread obesity and dental caries and to the great increase in heart disease. These problems and others are tied directly to the overabundance of empty calorie foods and a corresponding lack of traditional foods. The new foods have become accepted primarily because of advertising.

The Role of Advertising

Advertising is the chief source of nutritional information for most Americans, yet such advertising is not designed to provide nutritional information. As a leading advertising executive once said when talking about food products, "The job of product advertising is to persuade and sell, not to educate." It is this noninformative advertising that has been the prime mover in the proliferation of junk foods.

Advertisers agree that sales largely reflect the amount of money spent on advertising. With this in mind, we compared the advertising expenditures of the 100 most heavily promoted food brands against their relative nutritional value. The complete results of this analysis appear in Appendix III, but a summary of our findings may surprise you.

Of the one hundred brands we give only 7 a grade of "A"—indicating the food supplies substantial nutrients and has few questionable ingredients or additives.

On the other hand, 37 brands flunk our test with an "F" because they contain no nutrients other than calories!

Nineteen were graded "B," meaning they have high nutritional value, but contain questionable ingredients. The products whose value is due chiefly to the addition of vitamin-mineral supplements barely pass the test with a "C." (As we will see in later chapters, foods with such supplements are almost always objectionable on other grounds.)

This analysis clearly demonstrates the dominance of junk food advertising over the promotion of wholesome foods. The high-pressure huckstering of junk foods is most apparent when you look at those brands aimed primarily at children.

You need only look briefly at children's television to realize that the manufacturers are selling primarily sugar in the form of breakfast cereals, candy, gum, sweetened beverages and sugary desserts. We also made a check of one hundred food commercials picked at random during February and March 1975 from children's TV programs. Of the one hundred, seventy-seven were for products that had sugar as the first or second ingredient while ninety-eight had at least one additive such as unspecified artificial color or artificial flavor. The use of such chemical additives, in foods eaten by children, is a highly questionable practice.

What are the implications of the massive advertising expenditures for non-nutritive foods? The most obvious implication is that Americans, including children, are being subjected to a constant and large volume of nutritional misinformation that may be subverting their health. There is no doubt that many Americans do not have adequate nutrition. A Department of Agriculture study conducted in 1965 showed that 36 per cent of families with incomes under $3,000 had poor diets. Even among families with incomes over $10,000, 9 per cent had "poor" diets, while only 63 per cent had good diets. According to the same study, the nutritional status of Americans has declined; in 1965 the average person took in lesser amounts of five important nutrients than ten years previously, despite fortification of a wide variety of processed foods with these nutrients. There is little reason to believe that nutrient intake has improved substantially since 1965.

Natural food advocates have been talking for years about the adverse effects of junk food on health. They claim that the increase in popularity of junk foods has coincided with a spectacular rise in degenerative diseases. In terms of deaths per 100,000 population, cardiovascular disease increased by 37 per cent from 1900 to 1971. Cancer increased by 151 per cent and diabetes mellitus by 65 per cent in the same period. Cardiovascular disease and cancer are the two principal causes of death in the United States, accounting for 55 per cent and 16 per cent, respectively, of all deaths. By contrast, these diseases are relatively rare in undeveloped countries.

There is no conclusive proof, of course, that the modern American diet of refined foods is the major cause of degenerative diseases. Coincident with changes in diet have also been changes in the amount of exercise as a result of increasing dependence on the automobile and the trend to more sedentary occupations. As a result of cigarette smoking and exposure to industrial wastes, pesticides, automotive exhausts and other pollutants there has been a profound change in the chemical environment, exposing man to new and little understood health risks. The allegedly greater stress of modern living may also be a causative factor in cardiovascular disease. Diet is obviously only one of many influences on disease, but it seems likely that its role has been important.

Apologists for the food industry claim that Americans are the best fed people on the earth, and in support of this claim they point to the very high productivity of American farmers. In view of the extremely high consumption of empty calorie foods, it would be more accurate to describe Americans as the "most fed" rather than the "best fed."

A visit to any supermarket should dispel the industry claim that Americans are "best fed." In most supermarkets the relatively natural foods—fresh produce, meats and dairy products—occupy only the periphery of the store. Processed foods, most of which supply low or minimal nutrition, fill aisle upon aisle in the interior section of the supermarket and constitute the majority of the ten thousand or more items typically available.

The Economics of Junk Food

Junk foods are heavily advertised because they are profitable. Ordinarily, manufacturers find little profit in advertising traditional foods because such foods cannot usually be given a brand identity. To successfully promote a brand identity, the manufacturer needs something different and usually this is achieved with additives for these permit almost infinite variations in product characteristics.

Suppose that you are one of the many millers selling flour in a free market. You will not make much profit because competition will keep the price low. For example, wheat flour sells for about 15 cents per pound at retail. However, if you add a few cents worth of flour, hydrogenated oil, salt, sugar, some flavoring and artificial coloring, you can sell it to the retail customer at $3.30 a pound! How? You just put it in a fancy package, advertise it on TV, and call it "Shake 'n Bake."

An insight into the peculiar economics of the junk food industry is provided by information from the National Commission on Food Marketing appointed by President Lyndon Johnson. Among other information, the Commission provided detailed data on the cost structure of the cereal industry. Although the data are for 1964, they are still quite relevant to the situation in the seventies.

According to the Commission's information, a dollar spent at retail for breakfast cereal contains 10 cents worth of grain and 6 cents worth of additives, and also the vitamins, minerals and protein fortifiers used in some brands. Thus, only 16 cents out of each dollar spent for cereal goes to pay for the cost of ingredients. Twelve cents goes into packaging and 17 cents into advertising and promotion and the manufacturer's profit. The balance is expended on processing, transportation, wholesaling and retailing.

It is indeed bizarre that the retail customer should spend a dollar and get only 10 cents worth of grain. The absurdity of such economics is highlighted by comparison to a more rational industry such as beef. For every dollar that the consumer spends on beef at retail, 60 cents goes into raw materials while only 3 cents goes into advertising and 2 cents into packaging.

It is not difficult to imagine that high-nutrition cereals with a cost structure similar to beef's could be successfully produced and marketed, but no major food company has made an attempt to develop such a product, at least not since the end of World War II.

Cereals are not the only products with a distorted price structure. It is probable that most of the heavily advertised food products are priced high enough to provide sufficient margin for covering the cost of advertising and other promotion.

Health Foods

Millions of Americans, in disgust with the over-chemicalized, overprocessed foods which predominate in the supermarket, have turned to health food stores. There they have sometimes found more nutritious foods, but often they have not, and in either case they have paid more.

Health food stores typically carry a large assortment of nutritive supplements plus such foods as kelp, brewer's yeast, unrefined vegetable oils, unsalted nuts, yogurt, canned vegetarian meat analogs, sea salt, canned carrot juice, and even organically produced meat.

A snap judgment might be that these are largely

faddist foods. Such a judgment would be unfair unless the term "faddist" is also applied to heavily advertised supermarket foods. The dictionary defines "fad" as something that many people are interested in for a short period of time. "Faddists" who go to health food stores buy certain foods that are clearly here to stay, such as stone ground flour (used for at least 6,000 years), brown rice (goes back at least 3,000 years), unrefined oil (used milleniums ago) and organically grown fruits and vegetables (who can date their antiquity?). "Nonfaddists" who shop at supermarkets may buy foods of such recent origin as Carnation Instant Breakfast, Count Chocula breakfast cereal and Pillsbury Space Food Sticks. There are some curious products in both health food stores and supermarkets but although the latter have vastly more items that are questionable from a health standpoint, it is the health food stores that are thought of as deviant while the supermarkets are "normal."

Like the supermarkets, health food stores are dominated by brand names which results in considerable duplication of products. As in the supermarket, brand names are not always used for their value in communicating quality, but as a device for getting a higher price. Brand name manufacturers of some health store items, like their junk food counterparts, have built up significant economic interests by taking advantage of consumers' ignorance and fear. The most culpable are those manufacturers who, lacking adequate scientific justification, push large doses of a variety of vitamins and minerals. In this respect they are akin to the big food advertisers who, with a corresponding lack of scientific justification, push margarine for the prevention of heart disease. Both the vitamin and margarine processors may have some valid arguments, but we suspect that they may not be providing all the pertinent facts. In the meantime, both may be creating myths which could have adverse health consequences.

Junk foods are sold primarily through television advertising, health foods through the influence of health food writers. The patron saint of health foods is, of course, the late Adelle Davis. With over ten million copies of her books in print, including *Let's Eat Right to Keep Fit* and *Let's Get Well,* she has probably had more influence on the nutritional opinions of Americans than any other individual or, for that matter, any organization. She has quite correctly deplored the use of sugar and refined white bread and has engendered a healthy skepticism of junk food among millions. Despite her background in nutrition (she held an M.S. in biochemistry from the University of Southern California Medical School and worked for several years as a professional nutritionist), many of her statements are unsupported by facts. For example, she claims that drinking a quart of milk a day prevents cancer, a claim which, if true, would have been trumpeted *ad nauseum* by the American Dairy Association.

Dr. Edward Rynerson, Emeritus Professor of Medicine at The Mayo Clinic, says that some of the many factual errors in Adelle Davis's books are potentially harmful, such as her advice to take massive doses of vitamin A and the recommendation that a person with nephrosis take potassium chloride. Too much vitamin A can cause loss of appetite, extreme irritability, drying of skin, loss of hair, enlargement of the liver and other unpleasant consequences. Use of potassium chloride by patients with nephrosis is potentially lethal.

Given the widely diverse backgrounds of health food writers and their lack of objective standards of scientific judgment, it is not surprising that there is wide disagreement among them. In his informative book, *Natural Poisons in Natural Foods*, Albert Wertheim, who describes himself as a former food faddist, analyzed the dietary recommendations in twelve popular health books sold in health food stores with respect to thirty-eight types of food. He found, interestingly enough, that they disagreed on the value of twenty-two of the foods including soybeans, nuts and synthetic vitamins.

The consumer who wants authoritative answers may find this confusing Is it really important to take a multivitamin? Is unrefined oil worth the price premium over supermarket oils? Does sea salt really have more trace minerals than iodized salt? These are questions neither health food store personnel nor health food processors can answer with authority.

The Mystique of "Organic" and "Natural"

Organically grown foods—foods grown without synthetic fertilizers or pesticides—are an integral part of the health food mystique. Some agribusiness defenders seem to have overreacted against the organic food movement, denouncing it as a fad that could wreak irreparable damage on our agricultural system. One of the most vehement critics of organic foods is Professor Thomas H. Jukes, of the Donner Laboratory at the

University of California at Berkeley, who finds "a disturbing trend towards belief in the magic virtues of 'organic foods.' " Dr. Jukes is on firm ground when he claims that there is as yet no evidence for the nutritional superiority of organically grown foods, but he misses the significance of the organic movement as an ecological rather than a strictly nutritional alternative.

Other nutritionists, such as Joan Gussow, an instructor in nutrition at Teachers College, Columbia University, have a more thoughtful viewpoint. She points out that the usefulness of the organic farming movement should not be judged by whether it produces more nutritious food, but for its value as an alternative to chemical farming which, as she notes, is producing ominous ecological alterations on a global scale. Food without pesticide residues or other potentially harmful contaminants is obviously desirable, and it seems absurd to label anyone as a "faddist" for preferring such food.

On the other hand, if there is one basic myth in the health food movement, it is that "natural" is always good. Actually, many natural unprocessed foods contain substances that are inimical to health: for example, oxylates in rhubarb and spinach, phytic acid in whole grains, beans and nuts, and aflatoxins in raw peanuts. The first two could, under certain circumstances, cause severe malnourishment while the last is one of the most potent carcinogens known to man. Such natural flavorings as coumarin (from the tonka bean), oil of calamus (from the root of the calamus plant) and safrole (from sassafras) have been banned by the FDA as a possible cause of, respectively, liver damage, intestinal cancer, and liver cancer.

It is probable that most people will not be affected by toxic substances in natural foods but those who adhere to the myth that natural is always better may be depriving themselves of useful new foods. It is possible, for example, to fortify whole wheat with synthetic lysine, an amino acid that greatly improves protein value. When such products become widely available (and it seems likely that they will), hardline natural food advocates may be missing out on harmless low-cost, high-nutrition products.

To the extent that the better type health foods replace junk foods, particularly in the critical period of growth, pregnancy and lactation, such foods may indeed be beneficial.

Finding Nutritious Food

Somewhere between the distortions of the food advertisers and the inaccuracies of health food writers, it is possible to find tasty, nutritious foods. Unfortunately, identification of good food is often difficult because professional nutritionists, who should be our most authoritative source of information, are generally not effective in communicating useful facts to the public. At least in part, ineffectiveness stems from a reluctance to condemn some of the less desirable processed foods and failure to talk in terms of specific brands. No nutritionist from the U.S. Department of Agriculture or the Food and Drug Administration, for example, has ever issued a list of junk foods sold by the big advertisers, nor has there ever been any effective movement in these organizations to restrict the sale of junk foods.

The purpose of this book is to provide the type of specific nutritional and food-product information not ordinarily disseminated by professional nutritionists, physicians, or government agencies. Those who follow the suggestions given here will certainly find more nutritious food and may well save money in the process.

CHAPTER II

Dairy Products

Is Milk Necessary?

The dairy industry would like you to believe that milk is an essential food. The California Milk Producers Advisory Board, for example, claims that milk is needed by everyone and can be consumed in unlimited quantities. The opposite extreme is summed up by a long-forgotten health food writer who said "Cow's milk is a splendid food for calves, but it cannot be recommended very well for human beings."

Milk is a controversial product in part because of its saturated fat content. Many authorities, including the American Heart Association, recommend moderation in consumption of whole milk by adults but other experts do not concur.

Calcium in Milk

There has also been controversy over milk as a source of calcium, a nutrient which is essential for bone-building and maintenance in addition to other functions. Infants and young children, because of their rapid growth, need large amounts of calcium relative to body weight. Because the need for calcium decreases in adulthood, some authorities argue that adults need little or no milk. Milk and milk products constitute the primary source of dietary calcium, providing levels about double those of people who abstain from milk products. Vast numbers of the world's peoples, however, do not drink milk while maintaining adequate calcium in the body, apparently because the body is able to utilize the lower levels of calcium more efficiently. Indeed, for most of man's history, cow's milk has not been a staple of the diet. The earliest evidence of cow's milk as a human food goes back to only 9,000 B.C., and although it is easy to imagine that humans may have drunk cow's milk or the milk of other mammals at times before that, it is improbable that it was consumed very frequently before the advent of animal husbandry.

Authorities differ sharply on the amount of calcium needed throughout the stages of life. The U.S. National Academy of Sciences-National Research Council sets the adult allowance at about twice that of the United Nations' World Health Organization while agreeing on the same high levels for pregnant women. An adult following the WHO allowance could satisfy the requirement by drinking only one 12 ounce glass of milk per day.

Milk and milk-based products such as cheese and yogurt are the richest source of calcium, but it is possible to get substantial calcium by eating dark green vegetables such as collards, spinach, kale, and broccoli. Although such vegetables are high in calcium, the availability of the mineral is reduced by the presence of oxalic acid. (See "Oxalates in Vegetables" in Chapter III.) Some fish are quite high in calcium particularly sardines, smelts, lobster, oysters, salmon, and clams. Anyone, including children, who gets a sufficient quantity of these foods can dispense with milk and other dairy products completely. Indeed, strict vegetarians (no meat or dairy products) can get sufficient calcium for good health.

Lactose Intolerance

It is sometimes said that most of the world's peoples cannot drink milk without gastrointestinal disturbances. It would be more accurate to say that most people in the world cannot tolerate *large* quantities of milk.

Milk, of course, is the natural food of all infant mammals, including humans. Lactose, a complex sugar composed of molecules of glucose bound to molecules of galactose, is the main carbohydrate found in milk and occurs only in the milk of mammals and in no other foodstuff.

To digest this sugar, all infant mammals produce in their intestines an enzyme called lactase which hydrolyzes (splits) lactose into glucose and galactose, which are then absorbed. Unless it is split in this way, lactose cannot be utilized and instead passes into the lower intestinal tract where large quantities of fluids enter the bowel to dilute the sugar. This results in abdominal cramps, bloating or diarrhea.

Very high levels of lactase are produced throughout the normal suckling period, but after weaning the enzyme activity of most mammals decreases to about 10 per cent of its previous level. So-called "lactose intolerant" individuals, because they produce some lactase, can consume moderate amounts of milk particularly if spaced throughout the day and if consumed with meals. In the standard test for lactose intolerance, the subjects are given lactose equivalent to two quarts of milk. Thus, many people who are designated lactose intolerant when given this large amount may be fully capable of drinking several glasses of milk during the day.

Among Caucasian adults only 5 to 10 per cent are intolerant to large amounts of milk but among most other racial groups, intolerance is found among 70 per cent or more.

Many adults with reduced enzyme activity refuse to consume any amount of milk because of bad experience with large amounts that made them ill. Anyone with such unpleasant experiences might try smaller amounts at a time and taking it with meals. Because cold milk consumed alone passes relatively quickly through the intestinal tract, simply warming the milk first will, for some individuals, prevent the symptoms. Another way to avoid unpleasant symptoms is to replace fluid milk with fermented milk products such as cheese, yogurt and buttermilk, all of which are very low in lactose. Some "lactose intolerant" people, such as those in the Middle East, consume large quantities of fermented dairy products.

Milk Allergy

Milk allergy is a fairly common and important form of allergy especially in infants and young children. An infant who is allergic to his own mother's milk is considered a medical rarity, but many human infants are allergic to cow's milk. Milk allergy has been implicated in many diseases including chronic respiratory disease (such as recurrent pneumonia), circulatory insufficiency, chronic ulcerative colitis, thickened and painful bones, so-called "crib deaths," and even heart disease. Almost all children fed cow's milk show allergic reactions to some degree.

At least fifty-three separate signs and symptoms can be attributed to milk allergy, but the ten most common and important are eczema, cough, chronic nasal congestion, sneezing, asthma, colic, vomiting, diarrhea, refusal of milk, and failure to thrive. The incidence of milk allergy is not known exactly; estimates range from less than one per cent to seven per cent of the population or a minimum of two million people, quite a large number to be affected by a single food. Most children outgrow cow's milk allergy; 80 per cent get over it by one year of age, 95 per cent by two years and 97 per cent by six years. The preferred therapy consists of breast feeding the infant as well as reducing the amount of cow's milk.

Nutrients in Dairy Products

In addition to calcium and high-quality protein, dairy products are excellent sources of other nutrients including vitamin A and riboflavin (B_2) and vitamin B_{12}. They are, however, generally high in saturated fat, cholesterol and sodium. Products from which most of the fat has been removed, notably skim milk and cottage cheese, are low in saturated fat and cholesterol. Removal of fat results in loss of vitamin A (which is sometimes restored by adding the synthetic vitamin).

Dairy Products—A Listing

CHEESE

When milk is processed into cheese, some nutrients, principally the B-complex vitamins, are lost. Bacterial and mold activity synthesizes some B vitamins in the rind of aged cheese such as camembert, but this is of little benefit unless the rind is eaten. Except for the B-complex losses, most cheeses retain the original virtues of milk, including protein and calcium levels.

Most of the lactose in cheese is changed into lactic acid during the first fourteen days of ripening. Because all cheeses (except "fresh" cheese types such as cottage cheese) are ripened for at least two weeks, virtually no lactose remains in any cheese by the time it is consumed, making cheese readily digestible by even the lactose-intolerant.

So called "processed" cheeses, which are among the biggest sellers in the supermarket, have often been the target of both natural food advocates and gourmets. What are the facts? Are these cheeses made in a way which does indeed reduce nutritive value?

The basic difference between natural and processed cheese is the mixing-in of water and other ingredients, the removal of some fat, and heat treatment.

Processed cheeses are cooked at temperatures of at least 150°F to halt bacterial action and prolong the life of the cheese, while the natural varieties are made at temperatures below 130°F. The heat has little effect on nutrients in processed cheese. The real nutritional differences result from the dilution of the cheese with water.

The government classifies processed cheeses by their fat content, which is actually an index to the amount of dilution. Natural cheddar cheese usually has about 50 percent fat. This percentage is reduced in the three types of processed cheese according to the amount of water mixed in. Pasteurized Process Cheese, with 47 percent fat, is very similar to cheddar; Pasteurized Process Cheese Food has a minimum of 23 percent fat; while Pasteurized Process Cheese Spread has 20 percent fat. All nutrients in processed cheese are reduced in the same way as the fat. Thus, pasteurized process cheese loses very few nutrients and is comparable to natural cheddar, but the other two processed types (cheese food and cheese spread), suffer substantial losses of protein, calcium, iron, vitamin A, and the B vitamins.

Additives in Cheese

The cheese additive regulations are a model of bureaucratic illogicality. Cheddar cheese may be artificially colored but the label need not mention it; pasteurized process cheese spread may be artificially colored but the label must say so; mozarella may not be artificially colored. Fortunately one artificial coloring usually used is annatto, which has no known toxicity. Although harmless, artificial cheese colorings may not be a blessing. For example, mild cheddars are naturally white while sharp cheddars are yellow, yet in many supermarkets all types of cheddar are colored to the same yellow hue. The consumer is deprived of the opportunity to judge for himself the degree of mildness or sharpness.

Costs of Cheese

In terms of protein cost cottage cheese is the best buy. Except for a few blatantly overpackaged products such as Nabisco Snack Mate, which comes in an aerosol can, most domestic cheese provides good protein at moderate cost. Surprisingly, the protein in many types of cheese is less expensive than in milk.

Saturated Fat in Cheese

Cheese is one of the most concentrated sources of saturated fat available. Cheddar has 18 per cent saturated fat. By contrast, regular ground hamburger has 10 per cent and lean hamburger only 5 per cent. Cottage cheese is low in saturated fat with the creamed kind containing 2 per cent and the uncreamed virtually none.

Cheese Grading

The United States Department of Agriculture has a grading system for cheddar cheese. U.S. Grade AA is produced with special care in the quality of milk, processing and packaging. U.S. Grade A is of high quality but there may be some variation in flavor and texture. The grading is done by U.S.D.A. inspectors. The system sounds fine on paper, but is not very useful to the retail customer for the grade labels do not usually appear on retail packages, but only on wholesale packaging.

EGGS (SEE CHAPTER IX)

ICE CREAM

Ice cream and most other frozen desserts such as ice milk and frozen custard should provide substantially the same nutrition as an equal amount of the milk from which they are made. The big difference, nutritionally, is in the calories which can be more than twice as high as in milk. A half-pint serving of ice cream contains 270 or more calories.

Ice cream is, unfortunately, one of the most adulterated products in today's supermarkets, for at least twelve hundred different stabilizers, emulsifiers, neutralizers, artificial flavors, and artificial colors can legally be used in its manufacture. Most of the additives allowed in ice cream are artificial flavors. The recent proliferation of exotic flavors being offered (with names like "buttered pecan-maple fudge") has greatly expanded the use of chemical flavorings. Few of these have been thoroughly tested for safety and yet are allowed in any amount and combination the manufacturer wishes. The only sure way to avoid these chemicals in ice cream is to choose a brand which clearly declares on the label: "no artificial flavors added."

Under federal regulations, a product containing no artificial flavor is labelled with the common name of the flavor, such as "vanilla." If it contains both natural and artificial flavor, but the natural flavor predominates, the word "flavored" follows the common name, e.g., "vanilla flavored" or "peach flavored." If it contains both types of flavoring but the artificial flavor predominates, or if artificial flavor is used alone, then the label must read: "artificial" or "artificially flavored," e.g., "artificial vanilla" or "artificially flavored vanilla." Frozen dairy products must now list ingredients on the label, but the most questionable chemicals are still hidden behind the vague labeling terms "artificial color" and "artificial flavor."

Chocolate ice cream is the one flavor that rarely contains artificial color because cocoa, at levels giving a chocolate flavor, also imparts a deep color. Unfortunately, the coloring ability of chocolate is employed in the deceptive practice called "reworking." According to Consumers Union, reworking involves making chocolate ice cream from a lighter-flavored batch that is beginning to spoil, or from packaged ice cream returned from retail stores. The low-quality ice creams are mixed together and resold as chocolate. No law requires manufacturers to identify reworked ice cream on the label.

In addition to chemical additives, today's ice cream contains an extra measure of an old ingredient—air. Air has always been a major component of ice cream— even the home-made variety is more than one-third air—but today even greater quantities of air are being blended into the product. Air in ice cream would not be a problem for consumers if the ice cream were sold by weight like most other foods.

When buying ice cream, the wary shopper may wish to check the weight on the produce department scale. Any ice cream that weighs less than 2¼ pounds per half-gallon does not meet the federal minimum (which does not apply to products made and sold in-state). Better quality ice creams weigh around 2½ pounds, while the hand-packed variety available in specialty ice cream shops often tip the scales at 3½ or more pounds per half gallon.

Table I

AIR IN ICE CREAM—A BASIC GUIDE

If ½ gallon of ice cream weighs:	Approximate percentage of air is:
2 lb	56%
2¼ lb	50% (Federal legal minimum)
2½ lb	44%
2¾ lb	39%
3 lb	33%

SOURCE: Calculated from W. S. Arbuckle, *Ice Cream* (Westport, Conn.: Avi Pub. Co., 1966), p. 174, 217-218.

Ice cream was once made only from fresh sweet cream, but today other, cheaper dairy ingredients, such as evaporated or powdered milk and even skim milk are used instead. The label need not designate which of these or a variety of other permissible cream substitutes has been used.

"Natural" Ice Cream

Standard supermarket ice cream has acquired such a bad name that consumers are now willing to pay substantially higher prices for brands which claim to be more "natural."

While the term "all natural" should automatically exclude the most questionable additives in ice cream—artificial flavors and artificial colors—it does not necessarily mean that the product is made without other additives such as emulsifiers and stabilizers. Most ice cream brands contain stabilizers derived from natural sources such as carrageenan, agar-agar, gum acacia, guar seed gum, gum karaya, locust bean gum, oat gum, gum tragacanth, and gelatin, none of which, with the exception of carrageenan, has been seriously questioned for toxicity. Certain brands, such as Breyer's, provide quite complete information on the label, but the labels on some other "natural" ice creams fail to mention that they contain stabilizers.

White sugar (sucrose) is derived from natural sources, and thus the processor can claim: "only natural sweeteners added." The term "natural" is also no guarantee that the product does not contain excessive amounts of air as well. (In spot checks we found that one of the nationally distributed "natural" ice cream brands often weighs in at 2¼ pounds per half gallon, while the supermarket's own brand, selling at half the price, often weighed 2½ pounds or more.)

Soft Ice Cream

The soft ice cream sold at roadside stands is similar in composition to regular ice cream except that the soft variety has less air (around 34 per cent) and the sugar content may be 2 or 3 per cent less than regular ice cream. It generally contains greater amounts of emulsifiers and stabilizers than regular ice cream and is served at around 20° F instead of 0° F, the usual serving temperature of ice cream.

Frozen Custard

Frozen custard is similar to soft ice cream except that, if sold in interstate commerce, it must contain at least 1 per cent egg yolks, frozen egg yolks or dried egg yolks. State laws vary and since many frozen custard stands obtain their mixes locally, and therefore need not comply with the federal requirements, there is no assurance that the "frozen custard" bought at these stands is anything more than soft ice cream.

Ice Milk

Since ice cream may just as likely be made from milk as from cream, the term "ice milk" can be a misnomer. Ice milk, like flavored yogurt, has been deceptively promoted to the calorie-conscious on the basis of its low fat content. "Low-fat" ice milk cannot always be equated with "low-calorie," for like sherbet, this product often has extra sugar added which makes it just as high in calories as regular ice cream. The fat content of ice milk can legally run as high as 7 per cent (compared to 10 per cent for ice cream) although most brands average between 3 and 5 per cent fat.

Because it still contains dairy ingredients, ice milk compares favorably to ice cream in most nutrients.

Ice milk processors have also tried to capitalize on the public's fascination with "naturalness." An example is Sealtest Light N' Lively ice milk which emphasizes "all natural flavors." The package, however, notes that the product contains artificial color.

Sherbets and Ices

Sherbet, unlike ice cream, is low in milk solids and thus has about one-third as much protein and calcium. It also has virtually no fat, yet has so much sugar (over one pound of sucrose in each gallon) that caloric content is often equal to that of ice cream.

Ices are 30 per cent sugar and 70 per cent water and thus provide mainly calories and little or no protein, vitamins or minerals. Ices, like sherbets, rely heavily on additives to give them their texture, flavor and color.

MILK, CANNED

Canned milk comes in two basic forms: evaporated and sweetened condensed. In processing of evaporated milk, water is removed and the remaining milk is canned and sterilized at high temperatures. Condensed milk also has water removed, but a large amount of sugar is added as a preservative so that sterilization by heat is not necessary.

The high processing temperatures—240° for 17 minutes—used in making evaporated milk result in a somewhat cooked, burnt, or caramelized flavor and a slight brownish discoloration but, suprisingly, the effect on the nutritive value is moderate. The protein value is reduced only slightly, while of the vitamins, only two are affected, vitamin C and thiamin (B_1). As milk is not a particularly good source of either of these vitamins, the loss is not important.

Condensed milk is the result of a slightly different process in which a large amount of sugar is added. Because sweetened condensed milk undergoes less severe heat treatment than unsweetened evaporated milk, nutrient losses are even less.

According to federal law, evaporated milk must contain at least 7.9 per cent milk fat and 25.9 per cent total milk solids (protein, lactose, and minerals), while condensed milk must contain not less than 8.5 per cent fat and not less than 28 per cent total milk solids. This means that sweetened condensed milk has a slightly higher nutritional content than evaporated milk. The added sugar in condensed milk displaces water rather than fat or milk solids. Because of its high sugar content, however, sweetened condensed milk is not recommended by pediatricians for infant feeding despite its widespread use for this purpose.

Additives in Canned Milk

Most milk products thicken during storage but evaporated milk becomes thinner, losing up to 40 per cent of its original viscosity during the first few days of storage. This thinning eventually results in separation of the fat which rises to the surface and the settling of solid materials to the bottom of the container. To avoid this unsightly condition, manufacturers add stabilizers which maintain the dispersion of the ingredients. The most commonly used stabilizer in evaporated milk is carrageenan, an extract of the seaweed known as

Irish Moss. The smoother texture resulting from this stabilizer is often promoted in advertising of these products. (Carnation labels its stabilized evaporated milk as "Velvetized.") Because it has been shown to cause ulcers in animals. Dr. Michael Jacobson, Co-Director of the Center for Science in the Public Interest, declared: "The wisdom of exposing infants to carrageenan is highly questionable and deserves a thorough review by the Food and Drug Administration."

Lead in Canned Milk

Canned milk, both evaporated and condensed, has come under fire because it contains relatively large amounts of lead, a toxic metal which is introduced by the antiquated canning process unique to this industry.

Children are most susceptible to the effects of lead. Central nervous system involvement, including mental retardation, is frequently seen in ghetto children who ingest paint chips with a high lead content. These children are also exposed to high concentrations of atmospheric lead from automobile emissions along with lead in their food, especially canned milk. (Canned milk is used much more frequently for infant feeding in lower than in middle income groups, because it often sells for less than fresh milk.)

In 1973 Consumers Union found high lead levels in six well-known brands of canned milk—levels almost as high as the maximum daily permissible intake of lead from *all* sources for children one to three years old set by the Department of Health, Education and Welfare. (No guideline is given for infants under one year of age who presumably have an even lower tolerance.)

A CU test in 1974 found a drop in the lead content

of the same brands, but significant residues of the toxic metal were still present. Prudent parents may not want to feed the product to infants until the manufacturers switch to a safer canning process.

MILK, FLUID

Pasteurized vs. Raw Milk

The purpose of pasteurization is to destroy harmful organisms such as those that cause tuberculosis, undulant fever, diphtheria, typhoid fever, and other diseases. The process achieves its goal very effectively.

Advocates of raw milk correctly point out that by exercising proper sanitary procedures, along with regular inspection of cows and inoculation against disease, dairy farmers can reduce the occurrence of these diseases drastically. Milk undergoing this type of rigorous inspection is generally known as "certified raw milk" and for many years was available in most parts of the country. Today, however, certified milk is virtually impossible to find, as most states have either prohibited its retail sale or failed to continue support for the expensive and elaborate inspection and certification procedures required.

The recent upsurge of interest in natural foods has led many people to seek out farmers who sell raw uncertified milk. Most states have laws which give the farmer the right to sell unpasteurized milk at his farm, providing the customer goes there to purchase it. This is risky for without any government standards or regular inspection, the consumer has no way of determining the quality of the milk. Assurances from the farmer that his animals are "healthy" are, of course, no guarantee that they are indeed free from disease.

Advocates of raw milk often claim that it is more valuable because it retains naturally-occurring enzymes which are destroyed by the heat of pasteurization, yet they do not explain why such enzymes should be preserved. It is generally believed by scientists that the principal function of these enzymes is to carry on a multitude of biochemical activities in the milk-secreting cells of the mammary glands, and they simply remain in the milk after they have done their job. It is not clear whether the enzymes serve any purpose in human nutrition, and their destruction by pasteurization therefore appears to be of little consequence.

The large losses of vitamins attributed to pasteurization by raw milk advocates are misleading because the studies they cite for support are based on pasteurization by the inefficient "holder" method that has long since been replaced by the more efficient and nutritionally less destructive High Temperature, Short Time (HTST) method.

High temperatures for short periods are far less destructive than longer times at lower temperatures. Because of this phenomenon, HTST pasteurization of milk at 161° for fifteen seconds has virtually no effect at all on nutrients.

Homogenization

The cream in fresh cow's milk is in the form of fat globules which tend, upon standing, to separate from the non-fatty skim portion of the milk and float to the surface. Homogenization is a physical rather than a chemical process, in which the fat globules are broken up into such small particles that they remain suspended rather than float on the surface.

Because it is purely a mechanical process, homogenization does not affect the nutritional value of milk and, on the face of it, would seem to have no effect on health one way or the other. In 1970, however, Dr. Kurt Oster, chief of cardiology at Park City Hospital in Bridgeport, Connecticut propounded the rather startling theory that homogenization may be a cause of atherosclerosis.

Any such connection between homogenization and heart disease must be considered hypothetical, at least until additional studies are made, as Oster's theory is strongly criticized by other experts.

MILK, POWDERED

Powdered milk is a valuable food suitable for most purposes except infant feeding, where it should definitely not be used, because it lacks the polyunsaturated fats and vitamin E essential for infant nutrition. Powdered milk can also be hazardous to infants if it is not mixed with the required amount of water. Cow's milk is a fairly rich source of sodium and thus, if the mixture is too concentrated (i.e., too little water and too much dry milk), infants may develop dehydration. Critics of powdered milk believe that children are better fed with whole milk because it has all of the fat-soluble vitamins.

Some popular books on nutrition suggest that the consumer buy spray-dried powdered milk rather than the less nutritious roller-dried product. Roller drying is an obsolete process seldom used. Other books recommend low-heat rather than high heat powdered milk, which is somewhat less nutritious. Virtually all brands sold at retail are made by the low-heat process. There is little difference in nutrient value between instant and non-instant dry milk.

Powdered Milk and Food Poisoning

A potential hazard in nonfat dry milk powder is bacterial contamination. Over the years a number of cases of staphylococcal and salmonella food poisoning have been traced to contaminated dried milk. The symptoms in healthy adults are relatively mild but ailing persons, infants, and the elderly, are much more seriously affected and may even die from contamination that causes only an upset stomach in another individual. Food-poisoning bacteria are often present in animal products, especially poultry, but do not cause a serious problem because the bacteria are destroyed during cooking. The presence of such bacteria in dry milk is of special concern, however, because it is usually consumed unheated. Factory sealed packages are less apt to be contaminated than bulk packaged dry milk sold in many co-op stores.

Packaging and Storage of Powdered Milk

The most critical factor in maintaining nutritive value and also dissolving qualities is protection against moisture. An increase of only 3 per cent in the moisture during storage can cut the protein value by 20 per cent. It is also important to store at room temperature or below and in glass jars away from light. The factory-sealed boxes and particularly the individual quart serving packets provide excellent protection and, when unopened, allow long storage (up to one year) without loss of quality if stored at cool temperatures.

"NONDAIRY" PRODUCTS

Substitutes for dairy products are of two general types: those with one or more milk components as principal ingredients (along with sugar, vegetable fats, and additives) and those without milk components. The former are often called "non-dairy" products, despite the presence of dairy components, principally casein (milk protein) and lactose (milk sugar).

The presence of dairy ingredients in supposedly "nondairy" foods poses a problem to those who are allergic to milk products, intolerant of lactose, or who wish to avoid milk for religious reasons.

Recent interest in the possible connection between dietary saturated fat and heart disease has resulted in widespread criticism of whole milk (which is high in saturated fat). The possibility of replacing whole milk with a combination of skim milk and vegetable fat—known as filled milk or Melloream—may have some merit since most vegetable fats are unsaturated and do not adversely affect serum cholesterol levels.

Unfortunately, polyunsaturated vegetable fats do not have the chemical properties that are needed to create an appealing filled milk with a long shelf life, so manufacturers instead use coconut oil which is 86 per cent saturated—more saturated, in fact, than milk fat itself. (Milk fat is only 54 per cent saturated.) In addition, the coconut oil is also hydrogenated. Hydrogenation is a solidifying process that has been sharply criticized by many nutritionists because it alters the biological availability of the fat and may be implicated in the development of heart disease. Most milk substitutes containing hydrogenated coconut oil often list this questionable ingredient as "vegetable fat" on the label, a labelling practice potentially harmful to those who are advised by their physicians to substitute unsaturated vegetable fat for saturated animal fat. The percentage of saturated fat in "non-dairy" coffee whiteners and whipped cream substitutes is as follows:

Table II

SATURATED FAT IN "NON-DAIRY" PRODUCTS *

Coffee Whiteners		Whipped Cream Substitutes	
Coffee-Mate (1)	21.7%	Dream Whip (1)	26.6%
Cremora (1)	25.5%	Lucky Whip (1)	24.8%
Pream (1)	28.8%	D'Zerta Whipped	
Coffee Rich (2)	7.6%	Topping (1)	40.9%
		Cool Whip (2)	18.3%
		Rich's Whip	
(Whole milk	1.8%)	Topping (3)	13.4%
(Light cream	8.8%)	(Heavy whipping	
		cream	16.2%)

(1) Powder   (2) Frozen   (3) Aerosol

* Lauric, myristic and palmitic fatty acids only. Other saturated fatty acids are not included as they appear to have no effect on cholesterol level.

SOURCE: Percentage data for non-dairy creamers calculated from Monsen, E. R., & Adriaenssens, L., "Fatty acid composition and total lipid of cream and cream substitutes," *American Journal of Clinical Nutrition* 22:458-463 (1969).

Saturated fat in filled milks varies by brand and state, with amounts similar to whole milk. Filled milk has more real milk components than non-dairy coffee whiteners or whipped cream substitutes and hence is more nutritious. Imitation milk, because it does not contain any diary components, has inferior nutritive value and furthermore usually contains artificial color and flavor. In some states, filled milk must be labeled as "imitation milk" but can be distinguished from true imitation milk because it lists "fluid skim milk," "skim milk solids," or "non-fat dry milk" as components.

On the issue of filled and synthetic milks, professional nutritionists divide into two groups. One group sees the possibility of a future filled milk product that is less expensive yet as nutritionally sound as whole milk. This group argues that a properly fortified product would be an ideal food especially for disadvantaged population groups where price is critical.

The second group believes that the unique combination of proteins, fats, minerals, and vitamins in natural milk occurs in quantities and proportions which offer a biological advantage over substitute products with similar but not equal ingredients. Dr. Milton E. Rubini, editor-in-chief of the *American Journal of Clinical Nutrition,* says that, "There is concern that nondairy 'white beverages' offered to the public to date may be potentially hazardous. Because of their physical appearance and because their products are sold from the dairy counter in most stores, these products mislead the public into believing they are acceptable substitutes. This is certainly not the case with respect to the protein and calcium needed by infants and young children."

In 1972, the American Academy of Pediatrics' Committee on Nutrition, in a policy statement on the nutritional value of filled milks, imitation milks, and coffee whiteners in the diets of children, said that "most imitation milks on the market are totally unsuitable for infant feeding and constitute a public health risk." Because these products contain hydrogenated coconut fat, and are "inferior to milk in regard to their protein, vitamin and mineral contents," the Committee further declared that these products "cannot be considered as a suitable replacement for milk in the diet of young children" as well as infants. The Committee granted that older children on a mixed diet would be unlikely to suffer nutritional deficiencies if they used filled milk, but they advised parents and physicians to determine if a particular product was really "filled milk" rather than "imitation milk."

YOGURT

Yogurt is really soured or fermented milk, but it is made in a way that gives a pleasant, tart taste and thickish texture.

Flavored yogurt, which far outsells the plain variety, is made in two very different styles, which might be described as "natural" and "processed." Natural style yogurt, such as Dannon, is made from skim milk, and fermented by lactic acid bacterial cultures. For flavoring, a layer of fruit preserves on the bottom of the carton must be stirred up into the plain yogurt above.

Processed yogurt, called "Swiss Style" by the industry, more closely resembles canned pudding for the flavor is mixed in with the product. While tasty in its own way, it is shunned by experienced yogurt-eaters. In "Swiss Style" the yogurt and fruit preserves are mixed with other, often questionable ingredients and preservatives to maintain texture and flavor.

Yogurt is commonly promoted as a low-calorie food ("the dieter's delight," as Dannon says) with claims that it is "98 percent fat free." Plain yogurt has fairly low calories (130 per eight ounce cup), but the flavored varieties with up to 260 calories per cup (about the same as an average piece of Boston cream pie), are clearly not in the diet food class.

Because dry milk powder is added to most commercial yogurt to give it a thicker texture, the protein content is slightly higher than in plain milk. Vitamin and mineral content is about the same as in milk except for vitamin B_{12} which is considerably lower.

The Antibiotic Properties of Yogurt

Yogurt contains antibacterial properties which can kill most disease-causing bacteria which find their way into the product. For this reason, some health food writers have suggested that travellers to foreign countries can safely eat yogurt when the water and other foods are contaminated. Yogurt-making bacteria appear to produce an antibiotic effect similar to penicillin but at such a low level that it is extremely doubtful whether they exert any effect at all in humans. The antibiotic strength of an eight ounce cup of eight-day old yogurt is equal to nine units of penicillin, yet the usual adult dosage of oral penicillin ranges from 600,-000 to 2,400,00 units daily.

Although yogurt does not have enough antibiotic to be used as a drug by humans, it is generally a very inhospitable medium for harmful bacteria.

Therapeutic Effects of Yogurt

Galen, who was the personal physician to the emperor Marcus Aurelius, recommended yogurt for "burning and bilious stomachs," while a book published in seventh century Damascus claimed that "yogurt is good for strengthening the stomach and for refreshing and regulating the intestinal tract."

In more recent times the Nobel laureate and director of the Pasteur Institute, Elie Metchnikoff (1845-1916) advocated yogurt for longevity. Metchnikoff noted that an extraordinary large proportion of Bulgarian peasants lived to be over one hundred and that they consumed large quantities of yogurt. (However, he failed to mention that these people led an extremely active life and were not exposed to the environmental hazards of industrial society.)

Different strains of bacteria are used to make yogurt. During the 1920's there was widespread therapeutic use of "acidophilus milk"—a very sour, liquid-like yogurt made with the bacteria *lactobacillus acidophilus* —although to this day its therapeutic value has never been proven.

The myth of yogurt's great curative or disease preventative powers lingers on partly because some health food advocates mistakenly believe that today's commercial yogurt contains the supposedly beneficial *acidophilus* bacteria. Modern yogurt, such as Dannon, contains no acidophilus; only the strains *lactobacillus bulgaricus* and *streptococcus thermophilus*.

Recent experiments at the University of Nebraska have revived interest in yogurt's therapeutic value. The researchers reported in the *Journal of the National Cancer Institute* that cancerous tumor growth in mice was inhibited when the animals were fed a commercially available yogurt. Similar findings have been reported by foreign researchers, but most experts agree that it is still too early to judge the relevance of such experiments for humans.

The possibility has also been raised that yogurt may

be useful in lowering serum cholestrol levels. Dr. George V. Mann of the Vanderbilt University Medical School found that the Masai tribe of Africa enjoyed a low serum cholestrol level despite a diet high in cholesterol and saturated fat, much of which came from large quantities of whole milk yogurt. In an experiment in which young Masai warriors were fed with even larger amounts of whole milk yogurt, serum cholesterol levels were lowered even more. Dr. Mann concluded that yogurt supplies a factor that inhibits the formation of cholesterol. The beneficial factor has not yet been identified.

At this point it would seem premature to start eating very large quantities of yogurt with the expectation of preventing cancer and heart disease. Despite the dramatic effects seen in cancer experiments with mice, nothing indicates yet that a similar effect occurs in humans. Americans who adopt the Masai habit of eating extremely large amounts of yogurt—up to four quarts a day (2500 calories)—would have little room for other foods unless, of course, they adopted an extremely active lifestyle. The possibility of adverse consequences from relying too heavily on one food was suggested in a study in which rats fed an exclusive diet of yogurt made from skim milk developed cataracts. There is, of course, no evidence that yogurt in moderate amounts has any adverse effects on humans.

CHAPTER III

Fruits and Vegetables

Nothing is less controversial than fruits and vegetables. The most conservative academic nutritionists join with the freakiest of food faddists in praising the virtues of these foods. The only dissident voices are those of little children who balk at their broccoli. There is, however, a widespread feeling that frozen and canned fruits and vegetables are inferior to fresh produce. To a certain extent, the feeling is justified but there are important qualifications.

Processed Vegetables

Peas are processed by all of the generally used techniques—freezing, canning, and drying—and so provide a good example of the nutritional effects of processing for a variety of foods.

Freshly picked peas, properly cooked, are the most nutritious form of the vegetable, while frozen peas are only slightly less so. Canned peas are significantly below frozen nutritionally. Dried split peas are about equal in value to the canned but when equal caloric portions are compared, the dried form has less value. (See Table I.) This hierarchy of nutritional value—fresh picked, frozen, canned, and dried—applies to virtually all types of vegetables.

Table I

INDEX OF NUTRITIVE VALUE

PEAS	Per Ounce	Per 100 Calories
Fresh, cooked	100	100
Frozen, cooked	84	88
Canned, drained solids, warmed	62	55
Dried, split, cooked	63	39
APRICOTS		
Raw	100	100
Canned, juice pack, solids and liquid	85	80
Frozen, sweetened	78	41
Canned, water pack, solid and liquid	60	80
Canned, light syrup, solid and liquid	58	45
Canned, heavy syrup, solid and liquid	57	34
Canned, extra heavy syrup	56	28
Dried, sulphured, uncooked	195	38

Note: The index is computed by first calculating the per cent of Recommended Dietary Allowance provided by each product for nine major nutrients (protein, calcium, phosphorus, iron, vitamin A, thiamin, riboflavin, niacin, and vitamin C). These percentages are then averaged and the index computed by setting the average for the least-processed product equal to 100.

"Fresh-picked" is the key phrase here as storage losses in retail produce can be substantial. For example, asparagus refrigerated for one week at 32° F may lose 50 per cent of its vitamin C; if held at room temperature for only one day it may lose up to 40 per cent. By comparison, blanching, which is the only heat treatment in the processing of frozen asparagus, results in losses which average only 5 per cent. The losses in fresh produce are caused by naturally occurring enzymes which destroy certain vitamins, mainly A and C. Furthermore, much fresh produce found in retail stores is bred for toughness because this quality is desirable in handling and transport. Toughness is usually achieved at the expense of softer, juicier, more flavorful and more nutritious tissues. Much of the produce sold as fresh is harvested while still unripe and then is ripened during storage, a process which generally results in lower nutrient value than ripening on the plant. The fairly long interval after harvesting favors penetration of pesticide residues to the interior of the plant making washing or peeling less effective in removing residues.

Frozen and canned vegetables are not as apt to suffer the same indignities as "fresh" vegetables commonly found in supermarkets. They do not have to be bred for toughness because processing is done as soon as possible after harvesting. Immediate processing minimizes storage losses due to enzymatic action and also penetration of pesticide residues. While frozen produce must be somewhat resistant to handling because it has to be washed, sorted, blanched and packaged, the injuries are not as severe as those sustained by fresh produce during truck transport or in loading or unloading of shipping crates. Produce destined for canning and freezing is usually harvested when completely ripe.

In the processing of peas and other produce, the application of heat, particularly over extended periods, is the chief agent for reducing nutrient values. Frozen peas are subjected to heat at only one point, the steam blanching phase which lasts for only one to three minutes. Steam blanching destroys the enzymes that would otherwise destroy nutrient values, and because it is equivalent to partial precooking, it cuts the amount of time required for home cooking. Frozen peas are therefore subjected to about the same amount of total heat treatment as cooked fresh peas, which accounts for their small nutrient loss compared to fresh picked. Frozen peas that are kept at 0° F or lower in distribution and storage are often the equal, and even may surpass in flavor and nutritional value, the "fresh" vegetable bought in the supermarket.

Canned peas go through two additional high-temperature processing stages: heating in a vacuum to remove air from the can and sterilization in the can. The latter step particularly is destructive because temperatures are held at 250° for up to fifty-five minutes. The peas take three days to cool in the warehouse and during this period some cans, particularly those in the center of the packed cartons, which remain at relatively high temperatures, suffer further nutrient loss. Canned peas may also suffer significant additional nutrient losses during storage in stores and homes, particularly when kept in warm kitchen storage areas during summer months.

Dried peas lose nutrient value through the heat applied during the drying process. Peas and other dried legumes are nevertheless important foods, particularly for vegetarians, who value them for their protein. Even with processing losses, legumes retain substantial minerals and vitamins.

Fresh peas have virtually no salt, while a 3½-ounce portion of frozen peas have 115 mg and a portion of canned about 235 mg. Most canned vegetables have considerable salt but among frozen vegetables only peas and lima beans have substantial amounts. Canned peas may contain sugar and artificial coloring, both of which must be listed on the label. Sugar is allowed in other canned vegetables but artificial color is not.

Frozen vegetables are among the most nutritious convenience foods available anywhere. The latest wrinkle in frozen vegetables, Birds Eye "Five Minute Vegetables," is no exception. These vegetables, regardless of variety, can be cooked the same length of time. To achieve uniform cooking times, long cooking vegetables are blanched longer at the plant while shorter cooking ones are given a briefer blanch. This procedure does not lower nutrient value of the cooked vegetable.

Among the less desirable vegetables are those which come in sauces containing artificial color and flavor. Most combinations of vegetables are offered only in sauces, one of the few exceptions being those made by Seabrook Farms which contain no additives whatsoever, not even salt.

Processed Fruits

Fresh fruits in the supermarket suffer much the same indignities as fresh vegetables but as they are generally eaten raw, no loss from heat processing occurs. Frozen fruits are generally not as palatable as fresh because the characteristic crisp texture is lost. Ounce-for-ounce, they have moderately less nutrients but are heavily sugared and hence, in terms of vitamins and minerals per calorie are quite low in comparison to fresh fruit. (See Table I.)

Canned fruits packed in syrup (usually just sugar and water) are generally low in nutritive value compared to fresh fruit. These are commonly available in light syrup, heavy syrup, and extra heavy syrup, which differ only in the amount of sugar. Fruits canned in their own juice (no sugar) are surprisingly high in nutrients. (However, many that are labeled as being packed in juice also have added sucrose or corn syrup.) Those canned in water (usually sold as low calorie foods) are somewhat lower in value than the juice packs, but calorie-for-calorie, they have as much vitamins and minerals. Dried fruits, like dried vegetables, lose considerable nutrient value in processing. Fruit sauces such as apple sauce and cranberry sauce generally suffer greater losses in processing than fruit which has not been macerated.

Cost of Fruits and Vegetables

The cost of frozen produce may appear to be higher than fresh produce particularly when fresh is in season. However, the cost per portion of frozen food may be lower because it requires no trimming. Canned goods often appear to be less expensive than frozen, but

Much of the weight is in water. By law, the net weight designation on canned goods can include water.

Nutrients in Plant Foods

Most fruits and vegetables are rich sources of vitamin C wh le many are also sources of vitamin A. (See Appendix II.) Some vegetables have high concentrations of calcium and iron, but much of these minerals may be unavailable to the body because of binding with oxalic acid (see "Oxalates in Vegetables," page 64). With the exception of legumes, fruits and vegetables are usually not good protein sources but some such as potatoes and mushrooms provide small amounts of good quality protein. Fruits and vegetables are generally lower in trace minerals than grains, nuts, and seeds although calorie-for-calorie, they compare quite favorably. (See Appendix II, pages 329-334.)

Controlled Atmosphere Storage

Greatly increased storage life can be achieved by regulating the composition of air in which fruits and vegetables are stored. All fresh fruits "breathe" after harvest in a manner similar to animals; they take in oxygen and give off carbon dioxide (CO_2). Green plants in sunlight, of course, engage in the reverse process, giving off oxygen and taking in CO_2. The respiration of fruits is an integral part of the biochemical change which takes place during ripening and which leads eventually to decay. These changes can be slowed down considerably in cold storage, but even when refrigerated, fruit continues to "breathe" and the decay process slowly continues.

By lowering the oxygen content of the air and increasing the nitrogen content, respiration can be reduced, thus slowing the biochemical changes and leading to less ripening and decay. Nitrogen is one of the least toxic gases known and its use for storing fruits and vegetables should be an entirely safe process. Storage of some fruits and vegetables is also enhanced by increasing the level of carbon dioxide (also a harmless gas) instead of nitrogen.

Controlled atmosphere (CA) storage has been used most successfully with apples. Some varieties can be held for seven to eight months and yet appear just as crisp as the day they were picked. Virtually all apples sold between November and August have been stored by this method. Recently the industry has begun to use CA storage for other produce including pears, lettuce, and strawberries. Eventually, when the experts determine the optimum conditions for each variety, most fruits and vegetables may be stored and shipped by this method. The result will probably be beneficial in nutritional terms, for the evidence suggests that CA storage preserves vitamins considerably better than storage in air.

Many consumers object to produce that is prewrapped in plastic film because it is difficult to examine the underside for spoilage. The type of plastic film used by most supermarkets, however, does have an advantage for it allows the CO_2 to pass out of the package, thus significantly increasing storage life. For better storage at home, the plastic wrap should not be removed until the produce is to be used.

Ethylene Gas Ripening of Fruits and Vegetables

A wide variety of fruits give off ethylene (C_2H_4) as they ripen. While the production of this gas appears to occur as a result of the ripening process in the fruit, the gas that is given off can also stimulate ripening in other fruits. For example, bananas ripen faster when stored together with apples than when stored alone. Since so many fruits give off ethylene as a natural function of ripening, it seems doubtful that the use of ethylene to ripen fruits artificially is hazardous.

There is no evidence that *mature* fruits and vegetables stimulated to ripen more quickly because of added ethylene differ significantly in nutritional value from those ripened naturally. Ethylene is used, however, to turn *immature* green tomatoes red. Gas-reddened but immature tomatoes may have only one-half the vitamin C content of those naturally ripened. According to Consumers Union, about 80 per cent of tomatoes produced in Florida are picked while green and reddened with ethylene gas. Most Mexican tomatoes are not picked until ripening has begun. Over 95 per cent of the fresh tomatoes sold in the U.S. are from Florida or Mexico.

Hormone Sprays and "Gibbed" Fruit

In recent years a number of chemicals have been applied to a wide variety of fruits to increase their size. Fruits that have been treated this way include grapes, tomatoes, strawberries, figs, blueberries, cranberries, apricots, peaches, pears, apples, guavas, and cherries.

Herbicides such as 2,4,5-T have been found to act

as growth-stimulating hormones and allow some fruits to develop even when their flowers have not been pollinated. These are widely used by the fruit industry despite substantial evidence indicating that they cause birth defects. Because they are known teratogens, widespread use by fruit growers to increase the size of fruits is certainly a questionable practice.

Gibrellic acid occurs naturally in most seeds and fruits but in a synthetic form it is a commonly applied growth hormone. The size of Thompson seedless grapes sprayed with gibrellic acid for example, is increased by 28 per cent. Grapes such as Cardinal, Thompson Seedless and Black Monukka are sometimes labelled to indicate this treatment with the terms "Gibbed" or "Ungibbed" identifying the two types. There has been insufficient research on the possible adverse health effects of "gibbed" fruits.

Honey bees are the principal means of pollinating the flowers of fruit trees, but their numbers are dwindling due to the environmental contamination by pesticides. Because of this, use of synthetic hormone sprays will probably increase since these chemicals allow many fruits to "set" even when the flowers have not been pollinated.

Waxing of Fruits and Vegetables

Coating of fruits and vegetables with wax has become common. The primary purpose is to reduce shriveling from water lost through the tiny pores in the skin that allow the fruit or vegetable to "breathe."

As secondary benefits, flavor and texture do not deteriorate as rapidly as in unwaxed fruit, and the wax gives an attractive sheen to the surface. Fruits and vegetables that are commonly waxed include apples, oranges, tangerines, lemons, grapefruit, turnips, cantaloupes, green peppers, tomatoes, and cucumbers. Russet potatoes are also waxed.

The safety of such coatings has been questioned by several researchers. Dr. Wilhelm C. Hueper, former director of The Environmental Cancer Section of The National Cancer Institute, claims that such waxes may cause stomach cancer and that "consumers of food stuffs coated with paraffins or waxes are at risk."

The skins of produce such as citrus fruits, turnips and cantaloupes are not eaten and pose no hazard, cucumbers can be peeled (although this results in loss of nutrients in the skin), but tomatoes and green peppers present a particular problem. Federal regulations do not require produce to be labelled "wax added" and unfortunately it is often difficult to determine whether tomatoes or green peppers have such a coating.

Organic vs. Nonorganic Produce

To the chemist, the term "organic" simply means that a substance contains carbon. In this sense, "organic" can refer to anything from apples to corn to linoleum to polyethylene plastic. The term "organic food," according to advocates, refers to food that has been grown on naturally fertilized soil without the use of herbicides, pesticides or other potentially harmful synthetic chemicals.

Advocates of organic food claim that fertilization of soil with synthetic fertilizers depletes the soil of nutrients and that crops grown on such soils cannot produce optimal health. They claim that commercial farmers not only use pesticides which poison the food, but that they are concerned too much with the appearance and marketability of produce and ignore nutritive values.

On the other side, spokesmen for the food industry as well as U.S. Government officials declare that such talk is not only ridiculous but also dangerous because it undermines the public's confidence in the wholesomeness of the food supply. They claim that, except for an iodine deficiency which causes goiter, there is no evidence whatsoever that any nutritional deficiencies exist in America due to the quality of American soils. They insist that only by using pesticides can enough food be grown to feed the world's growing population, and that the remaining residues of such chemicals are well below harmful levels and, furthermore, that the government carefully inspects produce for these residues.

Who is right? As in most controversies, some truths and misrepresentations seemingly exist on both sides. There is little doubt that organic methods of farming are superior ecologically. Even individuals in the agribusiness establishment acknowledge the strictly ecological superiority of organic methods, but declare that organic farming is not a practical way to feed millions of people.

A more immediate problem is the possibility that pesticides may have unfavorable effects on human health. Despite the establishment by the federal government of "safe" limits for the amount of pesticide residues in produce, many scientists are concerned that such levels may not really be safe because not enough is known about their effects on humans. Other critics point out that the government only makes spot checks of produce and levels in excess of tolerance may appear in the uninspected portion.

According to a Ralph Nader study group report on the Food and Drug Administration, only 0.7 per cent of the 2.5 million produce shipments entering interstate commerce in the three year period between 1963 and 1966 were inspected, and the FDA's own statistics indicate that at least 75,000 shipments having residues in excess of tolerance went undetected.

Another problem is that even small amounts of residues in the allowable range can build up in the body over a period of time with consequences that cannot be foretold. A particularly disturbing development was the discovery several years ago that human mothers' milk in some parts of the country contained levels of DDT several times higher than allowed in cow's milk. One study showed that only eight of fifty-three nursing mothers had milk with less than the federal tolerance of DDT set for cow's milk.

Pesticide and herbicide residues are not distributed evenly among all food crops because of differing intensity of use, type used and thoroughness of washing. Vegetables grown underground have virtually no residues, while green leafy vegetables are apt to have significant amounts.

If advocates of organic foods seem to have the best of the argument regarding adverse effects of pesticides on the environment, their claims for superior nutritional value are somewhat less convincing. The most important factor affecting the nutritive value of produce is genetics. Plants can be bred for many kinds of desirable characteristics, but most breeders are interested solely in the commercially advantageous features, such as size, color, and juiciness, and ignore completely the possibilities for developing strains with improved nutrient value. Some commercial growing techniques, such as those for tomatoes, may result in the reduction of vitamin content. In most organic farming operations, the breeding has emphasized flavor and resistance to pests and disease. The possibilities for nutritive enhancement through genetic control has been largely ignored by organic farmers perhaps because it is assumed that high nutritive value would be assured by natural fertilization.

In addition to genetics, other factors affect the nutritive value of food, especially the amount or intensity of light. Vitamin C content of fruits and vegetables increases significantly when the plant is exposed to more sunlight. Temperature of the air is also important because heat speeds the rate of biochemical processes involved in the synthesis of vitamins. Adequate rainfall increases growth, but heavy rain leaches nutrients from the soil. Season of harvest or maturity also affects nutritive value. Some plants are highest in nutritive value when immature, others are highest when mature, and still others when overripe. Humidity affects transpiration (the giving off of moisture) which in turn affects the uptake of water and water-soluble nutrients from the soil. Wind velocity has a surprising effect on nutrient values, which decrease in high winds because some of the plant energy and nutrients go into structural support parts. These parts are generally inedible or indigestible.

The size of a fruit or vegetable is important. In most fruits the nutrients are concentrated near the surface, either in the skin or just under it. The smaller the fruit or vegetable, the more surface there is in relation to total mass. Hence, on a per pound basis, small fruits or vegetables have more nutrients than larger ones. Heavier fertilization will increase the size of produce but not necessarily the nutrient value.

The claims of organic farmers that their product tastes better are obviously subjective judgments. In many cases it is possible that nonorganic farmers who breed for taste characteristics may produce varieties that have more taste appeal. Fresh picked produce tastes better than that which is stored; to the extent that organic produce reaches the market faster, it can be better tasting.

The fertilizer used on crops is only one agent among many that influences nutrient value and is generally not the most important. Some organic farming advocates claim that the synthetic fertilizers result in less nutritious produce, but there is no valid evidence to support this claim.

Another objection to synthetic fertilizers voiced by

organic advocates is that they contain only the basic macro-nutrients—nitrogen, phosphorus and potassium —but no trace elements that are essential to plant nutrition. However, most commercially marketed brands of fertilizer are supplemented with a number of trace elements which favorably affect the growth and yield of crops. Whether all the nutrients essential to human health are added is questionable. The organic farmers claim that by adding back compost and manure to the soil, they return all the trace elements included in the synthetic mixes, as well as other less-known or even unknown elements which may also prove to be essential on the basis of future research. According to experts from the FDA's Division of Nutrition, little is known about the rate at which trace elements essential in human nutrition are either depleted from or added to heavily cropped soils in the U.S.

This is an important point in favor of organic farming and touches upon a potentially vulnerable aspect of synthetic chemical farming. However, the organic farmer who depends upon fertilizing his soil through composting of local waste materials may merely be reinforcing the natural deficiencies in the soil. There are over thirteen million acres in the U.S. which are naturally deficient in manganese, twelve million acres deficient in boron and six and one-half million deficient in molybdenum and copper. Land such as this, unless fortified, will grow less nutritious produce. Some organic farmers, recognizing these deficiencies, make up for them by fertilizing with seaweed, which is particularly high in trace elements.

There is no doubt that organic produce grown under optimum conditions is preferable to nonorganic produce. However, as anyone who has tried to buy organic food knows, the price is often two to three times as much as the comparable supermarket product, and there is usually no assurance that the produce is, in fact, organic. The federal government has no rules governing the production of organic food or use of the term in labelling or advertising, nor do state governments with the exception of Oregon.

Avoiding Pesticide Residues in Produce

Pesticide residues in produce are an important problem. Residues in meat may be more concentrated, but this is a small comfort to the vegetable and fruit eater because no one knows what level of pesticide intake may have adverse effects. Until the day that pesticides are eliminated, what can the cautious eater do? Here are five suggestions:

1. Buy Frozen Vegetables Rather Than Fresh Vegetables In The Supermarket.

The residues in frozen foods may be lower than in fresh because produce destined for freezing is washed shortly after harvesting before the pesticides have had time to penetrate and are also reduced by quick trimming of external parts before the pesticides can be absorbed into the inner surfaces.

2. Thoroughly Wash All Fresh Produce.

Rough or fuzzy textured produce (such as spinach, strawberries, endive and peaches) need extra attention. The use of a vegetable brush can increase the efficiency of the wash. Vegetables and fruits grown in city gardens or near busy roads should be washed very thoroughly. Avoid soaking, especially in warm water, as this leaches out nutrients.

3. Buy Union-Harvested Produce.

The Union Farm Workers (UFW) union headed by Cesar Chavez has fought for a reduction in the use of pesticides. While at the present time only a small fraction of American produce comes from UFW farms, more and more could be available in the future if consumers support this movement by making a special effort to seek out and buy the items that are available today. Be skeptical if the grocer claims his produce is "union" unless he can show you the shipping carton which displays the UFW's spread-eagle symbol.

4. Buy Organically Grown Produce.

Although seemingly the most obvious way to avoid pesticide residues, the consumer has no assurances that "organic" produce is indeed grown on naturally fertilized soil untouched by poison sprays.

5. Grow Your Own.

By carefully following organic gardening methods or by using a minimum of chemicals, the home garden can provide an inexpensive, nutritious and safe alternative to supermarket produce at far less cost for at least part of the year. One word of caution: until lead additives are totally banned from gasoline, experts advise that, due to the fallout of lead emissions, gardens should be located at least 300 feet from heavily travelled roadways, especially if produce from the garden will be consumed as a significant part of the diet. One study showed that vegetables harvested from home gardens located within 50 feet of a lightly traveled highway in Canandaigua, N.Y., contained lead levels 10,000 times higher than uncontaminated food. Lead is especially dangerous for children.

Nutrient Losses During Cooking

The home cooking process can be even more destructive of nutrients than commercial processing. In general, vitamins are the nutrients most affected by cooking while protein is affected to a much lesser degree. The essential fatty acids are only slightly affected while minerals are hardly affected at all by heating.

Because most nutrients are water-soluble, they leach out of food during cooking but remain nutritionally valuable. The cooking water may contain more of the water-soluble nutrients that the vegetable itself. The vitamins in the cooking water are, however, unstable and should be used at the same meal, if practical (in gravy, for example).

Nutrient losses during boiling increase as the amount of water is increased, therefore the minimum amount of water should be used. Losses also increase with time of boiling. Rapid cooking in vigorously boiling water is preferable to lengthy simmering. The smaller the pieces, the greater the loss of nutrients, and it is therefore desirable to reduce the number of cut surfaces exposed to the water. When possible, keep the vegetable whole with the skin on, while cooking. (This is the best way to boil potatoes).

An alternative to boiling is steaming by suspending the vegetable in a perforated basket above the boiling water in a covered pot. The food should not come in contact with the water. Vegetables cook faster by steaming than by boiling, and the quantity of nutrients leached into the water is reduced substantially, especially with green leafy vegetables.

The best nutrient retentions of all are obtained by pressure cooking. Most experts, however, hesitate to recommend this method for home cooking of most vegetables because the timing and pressure are very critical and home cookers are not designed to provide very accurate controls. The cooking times of most vegetables are so short that it is difficult not to over-cook but pressure cookers are suitable for long-cooking items such as rice. Some foods such as soybeans should never be pressure cooked because they foam and shed skins which can clog the safety vent, possibly leading to an explosion.

Cooking methods such as frying or baking that do not use water will, under certain circumstances, result in a higher retention of water-soluble nutrients. Ordinarily these methods subject the foods to higher temperatures than do boiling or steaming, and thus nutrients can be destroyed. Low-temperature frying can result in virtually no destruction of nutrients, while high-temperature frying can destroy 80 per cent or more. Similarly, baking can result in low or high losses depending upon temperature, length of time, and size of vegetable. (For example, large potatoes suffer a 59 per cent loss of thiamine as against only 22 per cent for small ones due to longer cooking time.)

Oxalates in Vegetables

Green leafy foods such as spinach and beet greens contain a substance called calcium oxalate. The calcium in this compound is so tightly bound that it cannot be absorbed by the body. Furthermore, there is some evidence that kidney and bladder stones may form when large amounts of calcium oxalate crystals must be excreted.

The binding of calcium in oxalate-containing greens such as spinach has led some experts to suggest that calcium deficiency may result when green leafy vegetables constitute a large part of the diet. The average American is unlikely to develop a calcium deficiency due to oxalate-binding in vegetables since milk and dairy products are included in most diets. Strict vegetarians, on the other hand, may develop calcium deficiency through overdependence on certain green leafy vegetables. Some provide large amounts of calcium in relation to their oxalic acid content and should not be a problem for vegetarians. These include turnip greens, kale, mustard greens, and collards.

Besides vegetarians, the group which may be most adversely affected by oxalate-containing vegetables is infants. Green leafy vegetables, especially spinach, should not be included in the infant's diet because he needs all the calcium he can get for bone growth. Oxalic acid, the unbound form of the compound, which is also present in these vegetables, may affect the mucous membrane lining the stomach and intestines of infants. Spinach should be omitted from infant diets not only because of the oxalates but also because of the possibility of nitrate poisoning. (See below.)

Nitrates and Nitrites in Vegetables

Although it is well-known that nitrates and nitrites are added to cured meats such as hot dogs and ham, few people realize that a number of vegetables naturally contain potentially hazardous levels of these substances also.

The presence of nitrites as well as nitrates in foods has long been considered potentially hazardous because such residues can cause methemoglobinemia—a condition in which nitrites combine with hemoglobin in the blood to prevent it from carrying oxygen to the tissues.

In older children and adults this condition has only been found when nitrites were ingested in large quantities—such as well water contaminated by fertilizer runoff. Infants, however, are extremely sensitive to even low levels of nitrites, leading the World Health Organization and the U.N. Food and Agriculture Organization to state categorically that nitrites should not be added to baby foods.

Infants under four months have much lower levels of stomach acidity than older children or adults, a condition which permits the growth of microorganisms in their stomachs that can change the normally nontoxic nitrate into dangerous nitrite.

There is widespread concern that nitrites may lead to cancer, but the possible danger from vegetables may be less than from meat treated with nitrites, because meat contains higher levels of the secondary amines that react with nitrite to create the carcinogenic nitrosamines.

Nitrate is converted to its more dangerous partner, nitrite, by the action of enzymes present in vegetables and by the work of certain naturally present molds and bacteria. The amount of nitrite produced depends heavily upon temperature. One study showed that in heavily fertilized spinach which contained 30 ppm of nitrite at harvesting, the amount jumped to 3,550 ppm in just four days at room temperature. The prudent eater may wish to retard formation of nitrites by refrigeration or by buying frozen spinach which, if properly processed and stored, provides fewer opportunities for nitrite formation. The nitrite in frozen spinach stays virtually the same for up to five months.

Botulism from Canned and Frozen Vegetables

Considered to be one of the most toxic substances known, botulinum toxin occurs only under special conditions, but conditions which are common to many types of canned vegetables. Botulism outbreaks in the U.S. have been caused by both commercial and home-canned string beans, beets, corn, chard, asparagus, olives, peas, figs, beet greens, chili peppers, beans, spinach and tomatoes. However, mushrooms are considered especially susceptible because of their shape and the methods used to grow them.

Botulin is produced when spores of the common microbe *clostridium botulinum* grow on food in an airless space. The inside of a sealed food container provides an ideal growth medium for these spores, especially in nonacidic foods. One of the primary purposes of heat treatment in canning is to kill the botulinum spores. They are tough, however, and are not destroyed until temperatures are far above boiling. Nonacidic foods must be heated under pressure long enough to permit penetration of the heat to the center of the can.

Failure to allow thorough heat-penetration appears to be one of the reasons for the so-called "mushroom epidemic" of 1973. Fortunately, the contaminated cans were found (quite by accident) before any deaths occurred. This was not the case ten years earlier, in 1963, when nine people died of botulism poisoning from contaminated canned tuna liver paste and smoked whitefish, and again in 1971, when one fatality resulted from botulin in a can of Bon Vivant vichyssoise. Although today the manufacturers are more careful about their processing techniques, the possibility always remains of this happening again, particularly in mushrooms, because they are especially likely to harbor large amounts of botulinum spores due to their very low acidity. Mushrooms are usually grown in horse manure (likely to be rich in spores), and the fluted undersides make thorough washing very difficult.

The Mushroom Processors Association, in apparent concern over consumer apprehension regarding botulism, has set up a program of certification and inspection. Cooperating processors can display the Association's bright blue "process certified" seal on their retail packages. Presumably this will afford protection to the consumer as the Association and its members have a strong interest in maintaining an effective program.

Where products with the Association's seal are not available, the cautious consumer will want to open the can, empty the contents into a saucepan and boil for ten minutes. Although boiling does not kill the spores, it does destroy any toxin that may have formed during storage. (This procedure is also recommended by experts as the safest way to treat *all* home-canned foods after opening, despite some destructive effects upon certain nutrients.) A safe alternative is to use fresh mushrooms, as exposure to air prevents the growth of the toxic bacteria. The public is often advised to avoid bulging cans which indicate that gases are being produced by spoilage inside. However, because a can does not bulge, one cannot assume freedom from botulism. Botulin toxins are the most potent poisons known. The lethal dose in man of botulin toxin is two micrograms; a gram (⅟₂₈ of an ounce) could kill 500,000 people.

Botulin can also occur in frozen boil-in-bag vegetables because such bags provide the vacuum necessary for growth. Researchers from General Foods disclosed the presence of *clostridium botulinum* in six packages of vacuum pouch packed spinach in butter sauce. The six packages were among one hundred packages of several types of vegetables selected at random. Boiling for 10 minutes eliminates the toxin, but what happens to those who undercook their vegetables?

Fruits and Vegetables—A Listing

BEANS

Dried mature legumes such as soy beans, mung beans, lima beans, peas, black beans, cow peas (black eye peas), broad beans, brown beans, kidney beans, garbanzos (chick peas), lentils, white beans, navy beans, and pinto beans are ancient vegetarian staples because they contain substantial protein. The protein is fairly low in quality with the exception of soybeans whose protein quality is almost as good as that of meat. The protein quality of beans can be markedly enhanced by combining with grains. The combination of brown beans and rice, for example, provides 56 percent more usable protein than the two foods taken separately.

Beans are low in fat and, unlike meat, contain virtually no saturated fat.

Beans are good sources of the B vitamins and fairly good sources of some minerals including iron. Beans contain phytic acid, a substance which binds minerals, making some of them unavailable to the system but the concentration is generally less than in grains and nuts. (See "The Phytic Acid Problem," page 100.)

Processing of Beans

Dried beans are one of the most lightly processed foods in the supermarket for they are not subject to intense heat and no preservatives or other chemicals are used in processing. Beans are protected by the pod and therefore are likely to have lower pesticide residues than leafy vegetables or fruits. Pesticides are usually not used as standard operating procedure, but only for specific insect problems.

Toxic Effects of Beans

Beans contain several toxic substances, most notably the trypsin inhibitors. The action of trypsin, the chief protein-digesting enzyme in the body, is impaired by these substances in such a way that the growth of young animals fed a diet of raw beans is retarded. Normal cooking eliminates the trypsin inhibitors and all other toxic factors found in beans generally available in the United States.

Flatulence

Of more concern to most people than possible toxic effects is the notorious tendency of legumes to cause flatulence. In order of decreasing flatus activity legumes rank as follows: kidney beans, California small white beans, pinto beans, mung beans, dried peas, Ventura lima beans, soy beans, fresh peas, Fordhook lima beans, and peanuts. Why beans produce gas is not yet understood and efforts to reduce the effect have been unsuccessful.

Buying, Storage and Cooking of Beans

Bright, uniform color in beans is a sign of freshness. Cracked seed coats and pin holes caused by insect damage are signs of low quality. Beans that are not uniform in size should be avoided as they will not cook at the same rate. Contents of packages bought several months apart should not be mixed because older beans may take longer to cook. Bulk beans, available in some co-op and health food stores, usually differ little in quality from the packaged product found in the supermarket. Quality can be maintained for several months by storing in a dry place at 50° to 70° F. and in a container with tight-fitting lid.

Beans require prolonged cooking time. One way to shorten cooking and also save energy is to soak the beans overnight and then freeze them solid. When ready to cook, add the frozen beans to a small amount of boiling water. This method can reduce cooking time from several hours to less than one hour.

FRUIT, DRIED

For many years, health food enthusiasts have been concerned about the use of certain forms of sulphur (sulphur dioxide or sulphite) as a color preservative in dried fruits. Recent evidence, however, suggests that the chemicals are safe, at least in the concentrations normally used in food, because the digestive system converts them into harmless substances. Nevertheless, the U.N. Joint FAO/WHO Committee on Food Additives does not give them a clean bill of health but calls for more study, including research into possible mutagenic effects.

Sulphited dried fruits are readily recognized by their light colors. During drying, the colors of fruit naturally darken in a process called "enzymatic browning" which can be prevented by sulphur compounds. The resulting light-colored dried fruits are often called "bleached" although the color is closer to that of the undried product. Sulphur is not used for dates, prunes, dark raisins and most figs but is used for apricots and golden seedless raisins. (Golden seedless may range in color from pale green through golden yellow to amber.)

Another additive used in dried fruit is sorbic acid, or potassium sorbate, considered completely safe. These are used as preservatives in dried fruits that have been partially rehydrated to make them softer and more palatable. (Completely dried fruit is extremely hard and tough and virtually impossible to chew unless soaked in water or cooked.) Both of these additives must be listed on the label.

Dark colored dried fruits (without sulphur) may be

partially rehydrated and then preserved by pasteuriza-iton, eliminating the need for preservative chemicals. Such "moist pack" dried fruits have no added preservatives.

According to the standard tables, dried fruits are good sources of iron and hence it is often recommended that women who are deficient in iron should eat these foods.

The high levels of iron in dried fruit may not be as beneficial as the standard tables indicate for iron is poorly absorbed by the intestine from most plant foods. More research will have to be done before the value of dried fruit as an iron source is clarified.

Dried fruits generally contain 67 to 77 per cent sugar and this, together with their tendency to stick to teeth make them highly cariogenic. Most dried fruits are fairly high in calories, averaging 255 to 275 for 3½ ounces.

FRUITS AND VEGETABLES, CANNED

Many believe that canned food will keep practically forever because it is completely sealed, and that storage temperature is unimportant because canned goods do not require refrigeration.

Both assumptions are false. Although canned food is heat-treated and sealed so as to prevent the growth of spoilage bacteria, other deteriorative changes can take place inside the sealed container. To keep these chemical changes to a minimum for long-term storage, temperatures just above the freezing point are best.

Grading the Produce

The U.S. Department of Agriculture has a grade labelling system for fruits and vegetables, but for several reasons it is of limited use to consumers. The grade labels are not based on nutritive value but solely on appearance—color, texture, gloss, absence of defects, and size. The second or third grade may therefore be a better buy nutritionally than the top grade.

Use of the grading system on retail products is optional and its use is not widespread. Furthermore, the system is a model of bureaucratic obfuscation. For example, U.S. No. 1 fresh asparagus are top grade while U.S. No. 1 carrots are second grade. To confuse matters even more, packers often use their own grade labels. These grades, although legal, have no significance except as promotional devices. To be official, "U.S." must appear on the label ("U.S. Grade A," for example).

In addition to buying second or third-grade products buyers of canned goods can save money by buying "mixed pieces" which are usually cheaper than "whole," "halves," or "slices."

FRUITS AND VEGETABLES, FROZEN

Frozen food is usually a very high quality product when it leaves the food processing plant but lack of care in handling and storage by shippers, warehouses and retail stores results in substantial reduction in quality by the time it reaches the dinner table. To retain most nutrients, frozen food must be kept at temperatures below 0° F.

Frozen vegetables appear to remain solid for some time even at temperatures in the 30's, and even when completely thawed can be refrozen without any outward indication of deterioration. Because of the difficulty of detecting improperly stored vegetables, they are often shipped in unrefrigerated trucks, left standing on loading docks in the sun, stored in coolers rather than freezers, and piled too high in open-topped supermarket freezer cases.

There is little a shopper can do to determine the quality of the frozen product while it is still in the package, other than to look for certain signs such as out-of-shape boxes and colored stains on the package which indicate that liquids leaked during thawing. "Pour and store" plastic bulk bags in which the vegetables are clumped together and do not flow freely have probably been thawed and then refrozen. Select frozen foods as the last items in your grocery shopping and ask the clerk for an insulated bag in which to carry them home.

Temperatures of home freezers may also hasten the destruction of nutrients because they are often not set properly to maintain 0° F throughout. For long-term storage, a good quality freezer thermometer should be used to monitor the temperature. Older refrigerator units which have the freezer located within the refrigerator compartment rarely go to below 20° F and thus should be used only for short-term storage of frozen food.

Thawing of Frozen Food

During thawing the number of microorganisms invariably present in frozen foods can increase rapidly to extremely high levels not only because of increased temperature but also because freezing breaks down many of the food tissues making them more susceptible to bacterial attack. Juices that leak out of thawing foods are rich in nutrients, providing ideal breeding grounds for bacteria. Fortunately, the thawing temperature which is safest from a bacteriological point of view—32° to 40°—is also the best for retention of nutrients. Frozen foods should be thawed at refrigerator temperature, not at room temperature.

FRUITS AND VEGETABLES, FRESH

A consumer will develop the ability to choose top quality produce only by experience but some general advice may be useful. To begin with, it's wise to open prepackaged produce and examine individual items for mold, overripeness, shriveling, and wilting.

Along with more specific buying advice, the following listing includes information on proper storage. For most of the fruits and vegetables listed, the *ideal* storage conditions are shown in parentheses, usually in terms of temperature and relative humidity (RII). A thermometer and a hygrometer are essential for finding the spot in the refrigerator that is closest to the ideal. By adjusting the refrigerator temperature, you should be able to approximate the ideal conditions in at least one area of your refrigerator. Where crushed ice is recommended as the ideal storage medium, the produce should be packed in the ice, not placed on top of it.

Apples

Look for firmness, crispness, and at least some bright-red color. Avoid those that yield to slight pressure on the skin. If buying in quantity, cut one open and if it is brown inside, reject the lot. Refrigerate. (32° F. and 90 per cent RH)

Apricots

Look for plump, juicy-looking fruit with uniform, golden-orange color. Ripe fruit will yield to gentle pressure on the skin. Avoid very firm dull-looking, pale-yellow or greenish-yellow fruit. Ripe apricots should be eaten as soon as possible or refrigerated for a day at most. (32° F. and 90 per cent RH)

Artichokes

Choose plump, globular artichokes, heavy for their size, with compact, thick, green, fresh-looking scales. Avoid those with spreading scales, large brown areas on scales, or grayish-black discoloration. Use as soon as possible, but if you must store them, keep in a plastic bag in the refrigerator. (35° F. and 90 per cent RH)

Asparagus

Buy those with closed, compact tips, smooth round spears, and rich green color covering most of the stalk.

The stalk should be tender down through most of the green part, should be almost round, and should not have vertical ridges. Avoid excessively sandy asparagus. Use as soon as possible, but if you must store, wrap the butt ends in a damp towel and keep in the crisper section of the refrigerator. (32° F. and 90 per cent RH)

Avocados

For immediate use, buy slightly soft avocados that yield to gentle pressure on the skin. Firm fruit will be ready to eat in a few days after ripening at room temperature. Avoid avocados with dark sunken spots. Ripe avocados will keep for several days in the refrigerator. (Unripe: 50° F. and 80-85 per cent RH)

Bananas

Buy bananas that are bright looking, firm, have green tips and are free of bruises. Bananas are best for eating when the yellow color is speckled with brown. Avoid those with dull, grayish appearance. Green-tipped bananas can be ripened at room temperature. Fully ripened bananas can be stored for several days in the refrigerator. (Green bananas: 50° F. and 80-85 per cent RH)

Beets

Beets should be firm, round, smooth over most of the surface, have a rich, deep-red color, and have slender main roots. Avoid elongated bulbs, those with scaly areas on top, and those with wilted greens. Beets can be stored briefly in the refrigerator but cut tops off first.

Beet Greens (See Spinach)

See spinach.

Blackberries

See raspberries.

Blueberries

Look for those with dark-blue color and a silvery bloom. Smaller berries tend to be tastier. Eat as soon as possible. (32° F. and 90 per cent RH)

Cauliflower

Curds should be creamy-white, compact, and clean. Slightly granular curd texture is not objectionable if surface is compact. Very small green leaflets extending through the curd are also not objectionable, but reject those that have begun to flower. Green color on the jacket leaves is a sign of freshness. Refrigerate in a plastic bag. (32° F. and 90 per cent RH)

Celery

Stalks should be fresh, crisp, rigid, glossy, and with light or medium green color. Leaflets should be mostly green and fresh or only slightly wilted. Avoid celery with discolored centers in branches. Refrigerate in plastic bag. (32° F. and 90 per cent RH)

Cherries

Look for bright, firm, glossy, plump-looking surface and fresh-looking stems. Sweet cherries should have a very dark color. Refrigerate. (32° F. and 90 per cent RH)

Chicory

See endive.

Collards

See spinach.

Corn

Look for fresh, succulent green husks, silk ends that are free from decay and stem ends that are not too discolored or dried. Plump but not over-large kernels are desirable. Eat corn the day you buy it, but if you must delay, refrigerate. (32° F. and 90 per cent RH)

Cucumbers

Cucumbers should be firm over their entire length, have many small lumps on the surface. Avoid very large cucumbers. Cucumbers can be stored in the refrigerator for a few days. (45° F. and 80-85 per cent RH)

Eggplant

Buy smooth, heavy, uniformly dark-purple plants, avoiding those with irregular dark-brown spots. Use as soon as possible, but if you can't, refrigerate for a day or two. (50° F. and 80-85 per cent RH)

Endive, Escarole and Chicory

Look for fresh, crisp yet tender plants with green outer leaves. Use within a day or two. Refrigerate in plastic bag. (32° F. and 80-85 per cent RH)

Figs

Ripe figs are best. Ripeness is indicated by degree of softness. Sour smell indicates overripeness. Figs are very perishable but will keep for a few days in refrigerator. (32° F. and 90 per cent RH)

Garlic

Choose large bulbs with big cloves. Store in cool, dark place away from onions and potatoes.

Grapefruit

Look for firm, bright-looking fruit, heavy for its size. Rough, ridged, or wrinkled skin may indicate pulpiness and lack of juice. Avoid those with soft discolored areas near the stem end. Grapefruit can be kept at room temperature for several days but longer if refrigerated. (50° F. and 80 to 85 per cent RH)

Pink grapefruit is not artificially colored. The color actually comes from a form of carotene, a vitamin A precursor that is naturally present in the fruit, making the red variety more desirable from a nutritional standpoint than the white which has insignificant amounts of this nutrient.

Grapes

Buy plump grapes that are firmly attached to the stem. White or green grapes are sweetest when the color has a greenish cast, or straw color with a tinge of amber. Red varieties are better when red predominates on all or most of the grapes. Avoid grapes with whitish areas around the stem. Refrigerate in plastic bag. (35° F. and 90 per cent RH)

Kale

See spinach.

Leeks, Shallots, Green Onions

Look for fresh, green, crisp tops with white portions extending two or three inches up from root end. Avoid those with yellowing tops. Refrigerate in a plastic bag. (32° F. and 90 per cent RH)

Lemons

Look for firmness, rich yellow color, reasonably smooth skin with a slight gloss. Coarse or rough texture indicates thick skin and less usable fruit. (50° F. and 80 to 85 per cent RH)

Lettuce

Iceberg and Romaine leaves should be crisp, while other varieties should have softer (but not wilted) leaves. Medium to dark-green color is desirable in most varieties. Avoid iceberg lettuce that is very hard, those with irregular shapes, and those that lack green color. Do not buy any lettuce with tan or brown area at margin of leaves. In storing, rinse, shake out excess water, and refrigerate in plastic bag. (Crushed ice storage is preferable.)

Limes

Buy limes with glossy skin that are heavy for their size. Avoid those with dry skin. Refrigerate. (50° F. and 80 to 85 per cent RH)

Loganberries

See raspberries.

Melons

There is no sure guide to determining quality of melons from the outside, but some indicators are fairly reliable. Cantaloupes (muskmelons) should have a delicate melon aroma and no traces of a stem but should have a pronounced cavity where the melon was cleanly pulled from the vine. Netting should cover the cantaloupe thickly, while background color under netting should be slightly golden or a light greenish-gray. Avoid dull, dark-green background color and lopsided or heavily indented melons. A slight rattling of the seeds is a sign of maturity. (However, loose, watery seeds indicate over-maturity.) Fully mature honeydews should have a pleasant fragrance, should be creamy-white or pale yellow, should be at least six and one-half inches in diameter, and should weigh about five to seven pounds. Avoid small honeydews with greenish-white exterior, for these do not usually ripen. If the honeydew is hard but otherwise acceptable, let it stand for several hours (or days) away from sunlight, pre-refably in high humidity, until mature. Both honeydews and cantaloupes are mature when characteristic aroma appears and when they are slightly soft at the blossom end. In watermelons, look for a dull rather than a shiny surface, with the underside turning a light yellowish color. Whole watermelons are chancy, so consider precut pieces. When buying, avoid those with hard white streaks running lengthwise, and look for red flesh and brown or black seeds.

Do not cut any melon before it has ripened. Ripe melons of any variety can be kept for up to a week in warmest part of refrigerator. (50° F. and 80 to 85 per cent RH)

Mushrooms

Mushrooms should be small to medium in size, with caps either closed or moderately open, with pink or light-tan gills. The surface of the cap should be white or creamy. Mushrooms grown in some areas are acceptable if cap is light brown. Avoid mushrooms with discolored gills or caps. Refrigerate in plastic bag but do not wash until ready to use. (32° F. and 90 per cent RH)

Nectarines

Look for bright, rich color, plumpness, and a slight softening on the seam. Nectarines can be ripened at room temperature and can be held for several days in refrigerator after ripening. (32° F. and 90 per cent RH)

Okra

Buy bright-green, blemish-free pods under four and one-half inches long, with tips that bend under very slight pressure. Avoid those with hard body. Refrigerate in a plastic bag. (50° F. and 80 to 85 per cent RH)

Onions

Onions should be hard, firm, dry, have small necks, be covered with papery scales, and be reasonably free from sunburn spots and other blemishes. Avoid sprouting onions. Store in a cool, dark cupboard away from potatoes. (50° F. and 80 to 85 per cent RH)

Onions, Green

See leeks.

Oranges

A greenish cast or green spots are not a sign of immaturity. Some Florida oranges are colored with the dye Citrus Red No. 2, despite the FAO/WHO Expert Committee's recommendation that "it should not be used as a food color." Dyed oranges (including temples and tangelos) need not be stamped "color added," and retailers rarely post a sign saying "artificially colored oranges" as required by law.

Russeting, which is a lacy, brownish blemish on the skin is not indictive of poor eating quality. Pick firm, heavy oranges with bright-looking skin. Avoid those with very rough surface, which indicates thick skin and lack of flesh. Store in refrigerator. (45° F. and 80 to 85 per cent RH)

Parsley

Look for fresh, crisp, bright green leaves. Refrigerate in plastic bag (Crushed ice storage is preferable.)

Peaches

Pick those that are fairly firm or becoming slightly soft and with yellow or creamy color between the red areas. Avoid those with green color and those that are very hard or very soft. Ripen at room temperature. If ripe, peaches can be refrigerated briefly. (32° F. and 90 per cent RH)

Pears

Look for firm pears that have begun to soften slightly. Bartletts should be pale to rich yellow. Bosc pears should be greenish-yellow to brownish in color. Anjous or Comice should be light green to yellowish green. Winter Nellis should be medium to light green. Avoid pears with spots on sides or blossom ends. Ripen pears in a warm place. Refrigerate ripened pears. (32° F. and 90 per cent RH)

Peppers

Peppers should be medium to dark green, glossy, relatively heavy for their size, and have firm walls. Store in refrigerator door shelf. (50° F. and 80 to 85 per cent RH)

Pineapples

Look for fragrant pineapple odor and "spikes" or leaves that are easy to pull out from the top. The fruit should be firm, heavy for their size, and the eyes should should be plump and glossy and show a slight separation. Avoid pineapples with slightly pointed eyes and dull yellowish-green color. Eat pineapple as soon as possible, but if you must store, keep in a plastic bag in the refrigerator.

Plums and Prunes

Choose fairly firm to slightly soft fruit, avoiding those with brown discoloration. Ripen firm fruit at room temperature. Refrigerate ripened fruit. (32° F. and 90 per cent RH)

Potatoes

Potatoes should be firm, clean, relatively smooth, reasonably well shaped, and with no splits, cuts, or cracks. New (immature) potatoes may look as if they are peeling, but this does not indicate poor quality. Mature potatoes should not be peeling or have sprouts. Some red potatoes are artificially colored and waxed.

Harmless green patches may develop on potatoes exposed to artificial light, but when exposed to sunlight such green areas are often high in solanine, a poisonous chemical related to nicotine and atropine. Several instances of poisoning have been attributed to eating green potatoes high in solanine. There is no way for the consumer to tell whether the green areas are caused by sunlight or artificial light. George Borgstrom, a leading expert on food products, declares that even potatoes packaged in bags with window openings are potentially poisonous unless turnover is rapid.

Store in cool, dry cupboard away from onions. 45° F. and 80 to 85 per cent RH)

Radishes

Buy firm, plump, round, medium sized radishes with strong red color. Remove tops and store in refrigerator crisper bin. (32° F. and 90 per cent RH)

Raspberries, Blackberries and Loganberries

Choose berries with bright, clean appearance, uniform color, and with no attached stem caps. The individual cells of the berry should be plump and tender but not mushy. Avoid those with stains on the container. Eat as soon as possible, but refrigerate if necessary for a day or two. 32° F. and 90 per cent RH)

Rhubarb

Stems should be tender, bright, and glossy looking and largely pink or red (although some of good quality are predominantly light green). Avoid fibrous stems and those very slender or very thick. Use as soon as possible, or refrigerate briefly if you must. (32° F. and 90 per cent RH)

Shallots

See leeks.

Spinach, Collards, Kale, Beet Greens, Swiss Chard

Look for young, tender, blemish-free leaves. Spinach leaves should be dark green, crisp and large. Beet greens and ruby chard should have a reddish color. If you cannot use as soon as possible, refrigerate in plastic bag. (Crushed ice storage is preferable.)

Squash, Summer

Summer squash varieties, such as crookneck, straightneck, and zucchini should be tender, firm, and with glossy skin. Use as soon as possible, but if you must store, refrigerate in a plastic bag. (32° F. and 90 per cent RH)

Squash, Winter

Winter squash, such as acorn, butternut, buttercup, and Hubbard, should have a tough rind and be heavy for its size. Keep in cool place. (50° F. and 80 to 85 per cent RH)

Strawberries

Choose those with bright-red lustrous color, firm, dry flesh, and with cap stem still attached. Avoid those with large uncolored areas. Don't judge solely on the appearance of berries at top of container, but examine those at the bottom also. Refrigerate for two or three days at most. (32° F. and 90 per cent RH)

Swiss Chard

See spinach.

Sweet Potatoes

Moist sweet potatoes, often called yams, have orange-colored flesh and are much more popular than the dry sweet potatoes that have paler flesh. In either type, look for firm, bright, uniformly colored skin, free from cuts. Store in cool, dark place. (50° F. and 80 to 85 per cent RH)

Tangerines

Look for deep-yellow or orange color and bright luster. Tangerines that don't feel quite firm are usually acceptable, but avoid those that are very soft. Avoid greenish or very pale yellow fruit. Store in refrigerator crisper bin. (32° F. and 90 per cent RH)

Tomatoes

As most supermarket shoppers have found to their annoyance, the old-fashioned jucy tomato has been largely replaced by the thick-skinned, cardboard-tough agribusiness product. These are grown with little regard for flavor, the major consideration being the yield per acre and the ease of handling. Cherry tomatoes, greenhouse tomatoes, and those imported from Mexico are usually more acceptable. Generally, the best will be found in roadside stands in season. "Vine-ripened" tomatoes are actually picked at the pink stage, before full ripening, and are usually as unacceptable as the non-vine-ripened. Tomatoes can be ripened at room temperature but only if they have not been refrigerated previously. (The ideal ripening conditions for mature green tomatoes are 65-70° F. and a relative humidity of 85-88 per cent.) After ripening, store in warmest part of refrigerator. (45° F. and 80 to 85 per cent RH)

Turnips

Turnips should be small or medium in size, smooth, fairly round, and firm. Store in cool humid place.

Watercress

Watercress should be fresh, crisp, and have a rich green color. Avoid those with yellow leaves. Store in plastic bag in refrigerator crisper bin. (Crushed ice storage is preferable.)

POTATOES, PROCESSED

The potato has suffered more maltreatment at the hands of processors than any other vegetable. Frozen french fried potatoes and potato chips are almost always cooked in hydrogenated fat, a questionable substance.

Dehydrated potatoes are less objectionable, but it seems likely that their nutritional value is less than in properly prepared fresh potatoes because of storage losses and because the peel and possibly some of the valuable nutrients under it are removed. Vitamin C is destroyed in the dehydration process and hence some products are fortified with synthetic vitamin C.

What little protein there is in potatoes is of surprisingly high quality; it is better than in soybeans, and equal to eggs! Calorie-for-calorie, potato chips and french fries have considerably less nutrients than freshly made potatoes or dehydrated potatoes. Nutritionally, baked potatoes are superior to mashed.

SOY PROTEIN, PROCESSED

An acre in soybeans will supply enough protein to last a man for over six years; an acre in wheat, rice or corn will keep a man for two or two and one-half years; an acre in poultry will keep him for six months; an acre in beef will keep him for two months. Natural soybeans have a very high protein content (34 per cent as compared to only 15 per cent for a choice grade beef carcass) and, moreover, the protein is of fairly high quality. For these reasons, there has been increasing interest in shifting from animal protein to soy protein.

Soy flour, soy grits and other processed soy products have been used for years at low levels in baked goods, in sausage and in other processed foods, not as protein extenders but as emulsifiers, binders and texture improvers. In recent years, however, many supermarkets have been selling meat that has been extended with textured soy protein while several food processors now sell a textured soy protein that the consumer himself can add to meat. There are at least half a dozen different types of processed soybean products now used in foods sold at retail:

Soy flour and soy grits are made by removing the hull and grinding the bean. Used primarily as ingredients in baked goods and meat products but also available as cooking ingredients in health food and co-op stores. The grits have the same composition as the flour but are more coarsely ground. Most flour and grits are defatted by solvent extraction. Protein content is 40 to 60 per cent.

Soybean concentrate, which is made by removing most of the oil and water soluble nonprotein parts of the beans, is used in processed meats and baby food. Protein content is at least 70 per cent.

Isolated soy protein is processed in a way that removes even more of the nonprotein parts of the bean. The phrase "isolated soy protein" rarely appears on retail food package labels because most of it is processed into textured protein. Protein content is 90 per cent or more.

Textured soy protein, also called **textured vegetable protein** and **textured spun soy protein,** is produced by a complex process of extrusion or spinning from soybean isolates, soybean concentrates, soy flakes or soy flour. It is the main ingredient in packaged meat extenders such as Plus Meat (J. H. Filbert Co.), in dry meat analogs such as BacOs (General Mills) and in canned meat analogs such as those sold by Worthington Foods. It can be mixed with hamburger sold at retail up to the 25 per cent level. Protein content of textured soy protein is 50 to 90 per cent. Textured soy protein, unlike canned beans or home processed beans, is devoid of flatus activity.

Hydrolized vegetable protein, a name that appears on many ingredients listings, is ordinarily not added for its protein value but to bring out the natural flavors in such foods as sauce mixes, instant soup, and canned meat products.

In soybean processing, the oil is extracted from the solid part with the use of a solvent, usually hexane, residues of which may remain. Although hexane is chemically inert, the Food and Agriculture Oraganization of the U.N. believes that more information is needed before its safety can be judged.

Processed soybeans may, like unprocessed legumes, contain phytic acid, a substance that can decrease the availability of magnesium, calcium, zinc, iron, manganese, copper, molybdenum, and possibly other minerals. At least one expert on plant protein has noted the possibility of improving the availability of minerals in processed soybeans by combination of steaming under pressure and the addition of stubstances called chelating agents. Much work, however, remains to be done in order to develop this processing method.

Processed soybean does not equal meat in protein value, has somewhat lower vitamin content, and because of phytic acid may be considerably inferior in mineral availability. Meat is the principal source of trace minerals in the American diet and thus its replacement with soy products could adversely affect trace mineral intake unless substantial amounts of vegetables which also contain trace minerals are consumed.

SPROUTS

Sprouts from such seeds as soybeans, mung beans, and alfalfa have long been regarded as miracle foods by some health food advocates because they are still growing when consumed and hence supposedly contain "life force." Sprouts are not exactly miracle foods but are quite nutritious.

An extensive investigation of vitamin content in sprouts from a variety of seeds was conducted in the late forties and early fifties by a group of Indian researchers who found that the content of every vitamin, with the exception of folic acid, increased significantly two days after germination and continued to increase until at least the fourth day.

Much of the mineral content in cooked beans is bound up by phytic acid and hence is unavailable to the system. In sprouts, however, this is less of a problem because much of the phytic acid is eliminated in the sprouting process.

Sprouts can be grown at any season, need very little space and do not require much expertise. For beginners, the easiest beans to sprout are mung beans, which are available in most health food stores. The beans should first be soaked in warm water for eight hours in a warm place such as a kitchen. Use four times as much water as beans (e.g. one-half cup beans to two cups water). Rinse in cool water and place the drained beans in an opaque container, with a wide diameter opening (containers made of unglazed pottery, china and plastic are suitable but avoid metal and wood). Cover container loosely and let stand at room temperature with only the water clinging to the beans. Every eight hours or more often, if practical, rinse seeds and pour off water. The sprouts are usually harvested when they are between ½″ to 4″ long or three to six days after initial soaking.

Among the seeds suitable for sprouting are alfalfa, garbanzo, lentil, millet, rye, wheat, sunflower and soybean, each of which has its distinctive flavor.

Sprouts from these seeds are suitable for eating raw or cooked and can be used in salads, soups, breads, and a variety of recipes.

TOMATO-BASED PRODUCTS

Like fresh tomatoes, canned tomatoes and other packaged tomato products supply appreciable amounts of vitamin A and C, although there is some loss in processing and storage. Prolonged storage, particularly under high temperatures, reduces vitamin content.

Much more worrisome than losses in processing and storage is possible lead contamination in canned tomato products. Tomatoes are highly acidic and hence can leach large amounts of lead from the soldered seam in the can. Enamel lined cans offer some protection if the linings are perfect. Dr. Beverly Paigen, author of *Toxic Metals: The Persistent Poison* (in press) feels that the overall exposure to lead is so high that it is important to reduce exposure wherever possible, for example, by choosing tomato products in glass jars rather than cans. (The advice applies to canned citrus products, which are also highly acidic.)

Canned and jarred tomato products differ primarily in their concentration of tomato and in seasoning. These products do not usually contain any questionable additives, but depend upon salt, spices, vinegar and other such traditional ingredients for their flavor. However, in recent years processors have introduced several products with questionable additives such as Mott's Clamato Juice, the only widely distributed tomato product with artificial color.

CHAPTER IV

Cereals

The Great Bread War

Whole wheat bread is no better than white enriched, says Dr. Fredrick J. Stare, Emeritus Professor of Nutrition at the Harvard School of Public Health, while the consumer writer Sidney Margolius claims that white bread provides more nutrients per dollar. On the other hand, numerous critics of white bread call it "absorbent cotton" or "balloon bread," pointing to the heavy nutrient loss in processing. Recently the well-known British cancer expert, Dr. Dennis Burkitt, suggested that white bread is associated with a host of diseases, including cancer of the bowel and heart disease.

The almost theological nature of this controversy is suggested by its vocabulary. In the lexicon of health food enthusiasts terms like "whole," "unrefined," and "natural," are opposed to "unnatural," "depleted," "plastic," "dead," or "robbed," words which accurately describe, according to these individuals, common white bread.

To understand the controversy, we must first know what happens to wheat when it is milled. Wheat consists of three parts: the bran coat, which protects the seed and which accounts for 12 per cent of the grain by weight; the germ or embryo, which accounts for 3 per cent; and the endosperm, the starchy segment which accounts for 85 per cent. The objective of conventional wheat milling is to extract as much pure endosperm as possible. The endosperm, crushed and sifted, is what we know as white flour while most of the bran and germ becomes animal feed.

Enrichment

Some of the strongest attacks by natural food advocates are not made on plain refined flour and bread but on products that have been enriched. Enriched products are seen as even more pernicious, since they give the illusion of being as nutritious as the whole grain, but actually lack some of its nutrients, especially some of the B complex and trace minerals.

The criticism is well taken for enrichment is a halfway measure. Under FDA regulations, flour may be enriched with vitamins B_1, B_2, niacin, and iron. Vitamin D, calcium and wheat germ may also be added, but since they are usually omitted most of the nutrients lost in milling are not restored to "enriched" flour.

The milling of white flour results in a loss of more than two thirds of the thiamin (B_1), riboflavin (B_2), niacin, vitamin B_6, folacin, vitamin E, iron, phosphorus, magnesium, potassium, copper, manganese, and zinc found in the whole grain. In addition, 40 to 60 per cent of the pantothenic acid, calcium, molybdenum, and chrominum are lost. Selenium is the only nutrient for which losses are less than 2 per cent.

Health Improvements Due to Whole Wheat Bread?

Due to shortages during World War II, several European governments decreed that bread be made from relatively unrefined flour. Advocates of whole grains often cite improvements in health which they claim are due to an increased consumption of whole wheat bread. Although it is true that the incidence of coronary heart disease decreased during this period in several northern European countries, the role of whole wheat bread is not clear. Decreased consumption of sugar and animal fat and the increased exercise necessary during wartime may well have had more influence on the rate of heart disease than any increase in whole grain consumption.

A substantial reduction in the incidence of dental caries (cavities) also occurred during and following World War II, as indicated by studies done in England, Norway, and Japan. The reduced availability of sugar, candy and other sweets is cited as the primary cause, but a corresponding increase in other less cariogenic foods, such as whole wheat bread, might have been beneficial. Some evidence indicates that whole grains help reduce the incidence of tooth decay in animals.

On the other hand, ill-health due to an increase in the consumption of whole wheat bread has also occurred. During World War II, the government of Ireland introduced whole wheat flour as a replacement for white flour, but unlike the English national flour, it was not enriched with calcium, with the result that rickets increased considerably among children. (Rickets resulted from insufficient calcium for building bones during growth, thereby producing deformities of the legs, arms, and even the skull.) Apparently, the calcium in the whole wheat was bound by phytic acid, which is milled out of white bread.

The Phytic Acid Problem

Unless measures are taken to lessen its effect, phytic acid can bind up not only calcium, but other minerals as well and can, under certain circumstances, cause iron deficiency anemia, and retarded growth from zinc deficiency.

Phytic acid is found in the seeds of a wide variety of plant foods, including not only grains but also nuts and legumes (but not to any extent in leafy vegetables, roots, or fruits).

Dr. Robert S. Harris, a leading authority on food products, has called phytic acid "the most important of the substances present in edible plants which interfere with nutrition." The detrimental effects of phytic acid have been apparent for many years in India and the Middle East, but up to now there has been little concern regarding American diets, which are rich in such phytate-free foods as meats, eggs, and dairy products. Recently, however, American scientists have become concerned because increasing number of people are adopting "natural" food and vegetarian diets including large amounts of whole grains, nuts, seeds, and legumes. A leading text on cereal chemistry notes that a possibly serious calcium deficiency might result if brown bread (high in phytic acid) is substituted for white bread (low in phytic acid) at the same time that calcium-rich milk and cheese are severely restricted.

The seriousness of the problem in one of its extreme forms is indicated by the case of Iranians and Egyptians who consume large quantities of a type of unleavened whole wheat bread high in phytic acid. The phytic acid combines with iron and zinc, causing anemia, arrested sexual development and dwarfism. Following World War II, Japanese children experienced increased heights and weights. These increases were attributed to greater intake of animal protein, but now it has been suggested that a more likely explanation is the reduction of phytic acid and a consequent increase in the zinc content of the postwar diet.

The quantity of minerals made unavailable by phytic acid varies. The maximum amount of phosphorus tied up may vary up to 90 per cent in grains, 72 per cent in legumes, 59 per cent in chocolate, 50 per cent in nuts, and 16 per cent in fruit.

A given amount of phytic acid can only tie up so much mineral, and therefore a large supply of minerals in the diet can overcome the harmful effects of phytic acid. Thus calcium, which is quite abundant in most Western diets containing milk or milk products, is supplied in sufficient quantity to overcome the effect of phytic acid. This is not so, however, for other minerals such as iron, zinc and magnesium which are widely undersupplied in the American diet. Intake of iron, for example, is marginal in the diets of many women of childbearing age, and thus increased phytic acid could result in serious problems. Phytic acid may tie up other trace minerals such as chromium, manganese and molybdenum.

Under the right conditions, whole grains and seeds can themselves reduce their own phytic acid content by the formation of the enzyme phytase which breaks down the phytic acid, releasing the minerals.

As a general rule, phytase forms only during sprouting. However, wheat, rye, and to a certain extent barley and buckwheat, are exceptions. If these four grains are moistened and kept warm for several hours (e.g., 100° F for two hours) most phytic acid will be eliminated in the rye and wheat, and a considerable amount from barley and buckwheat. Since these conditions occur during the yeast fermentation step in breadmaking, many breads made with these grains will not bind up minerals to an appreciable extent.

The phytic acid in other foods such as oats, corn, peanuts, sunflower seeds, and soybeans may be reduced by eating these foods in sprouted form when practical.

The phytase enzyme can withstand more heat than many other enzymes and is not destroyed until temperatures go above 180°F. Wheat bran contains extremely high levels of phytic acid, but it also contains substantial quantities of phytase, and by soaking overnight at room temperature, phytic acid is significantly reduced. Soaking in warm water (104° F) for only two hours may destroy 100 per cent of the phytic acid present in wheat bran. A yogurt maker can be exceptionally convenient for this purpose because it can maintain the soaked grain at about the optimal temperature for an extended period.

Vegetarians should emphasize a balanced diet from a variety of sources including dairy products and leafy vegetables, both of which are good sources of some minerals. Variety, in conjunction with known methods of reducing phytic acid, should prevent the development of possible mineral deficiencies. Strict vegetarians (no dairy products) should be particularly on guard against possible deficiencies due to phytic acid.

As a group, vegetarians in America and Europe enjoy health at least equal to that of meat eaters and have no apparent problems that can be attributed specifically to a high intake of phytic acid. There has not, however, been any study which focuses specifically on the problem of phytic acid among vegetarians. Future studies may well reveal some vegetarian eating patterns in which the compound plays a detrimental role.

High-Fiber Bread

Widespread interest in the possible value of fiber in the diet led to the marketing of at least one "high-fiber" bread by most of the nation's leading bakeries. Many of these breads are similar to the makers' usual whole grain bread, but with added fiber in the form of wheat, soy or corn bran.

Many consumers, however, do not like the resulting coarse, dark whole grain bread. To appeal to those who prefer "white" bread, the ITT Continental Baking Company (makers of Wonder Bread), introduced Fresh Horizons, a white bread with two grams of fiber per slice and reduced calories. Fresh Horizons was the first commercial bread to use powdered cellulose (from wood pulp) as a fiber source. Powdered cellulose is bland and white and thus can be added in large amounts without significantly affecting the flavor or texture of the bread.

Wood cellulose does not appear to be harmful, but it is not very beneficial either. Cellulose is only one form of a complex group of substances known collectively as "fiber," and has far less effect on the body when compared to other sources of fiber such as the hemicellulose in bran or the pectin in fruits. Cellulose absorbs water and thus can be beneficial in preventing constipation. However, grinding cellulose into a fine powder (necessary to make it palatable in bread), reduces this ability to absorb water, making cellulose-containing breads of marginal value.

Studies done with student volunteers at Cornell University by Dr. Peter Van Soest, a noted expert on dietary fiber, indicated that breads made with coarse natural bran were a far more effective source of fiber than the powdered cellulose breads.

The Nutritive Value of Grain

The protein in grains is generally considered of lower quality than in meat, poultry, fish, eggs, and dairy products. Protein quality is measured by the pattern of the eight essential amino acids; the pattern in the egg is often taken as the ideal because the body is able to utilize its particular combination of the amino acids more efficiently than of any other food. Grains and cereals, as compared to the egg, are particularly deficient in the amino acid lysine. Because of this deficiency, cereals alone are not a good source of protein for the growing child, but some studies suggest that they are adequate for adults. Grains are good sources of minerals, the B vitamins, and fiber.

One way to improve the protein quality of cereals is to eat them with foods high in lysine, such as fish, meat, dairy products and beans. Several breakfast cereals now on the market are fortified with soybean mixtures and thus have superior protein.

Cereals—A Listing

BARLEY

Whole grain barley is comparable in nutrient value to whole grain wheat and rye. Although barley flour is sometimes called for in recipes, the whole grain or the "pearled" form is most often used.

Pearled Barley

Pearled barley, also called "pot barley," has had the outer husk removed by abrasion. Since the vitamins are concentrated in the husk, this form has substantially lower levels of vitamins than whole barley. Surprisingly, however, the protein value for pearled barley is virtually identical to that of the whole grain since the important amino acids are concentrated in the endosperm rather than the husk.

The differences in vitamin values between whole and pearled barley are not significant in the small amounts of the grain that are called for in most recipes. Many of the natural foods cookbooks, however, offer recipes that feature barley as the main ingredient and for these dishes whole barley is preferable.

Malted Barley

Malted barley, which is barley that has been sprouted, forms the basic raw material for beer and whiskey production but little of the nutrients survive alcohol processing. Liquid extracts of malt, which retain much of the nutrients of the sprouted seeds, are used in malted milk and as flavoring in certain breakfast cereals.

Sprouting of grains and seeds results in increased levels of most nutrients, and while the changes are not as spectacular in barley as in some other grains (such as oats) they are still significant. Most amino acids also increase in the malting process, notably lysine, which reaches a level in malt double that in an equal amount of whole wheat. Malting also eliminates the phytic acid in barley, making the minerals more available.

Malted barley has a distinctive sweet flavor that can add new interest and nutritional value to many dishes that call for rice, millet or buckwheat. Many find it appetizing as an ingredient in homemade granola.

BREAKFAST CEREALS

Breakfast cereals lose most of their vitamins and minerals through over-refining of the grain. In addition, by discarding the lysine-rich germ, the refining process lowers the protein quality.

Perhaps most important in the lowering of protein quality are the losses of lysine due to the browning process. In the presence of heat and moisture, a reaction takes place between lysine and sugar which is called the "Maillard Reaction," commonly known as "toasting." The reaction can be so severe, particularly in flaked, puffed and expanded cereals, that virtually all the lysine is destroyed. This means that most breakfast cereals containing sugar are apt to have very little usable protein. The package labels show the gross protein, a figure which can be extremely misleading if most of the lysine is destroyed.

The low nutritive value of most cereals was dramatized in a study conducted by Dr. Constance Kies of the University of Nebraska and Dr. William Caster of the University of Georgia. In this study thirty-eight packaged breakfast cereals were fed to rats as their sole source of nutrients. Twenty of the cereals failed to keep the rats alive while an additional twelve resulted in little or no growth. Only two of the cereals, Quaker Life and Post Oat Flakes, promoted excellent tissue growth. These two brands probably tested well because of lysine in the grains. The low nutritive value of most cereals as revealed by the Kies-Caster study was corroborated by a somewhat similar study published by Consumers Union.*

The Enrichment of Cereals

In an effort to make up for losses in the milling process and also to provide extra nutritive value, the cereal manufacturers usually add up to eleven synthetic nutrients: vitamins A, B_1, B_2, B_6, B_{12}, folic acid, C, D, E, niacin and iron. These are usually added to a level to provide either one-third or 100 per cent of the minimum daily requirement in a one-ounce serving.

* Unfortunately, CU made growth the sole basis for recommendations to their readers and ignored other relevant criteria such as the presence of questionable additives or the absence of deficiency symptoms. All cereals tested by CU, with the exception of Kretchmer's Wheat Germ, produced deficiency symptoms. Using growth as the sole criteria, CU ended by recommending three cereals with questionable additives while downgrading wheat germ, which is probably the single most nutritious food in the supermarket.

In one sense, fortified cereals are deceptive for you are given the comforting illusion that your cereal is superior to the original grain while in actuality you are denied many nutrients lost in processing including others in the B complex, magnesium, zinc, and trace minerals. It is true that those whose diets are largely refined foods are better off with the added nutrients than without them but it is likely that they would benefit from getting the entire range of nutrients found in the whole grain.

"High Nutrition" Cereals

In recent years, the cereal industry has realized the promotional value of protein, vitamins and minerals and has tried to exploit consumer fears about the absence of these nutrients in the diet while providing a minimum of nutritional improvements in their product. Perhaps the most blatant examples of this practice are Product 19 and King Vitamin, both of which placed in the bottom group in the animal feeding tests referred to previously. Both have artificial color while King Vitamin also has artificial flavor. (King Vitamin is 47 per cent sugar and only 33 per cent grain!) Total (contains artificial color) fared only moderately better than these two cereals in the animal studies.

Special K is the only cereal in this group which received good ratings in both of the animal feeding tests. Although not made from whole grains, it has some of the nutrients restored by the addition of wheat germ.

Children's Cereals

At the bottom of the nutritional barrel are the cereals designed especially for children. Virtually all have over 30 per cent sugar and many have close to 50 per cent. Fruity Pebbles has 47 per cent, Captain Crunch has 41 per cent, Alpha Bits has 42 per cent, while Super Sugar Crisp has 43 per cent, which is greater than the grain content. Needless to say, children's cereals are laced with unspecified artificial colors and flavors.

Bran Cereals

Crude bran of the type commonly available from health food stores is being increasingly used for its fiber content. The wisdom of using large amounts of crude bran has been questioned, as it is very high in phytic acid. The phytic acid in one ounce of crude bran ties up 387 mg. of calcium or almost half the Recommended Dietary Allowance for an adult male. Wheat bread fortified with as little as 7 per cent bran cuts absorption of iron in half. Although this does not indicate that whole wheat bread in moderate quantities is inimical to health, it does strongly suggest that large quantities of bran should not be taken, particularly by those who may be deficient in iron, for example, very young children and women of childbearing age. Other minerals, such as zinc, may be deficient in many American diets, and may also be affected by bran.

The Kellogg Company has promoted its All Bran cereal as a good source of dietary fiber. The arguments against crude bran should logically apply to this type of product also, but with less force because, not being 100 per cent bran, it has less phytic acid. It would nevertheless seem unwise to depend on large amounts of either product as the principal source of fiber if only because it is advantageous to get substantial fiber from a variety of plant foods.

It is possible to eliminate much of the phytic acid in bran, since it also contains large amounts of the enzyme phytase, which under the right conditions readily breaks down the phytic acid. (See "The Phytic Acid Problem," page 102.)

Granola and "Natural" Type Cereals

Granola is not a standardized commodity like corn flakes, but it is a loosely defined group of products based on lightly processed grain, usually rolled oats, and containing in addition such ingredients as wheat germ, dried fruit, nuts, oil, non-fat dry milk and a sweetener, which may be honey, molasses, sugar or some combination of these.

In revulsion against the flaked and puffed products of the major cereal companies, many have switched to granola, either homemade or store bought. Most of the commercially made brands are less than ideal from a health standpoint for they contain substantial amounts of sugar. Brown sugar is the second leading ingredient in Kellogg's Country Morning ("The All Natural Cereal"), General Mill's Nature Valley Granola Cereal ("100 per cent Natural"), Quaker 100% Natural Cereal, and Pet's Heartland Natural Cereal. Brown sugar, of course, has virtually no more nutrient value than white sugar. Several products, such as Familia, imported from Switzerland, have a very low sugar level.

Most of the granola-type cereals contain saturated (but unhydrogenated) vegetable fat, usually about 15 to 25 per cent. Familia, with only 7 per cent, has less than other widely available "natural" cereals.

Some recipes for homemade granola call for honey to be added before baking to a golden brown. The browning process, which occurs through the interaction of lysine and sugar or honey, results in the loss of lysine, a loss that can be avoided by adding the sweetener after baking.

Hot Cereals

Roman Meal (both instant and five minute types) and Wheatena are made from whole grains and hence are superior to other hot cereals made from refined grains such as farina. Farina is made of wheat from which the bran and germ have been removed but some brands, such as Nabisco Cream of Wheat, are fortified with wheat germ and hence are preferable to plain farina. Cream of Rice, is based on white rice. Rolled oats, including the "old fashioned," quick and instant types are very lightly processed cereals which retain most of the nutrients of the original grain. However, because they have a particularly high phytic acid content, most of the minerals are not available and hence these would be a poor choice for children to eat on an everyday basis. For adults, on the other hand, they may be beneficial because of the ability to lower serum cholesterol. (See "Oats," page 118.)

Maypo 30 Second Oatmeal with Maple Flavor was rated first among forty-four cereals by Consumers Union on the basis of its ability to promote growth in rats and, presumably, children. Nonetheless, Maypo is a questionable product for children, because of its sugar content and artificial flavor. (Growth-promoting ability should not be the only criterion for evaluating a cereal in mixed diets.) Other flavored hot cereals such as Instant Quaker Oatmeal and Nabisco Mix and Eat Cream of Wheat have considerable sugar and contain artificial flavor.

Choosing a Breakfast Cereal

In choosing a breakfast cereal it would seem wise to ignore the claims for vitamin and mineral enrichment and instead concentrate on cereal's unique quality as a good source of certain trace minerals and of fiber. On this basis, overmilled cereals such as farina or corn flakes, which lose much of their minerals and fiber in processing, would be eliminated. Flaked and puffed cereals, even though made from whole grains, are suspect because of severe heat processing; when made with sugar, the protein losses are particularly severe. Most children's cereals and some adult cereals are suspect not only because of sugar content but because of artificial color and artificial flavor.

When these considerations are applied, most cereals are found wanting. Among a few good cereals widely available are oatmeal, Ralston (regular or instant), Roman Meal, Wheatena, Familia, Kellogg's All Bran, Kretchmer Wheat Germ, and Shredded Wheat. (Shredded Wheat may look highly processed, but actually it is very lightly processed and, moreover, contains no sugar.)

BUCKWHEAT

Despite its name, buckwheat is not botanically related to wheat and technically is not even a cereal grain but rather a herbaceous plant.

Buckwheat Flour

Most buckwheat consumed in the United States is in the form of flour. Twenty per cent of the husk and germ is removed to produce "dark" buckwheat flour while about 50 per cent is removed for "light" buckwheat flour. Dark buckwheat flour thus retains many of the vitamins and minerals of the whole grain but the light flour loses much more of these nutrients.

Dark flour has about twice the protein of light flour and contains almost three times as much lysine as whole wheat flour. Dark buckwheat flour is also unusually high in the amino acid tryptophan, making it a good complementary protein for corn, which is low in both trytophan and lysine (most buckwheat pancake recipes call for a combination of these two flours).

Buckwheat flour is most frequently used to make buckwheat pancakes. Some health food stores carry pancake flour made from dark buckwheat flour. Although made with light flour, "Aunt Jemima Buckwheat Pancake and Waffle" mix is unusual for the supermarket as it contains no artificial flavors, colors, antioxidants or other questionable additives.

Buckwheat Groats

Buckwheat groats come from chopped whole buckwheat kernels and are even higher in nutritive value than dark buckwheat flour. When sauteed in oil and then simmered in water, buckwheat groats are called kasha and are used in various Jewish and Middle Eastern dishes. A slightly milder flavor results if buckwheat groats are simply added to boiling water and cooked like rice.

CORN PRODUCTS

Corn is milled in much the same way as wheat to produce several products including corn meal, hominy, and hominy grits. It is considerably lower in nutrient value than wheat, rye, oats, and the other grains.

Corn Meal

Corn meal contains almost all of the germ and bran portion of the corn kernel, retaining most of the nutrients of the whole corn from which it is milled. It is often referred to as "old-fashioned," "stone-ground," or "water ground" corn meal.

Yellow corn meal is higher in vitamin A than white corn meal, but other nutrients are similar. Bolted corn meal has had much of the hull removed with sieves and contains about three-fourths of the nutrients in whole corn meal while degermed corn meal contains less than half the nutrients of whole meal.

Hominy Grits

Hominy grits, also called "corn grits," are processed similarly to coarsely ground white wheat flour. In the Southern U.S., hominy grits, or just plain "grits" as they are often called, are popular in a variety of dishes.

Hominy grits are a highly refined product, almost completely free of the corn germ and bran, and contain about one-third to one-half of the B-vitamins found in the whole corn.

Hominy

Hominy, which is usually consumed as a canned white corn, has even less nutritional value than hominy grits. White field corn is boiled in a two per cent lye solution for about twenty-five minutes to loosen the skins from the kernels. It is then washed to check the action of the lye and bleached with a dilute solution of sodium bisulfite, which in turn is removed by boiling in water. After packing in cans, hominy is processed at 240° F for about one and one-half hours. Virtually no nutritional value remains other than calories following such arduous processing.

MACARONI

Refined macaroni products such as spaghetti and noodles lose so much of the nutrients in processing that eating them every day for a main dish, as in some Italian-American households, is a questionable practice.

Macaroni is made from semolina, the coarse granular product obtained from the endosperm of durum wheat. In processing, the product is enriched with iron, niacin, thiamine, and riboflavin, but other nutrients lost in bran and germ are not restored. A pound (cooked) has less than 0.5 grams of fiber as compared to about 8 grams for a pound loaf of whole wheat bread.

The FDA has issued standards of identity for whole wheat macaroni products, but these products are ordinarily available only in health food stores and at a premium price. Whole wheat macaroni, like other unleavened whole grain products, probably has considerable phytic acid and thus much of its mineral content is probably not available to the body.

A considerable amount of lysine is lost in the processing of macaroni, making its protein value inferior to the whole grain. Egg noodles, an exception, have protein quality equal to the whole grain. The protein quality of macaroni could be improved by the addition of soy flour or synthetic lysine. The FDA has established a standard of identity for soy reinforced macaroni products, but such products are not widely available.

The packages often suggest a range of cooking time, e.g., ten to fourteen minutes. With the minimum time less of the water-soluble B vitamins will be lost.

The keeping qualities of both regular and whole wheat macaroni are excellent.

MILLET

Millet, a strongly flavored grain, is of little importance in Western diets, but is popular in the Orient and Middle East. In terms of vitamin and mineral content, it is the richest grain available. In protein quality it ranks somewhat below wheat and rye, but in other essential amino acids it closely resembles the ideal proportions of eggs. For this reason, it is exceptionally good as a complementary protein with legumes and dairy products which are high in lysine but low in methionine.

OATS

Oats are somewhat higher than wheat in protein quality. Like other cereal grains, they have low levels of lysine, although recent studies show that methionine is the limiting amino acid in oat protein. Since milk is also low in methionine, the combination of the two does not significantly increase the total value.

Although oats also contain substantial quantities of minerals, especially calcium, phosphorus and iron, the high levels of phytic acid in rolled oats reduces the availability of these minerals. In moderate amounts this should not be a problem, but it would be unwise to feed this cereal to children as a staple. However, oatmeal may be of value to those with elevated blood cholesterol levels. The addition of rolled oats to the diet has been shown to reduce blood cholesterol significantly in both animals and humans.

Whole Oat Grain

Whole oat grain is the unprocessed form as harvested. The tough, inedible outer hull is of little nutritional value, and this form of oats is valuable only for sprouting.

Sprouting substantially increases the levels of certain B-vitamins, including an amazing 2000 per cent increase in riboflavin (B_2) and a 436 per cent increase in the niacin content. Sprouting also activates the destruction of phytic acid by oat phytase, thus releasing the minerals in oatmeal for use by the human body. (Directions for sprouting seeds and grains will be found in Chapter III, "Fruits and Vegetables," page 95.)

Oat Groats

The oat groat is produced by removing the outer hull which contains few nutrients. Thus the groat, which contains the germ, bran and endosperm, has virtually the same nutrients as the whole grain.

Steel Cut Oats

Steel cut oats (or "Scotch oats," as they are often called), are made by cutting the groats into granular pieces with steel rollers. They have essentially the same nutritive value as groats. To be palatable they require longer cooking than rolled oats.

Rolled Oats

Rolled oats, the form most often used as a breakfast cereal, are made by flaking the groats. They are made in two varieties, the regular and the quick-cooking which has smaller flakes to facilitate water absorption. Nutritive value of the two varieties is identical. Rolled oats are incorrectly called "oatmeal." The vitamin value of rolled oats and steel cut oats is identical; their protein value is also similar.

Oat Flour

Much of the germ and bran of the groat remains in the flour and, therefore, this product is almost as nutritious as whole groats or rolled oats.

PUMPERNICKEL

See Rye.

RICE

Brown Rice

Unprocessed rice is known as "paddy" or rough rice. To make brown rice, the hull is removed by abrasion between rubber-covered rollers, This very mild processing preserves virtually all of the nutrients.

According to the statistics on nutrient value, brown rice would seem to be superior to other types. Like other whole grains, however, it has a high phytic acid content which binds much of its minerals, making them unavailable to the body

Another problem with brown rice is rancidity. Brown rice contains more oil than the highly-milled rice and hence is more susceptible. Rancidity can be delayed by keeping the product tightly capped in the refrigerator.

White Rice

White rice goes through processing which removes nutritionally valuable bran and germ. Most white rice is enriched with thiamine, niacin and iron, but this does not make up for more than a dozen other nutrients lost in processing. The FDA regulations permit riboflavin enrichment but this nutrient is usually not added because it turns the rice yellow. White rice has far less phytic acid than either brown or converted rice.

The nutritious parts which are milled out of white rice are the rice bran and rice polish. The rice bran contains the outer cuticle of the bran and the germ, while the polish contains the inner cuticle layer of the bran. These products, which have very high levels of nutrients, are used mostly as animal feed although some are sold through health food stores. Because of the high phytic acid content, particularly in the bran, much of the mineral in these products is unavailable to the body.

Converted Rice

Parboiled, or converted, rice is made by placing rough rice in a vacuum tank, running hot water through it at high pressure to dissolve the nutrients from the bran and germ and draw them into the center of the grain. The rice is then dried and milled similarly to white rice. Converted rice lies midway between brown and white rice in nutrient value. Converted rice, because it loses the bran coating, is probably lower in phytic acid than brown rice. It will not go rancid as quickly as brown rice and also has greater resistance to insects because the processing destroys the insects, eggs and larvae and hardens the shell for protection against pests.

Quick-Cooking Rice

Quick-cooking rice is made by soaking, cooking, and then dehydrating the grain. The grain is dried so that it has a porous open structure that facilitates quick rehydration when it is added to boiling water. The nutritive value is somewhat less than enriched white rice, making this the least nutritious form of the grain.

Rye

Rye Flour and Bread

Rye is comparable to wheat in nutritional value but the milling is so mild that dark rye flour has more vitamin and mineral content than whole wheat flour. According to the standard tables, the protein in rye is about the same as in wheat, but some studies done with laboratory animals suggest that its quality may be considerably higher than that of wheat.

Rye contains such an active phytase that under common baking conditions almost all the phytic acid is eliminated, even though dark rye flour contains substantial amounts of rye bran. Thus the minerals in whole rye bread, which are at a higher level than in wheat, are more available to the body than those in whole wheat bread.

In selecting rye bread, look for those which list rye flour as the primary ingredient, especially if it is "whole rye flour" or "dark rye flour." A unique rye bread currently available is Pepperidge Farm Sprouted Rye, which contains, in addition to rye flour as the primary ingredient, stone ground 100 per cent whole wheat flour, sprouted rye kernels, sesame seeds, sunflower seeds, raw wheat germ, molasses and honey, along with other ingredients.

Rye is susceptible to the growth of a poisonous mold known as "ergot." Symptoms of ergot poisoning, also known as "St. Anthony's Fire," include spasmodic contracting of the arm and leg muscles leading eventually to gangrene and other effects. A less severe form produces headache, giddiness, cramps, weakness and constipation. The use of the chemical preservatives calcium propionate or sodium propionate prevents the growth of ergot and other molds. This is one of the few cases where the "risk-benefit ratio" is decidedly in favor of the additives. Opened packages of whole rye bread which do not contain preservatives should be consumed in a few days, especially under humid conditions. Rye bread that has become hard and dry does not foster mold growth and will keep for long periods.

Pumpernickel Bread

In Europe, pumpernickel bread is made from unground whole rye kernels which undergo a long steaming process to make them edible. This method produces an extremely dense and very nutritious bread. In the United States, most "pumpernickel" bread available today is made from white wheat flour mixed with some rye flour and then colored dark brown with caramel coloring. Such bread has little nutritional advantage over regular white bread. A dense pumpernickel loaf made from dark rye flour without added coloring is available at stores in certain ethnic communities or even in the delicatessen section of supermarkets.

Rye Grits

Rye grits, coarsely-ground whole rye grain, were formerly used in the manufacture of pumpernickel bread and are very nutritious compared to corn or wheat grits.

WHEAT

Wheat Berries

Whole wheat grains, often called "wheat berries," are sold through health food stores and food co-ops for sprouting, cooking, and home-grinding of flour.

Wheat berries are high in phytic acid, but most of this can be eliminated either by sprouting, or by soaking the grain (several hours in warm water), then spreading it out to dry in the sun, on a radiator, or in a just-warm oven. The heat treatment keeps the grain from sprouting or molding.

When buying wheat berries that are not factory prepackaged, be certain that the original container (sack or drum) is displayed and is labelled specifically for human consumption. Wheat intended for planting is usually coated with a mercury-based fungicide that is extremely toxic.

Bulgur

Bulgur (also called bulgar, bulgor, or "cracked wheat") is simply precooked whole wheat, processed similarly to converted rice and therefore sometimes called "parboiled wheat." The parboiling conserves most of the nutrients by leaching them from the outer layer to the center of the grain. Much of the phytic acid is apparently eliminated through the steeping and the removal of part of the bran.

Bulgur is usually available through health food stores or natural foods co-ops either as whole parboiled grains or in the coarsely milled form called "cracked wheat." It is often used in salads and other cold dishes without further cooking, or it may be cooked as is rice.

In home cooking, bulgur is boiled in just enough water for all of it to be absorbed in 15 to 20 minutes.

Wheat Germ

The most nutritious cereal product obtainable is wheat germ. In the milling of white flour, the germ (or embryo) of the wheat kernel is removed primarily to increase the storage life of the flour (the oily germ becomes rancid quickly and its high levels of nutrients attract insects and rodents).

Although the germ constitutes only about 3 per cent of the weight of the whole wheat kernel, it contains higher levels of virtually all vitamins and minerals than are present in the remaining 97 per cent of the grain. The protein quality of wheat germ is also excellent, with an amino acid pattern approaching that of animal proteins. Because of its high nutritive value, wheat germ is an important component of animal feeds and is appearing increasingly as a breakfast cereal with milk and as a recipe ingredient.

Health food advocates usually extol the virtues of raw wheat germ, yet experiments have shown that toasting actually increases its nutritive value. Since plain wheat germ does not contain any sugar, lysine is not lost through the Maillard reaction during toasting as it is in most breakfast cereals nor is it lost in the processing of sugared wheat germ such as Kretchmer Cinnamon Raisin for the sugar is added after toasting.

White Flour and White Bread

The two principal types of white flour available in the supermarkets are all purpose flour, which is bleached and contains no leavening, and self-rising flour, which is also bleached but contains leavening.

The traditional method of making raised baked goods, such as bread or biscuits, relies on yeast fermentation. In this process active dry yeast organisms are added to a flour-water mixture and under the proper conditions of warmth and moisture the yeasts grow, giving off carbon dioxide gas in the process. In self-rising flour, the carbon dioxide gas is produced not by natural yeast fermentation but instead by the relatively instantaneous chemical reaction of an acid with sodium bicarbonate (baking soda) when the dough is baked. Self-rising flour has made possible the phenomenal rise in the sales of prepared biscuit, pancake and cakes mixes.

There are problems with self-rising flour. The resulting chemically-raised baked goods have a "spongy" texture compared to yeast-raised. More importantly, the nutritional value of the product is also affected. Chemically-raised baked goods are more alkaline than yeast-raised which causes appreciable destruction of certain vitamins, such as thiamine (B_1). Self-rising flour is also invariably bleached and thus devoid of vitamin E.

There is also some concern about the presence of harmful impurities in the chemicals used in self-rising flour. Low levels of arsenic, lead, and fluorine, are commonly present.

Aside from these impurities, the chemicals used in self-rising flour (sodium bicarbonate and sodium acid pyrophosphate) do not appear harmful, except that their presence further increases the intake of sodium, a mineral that is overabundant in the American diet.

"White" flour has a slightly cream-colored tinge even after milling has removed all the darker bran and germ. This is due to the presence of a yellow pigment called xanthophyll. Because this pigment is regarded as undesirable by some, the flour is chemically bleached. In recent years the major flour producing companies have been marketing unbleached white flour along with their traditional bleached product.

The two most widely used chemicals for bleaching flour, chlorine dioxide and benzoyl peroxide, appear to be harmless in the quantities usually used but they destroy the vitamin E. The loss of vitamin E is probably not significant in a mixed diet, since the whole grain itself is a poor source of this nutrient. The bleaching of flour serves no nutritional need but neither is it a menace, as some food purists claim.

The Production of White Bread

The essential elements in bread are flour, yeast, milk, water, shortening, salt and a sweetening agent. The large scale bakers of white bread are not geared to make a simple product based on these ingredients alone because their marketing system demands extended shelf life and uniformity of product, characteristics that can only be achieved through use of many additives. The bakers begin with a white flour of low nutritive value which is aged, perhaps with chlorine, an inadequately tested chemical. Aging is necessary to avoid sticky, poor rising dough. The handling characteristics of the dough may then be improved with potassium iodate, the use of which has been termed "highly undesirable" for use in bread by the Food and Agriculture Organization of the U.N. Carrageenan may be added as a thickener in milk added to the dough. The dough may then be bleached with any one of several chemicals that reduce what little vitamin E is present. The resulting loaf is then preserved usually with calcium propionate, which is harmless. The FDA regulations permit more than forty additives, most of which, including the questionable ones, need not be listed on the label. Most of these, with the exception of vitamins, soy flour (seldom used) and preservatives are of little value to consumers but are used for the convenience of the bakers or for cosmetic purposes.

Whole Wheat Flour and Bread

Whole wheat flour is generally made by one of two methods. In the most prevalent method, the miller takes the bran and germ and adds it back to the endosperm flour. If all the bran and germ are added back, the product is 100 per cent whole wheat flour. Some object to making the whole wheat flour in this way, claiming that the machinery destroys taste and/or nutritional values through the heat of friction. Stone ground whole wheat flour is made by the age old process in which the grain is ground between two stones at relatively low temperatures. No reliable studies have been made to show the comparative nutritional value of whole wheat made by the two methods.

The term "stone ground whole wheat flour" can be deceptive. If the whole wheat grain is fed to a stone-grinding mill and all of the resulting ground flour is collected and bagged, an extremely coarse textured flour results. This is what "100 per cent stone ground flour" should ideally consist of. Such flour, however, has poor baking characteristics and hence millers have long desired to produce a "whiter" product which contains less bran and germ. To produce such a flour before the advent of the steel rolling mill (or even today in those mills that use stone grinders), the miller can screen the flour to remove the larger pieces of bran and germ, then run the screened flour through another grinding with the stones set closer together, followed by more sieving. The resulting flour, while still dark in color due to the presence of finely ground bran and germ that cannot be filtered out, does not contain all the original material.

It is difficult for the consumer to determine when this type of flour is used, especially in bread, since the label might read "stone ground whole wheat flour," a term which gives no indication of how much of the original grain remains.

To further complicate matters, flour that has not been stone ground (e.g., steel roller milled) and is labeled "100 per cent whole wheat flour," may actually contain more of the original grain than "100 per cent stone ground whole wheat flour" that has been screened, since the former consists of white flour with bran and germ added back to equal the percentages found in the original wheat grain. Then again it may not.

Much whole wheat flour, particularly that sold in health food stores or in the health food section of supermarkets, does not contain preservatives. Whether stone ground flour without preservatives will keep well is a subject of controversy among millers. It would seem wise to keep stone ground flour in the refrigerator and use it as soon as possible after opening to prevent rancidity.

Genuine whole wheat bread is not necessarily the best possible. Dr. Roger Williams, the noted biochemist and a thoughtful critic of the food industry, significantly does not call for a return to whole wheat bread, nor does he propose that white bread be "enriched" to make it the equivalent of whole wheat, Instead, he advocates the application of scientific knowledge in nutrition to produce, through added vitamins, minerals, and amino acids, a "modern bread vastly *better* than old fashioned whole wheat bread."

CHAPTER V

Meat, Poultry, and Fish

The Ecology of Meat

Farm animals are machines for converting the protein in grass, alfalfa, corn, oats, soybeans, barley and other grains and legumes into animal protein. The machines are unfortunately very inefficient; it takes 5 and one-half pounds of grain protein to produce 1 pound of poultry protein, 8 pounds to produce 1 pound of pork protein, and 22 pounds of produce 1 pound of beef protein.

Not only is meat inefficient to produce, but most Americans consume far more than they need to satisfy their protein requirements. Most of the world's people consume about 500 pounds of grain per year directly as food, but Americans consume almost 2000 pounds a year, most of it indirectly in the form of grain-fed beef, pork and chicken.

Georg Borgstrom of Michigan State University, one of the leading authorities of the world food problem, points out that America must feed not only its two hundred million people, but also its livestock which consume enough protein to feed an additional 1.3 billion humans. On a global scale, cattle eat enough to feed almost nine billion people or nearly three times the world's human population. If all the cattle in the world could be put on a giant scale, they would outweigh all the people in the world by five to one.

Spokesmen for American agribusiness deny the evidence favoring a reduction in meat consumption. Yet according to Jean Mayer, the Harvard nutritionist, a 10 per cent cut in meat eating by Americans would release enough grain to feed sixty million people.

The Need for Meat

Whether meat-eating or vegetarian, we must get protein in order to survive. By weight, humans are 18 to 20 per cent protein, its bulk distributed in the muscles, skeleton, skin, adipose tissue and the blood. All body cells and most body fluids contain protein. Protein is essential for growth and is related to such vital functions as carrying oxygen to the tissues.

The quality of protein is measured largely by the balance of its constituent amino acids. There are eight essential amino acids which must be obtained through food to maintain life: tryptophan, threonine, isoleucine, leucine, lysine, valine, the sulphur-containing amino acids (methionine and cystine), and the aromatic amino acids (phenylalanine and tyrosine). In addition, histadine is essential for infants. The essential amino acids are utilized by the body as a group.

Our bodies not only require that all of the essential amino acids be consumed simultaneously (or at least at the same meal), but that they be provided in roughly the proportions found in the egg. The egg, at least from the protein standpoint, comes close to being the perfect food. Conformity to the proportions of amino acids in the egg and, to a lesser extent, digestibility of the food, are used as a measure of protein quality.

Meat, poultry, and particularly fish have amino acid patterns that are well balanced and hence these foods are considered to have high protein quality. Plant foods, on the other hand, are generally low in at least one amino acid. Cereals, for example, are low in lysine while legumes are low in the sulphur-containing amino acids. Some plant foods, however, such as soybeans and potatoes, have protein quality almost as good as that of beef. Moreover, when plant foods are combined the protein quality may be enhanced. A combination of cereals and legumes will supply better quality protein than either one separately, since the extra sulphur-containing amino acids in the cereals make up for the deficiency in the legumes while the extra lysine in the legumes makes up for the deficiency in the cereals.

The protein in plant foods is sufficient for health as evidenced by the experience of many vegetarians who do not eat even dairy products or eggs. Harvard nutritionist Mark Hegsted, an authority on vegetarian diets, puts it this way: "It is difficult to obtain a mixed vegetable diet which will produce an appreciable loss of body nitrogen [protein] without resorting to high levels of sugar, jams and jellies, and other essentially protein-free foods."

Meat, poultry, and fish provide substantial vitamins and minerals but with the exception of vitamin B_{12}, adequate quantities of these nutrients are provided by plant foods. On the other hand, only plant foods provide fiber. Meats, even lean cuts, tend to have substantial amounts of saturated fat while all animal foods contain cholesterol. Meat, fish and poultry are good sources of certain trace minerals but plant foods and particularly grains also have substantial amounts.

Nutrients in Meat, Poultry and Seafood

Meat products, particularly processed pork and all cuts of fresh meat that are not well trimmed, are high in fat and hence high in saturated fat and calories. Poultry and seafood, particularly shellfish, are, on the other hand, low in fat. Meat, poultry, and seafood generally are high in iron and the B vitamins while liver from any animal is an outstanding source of these nutrients as well as vitamins A and C.

Meat Inspection

Harvard nutritionist Jean Mayer has said that if he were looking for fraud in the food industry, he would start with meat inspection. "It is a scandal. It's never worked. For seventy years, we've had a movement to clean up the slaughterhouse and it's not working yet.

Best proof of it is Massachusetts, where most of the [state] government inspectors are under indictment for bribery."

Federal inspection, which is mandatory for all meat plants engaged in interstate commerce, is fairly effective in preventing contamination at the slaughterhouse and processing plant level, but only 80 per cent of all meat is covered. State inspection, which covers most of the remaining meat processing plants, is not as effective, primarily because it is considerably more susceptible to political pressure by the processors. The retail supermarkets and independent butcher shops, which are state or municipally regulated, are inspected even less thoroughly. Federal inspectors are in the plant as long as it operates, but state inspectors generally go home at the end of seven hours, leaving any unscrupulous processors free to subvert the law after hours. Retail inspectors may make as few as six visits a year to a large supermarket, often announcing their arrival in advance. There is little you can do to insure that the meat you buy is adequately inspected.

Pesticide Residues

All food contains pesticide residues, but animal products—beef, pork, poultry, dairy and fish—tend to concentrate the chemicals. Big fish eat many smaller fish, cattle eat enormous quantities of grass or feed, and with each meal the concentration of pesticides stored in their tissues increases. A 1969 report showed that meat, fish, and poultry as a group had ten times as much residue of DDT and its breakdown products as green leafy vegetables, eight times as much as fruit, seventeen times as much as legumes, ten times as much as grains and twenty-four times as much as root vegetables. When we eat animal products we become, in effect, the ultimate concentrator of such residues.

While some pesticides have caused cancer in laboratory animals, many experts doubt the chemicals are carcinogenic to humans at the relatively low levels found in food. Other equally qualified scientists strongly disagree.

Even those skeptical of the adverse effects of pesticide residues believe that it is still important to intensify research into possible relationships of these chemicals to cancer, birth defects, nervous disorders and many other diseases.

Pesticides have their most dramatic effect not on man, but on wildlife. Several species at the top of the food chain such as the American bald eagle are threatened with extinction, but the mosquito, which is the prime target of DDT in malaria control, is fast becoming resistant. The ecological problems of pesticide use appear, at the moment, to be far more threatening than the problem of toxicity in meat and other food.

Antibiotics

The modern system of fattening cattle is based upon confining the animals to feedlots where their food can be controlled precisely and where their movements are restricted to enhance accumulation of fat. The unsanitary conditions of the feedlots would not be possible without the use of antibiotics. Modern chicken growing, with its confinement of thousands of chicken in a limited space—often three or four to a small cage—also depends upon antibiotics. Both cattle and poultry are given antibiotics primarily to prevent, not cure disease and, more importantly from the feeder's viewpoint, to promote increased growth. The antibiotics are given continuously in the feed at considerably lower levels than would be used in curing disease.

The practice, which started in 1950 on a commercial basis, began to generate controversy in the early sixties when a British fact-finding committee reported evidence that antibiotic-resistant strains of salmonella and other pathogens had become established. Since then much of the controversy has centered on the question of whether antibiotics used in animal feeding are becoming less effective in treatment of human disease. Of eight antibiotics widely used for animal feeding, six are used in treatment of humans (chlortetracycline, oxytetracycline, penicillin, bacitracine, neomycin sulphate and erythromycin). Despite this, proponents of antibiotics in animal feeding claim that efficacy in human use has not declined.

Over 75 per cent of the meat and meat products in the U.S. comes from animals that have been treated with antibiotics. Many of these animals have illegal residues at the time of slaughter. According to a 1969 study, such residues may possibly account for the apparently widespread hypersensitivity to antibiotics. Undercooked meat is most likely to contain residues as all but one of these antibiotics are destroyed in cooking.

Hormones

Since 1947 the synthetic hormone DES (diethystil-bestrol) has been used in chicken feed and since 1954, in cattle feed because of its ability to promote greater weight gains on less feed. In laboratory tests with several varieties of animals, DES has caused cancer of the breast. Ordinarily, a chemical shown to be carcinogenic in animal tests would be banned under the Delaney Amendment to the 1958 Food, Drug and Cosmetic Act, but the Amendment was revised in 1962 to permit carcinogenic drugs for animal use if no residues are found after slaughter.

In 1971, several cases of a rare type of vaginal cancer among young women were found to be caused by their mothers' use of stilbestrol to prevent miscarriage fifteen to twenty years earlier. This finding, together with the revelation that residues in meat were more widespread than believed, created a public outcry that led to the banning of DES by the FDA in 1973. In early 1974, the ban was overturned in federal court on a technicality, again making its use legal.

Despite strong opposition from the meat industry, the FDA managed to finally ban the use of DES, as an additive to animal feed and as a subcutaneous (under the skin) implant, on July 20, 1979.

Even though DES was banned, other hormones, some of which may be carcinogenic, are still permitted.

Most experts believe no threshold exists below which a carcinogenic substance can be declared safe. Because of the carcinogenic risk, many countries including Argentina, France, Germany, Sweden, and Italy have banned use of hormones in livestock. Unless federal action is taken to ban all hormones, the only way for meat eaters to avoid possible exposure to potentially harmful residues is to buy organically produced meat. However, this may not be the easiest course of action because of the difficulty of finding organic producers.

The meat industry has frequently argued that if hormones are banned, the cost of meat to the consumer would increase significantly. According to the USDA's own figures, banning of DES will cost the average consumer less than 2 cents a week.

Toxoplasmosis

Perhaps the most serious consequence of eating undercooked meat is the occurrence of toxoplasmosis, a disease considered to be one of the leading causes of birth defects, outranking rubella, cystic fibrosis, muscular dystrophy, congenital syphilis or phenylketonuria (PKU).

Toxoplasmosis has been overlooked by physicians until recently, but the disease is now called "the commonest infection in the world" and is believed to affect over seventy-five million Americans, most of whom are unaware that they have it.

Toxoplasmosis results from the action of a protozoan parasite which enters the body and lodges in the tissues in much the same way as trichinosis. During its life cycle, the protozoa lives in the bodies of several animal hosts. Housecats are the principal transmitters of the disease to humans, but it can also be transmitted by pork and lamb (but rarely by beef). Unless thoroughly cooked, pork and lamb are likely to transmit toxoplasmosis to humans. In most persons such an infection has little noticable effect except symptoms of minor infection (rash, swollen lymph glands, etc.), but some individuals suffer severe reactions leading to complications which resemble typhoid fever. Death may occur in rare cases.

Of particular concern is congenital infection—the transmission of the protozoa from the pregnant mother to her fetus. Infected in this way, there is a strong likelihood that this causes birth defects and in particular, blindness and brain damage. Even when the infant is born normal, the protozoa can remain dormant for twenty to thirty years and then become active, causing brain damage and blindness.

The most critical time for infection of the pregnant woman either from cats or undercooked meat is in the first trimester. In animal experiments, mothers exposed to toxoplasma soon after conception transmitted the disease to their offspring over 80 per cent of the time.

Everyone, but particularly pregnant women, should scrupulously avoid eating undercooked pork or lamb, and also rare hamburger as some hamburger contains pork or is put through the same grinder as pork.

Meat and Cancer

Cancer as a result of heavy meat eating? Some researchers suggest there may be a connection.

In areas where beef consumption is high such as Scotland, North America, Australia and New Zealand, the incidence of large bowel cancer is considerably greater than in areas of low beef consumption such as Central America, sub-Sahara Africa and Japan. Moreover, the incidence of large bowel cancer has declined in Australia coincident with a decline in beef consumption. Among Japanese immigrants to the U. S. there has been an increase in bowel cancer coincident with an increase in meat eating.

Another study based on statistics from twenty-eight countries found a correlation between high animal protein intake in general and cancer of the colon. Still another analysis, this one based on data from thirty-seven countries, found a significant correlation between cancer of the colon and breast cancer with a high fat, high animal protein diet.

Experiments with laboratory animals lend weight to evidence from these statistical correlations. Dr. Roy L. Walford of the University of California School of Medicine reported in 1971 that rats and mice fed at one third the normal level of calories and protein lived up to twice as long as normal and developed 10 per cent to 60 per cent fewer cancers than better-fed animals. Dr. Robert Good, a leading immunologist and director of the Sloan-Kettering Cancer Research Center, working with Dr. David G. Jose of the University of Minnesota, found that laboratory rats and mice fed a reduced protein diet enjoyed increased resistance to certain types of breast and blood cancer. However, their experiments indicate that too great a protein deprivation creates susceptibility to cancer.

A possible explanation has been advanced by a group of British researchers who, pointing to the apparent correlation between cancer of the colon and dietary fat, suggest that fats provide an environment in the intestines that favors the growth of carcinogen-producing bacteria.

Another explanation has been advanced by Dr. Willard J. Visek of Cornell University, who believes that protein in excess of bodily needs results in the formation of ammonia at potentially harmful levels. Because ammonia accumulates in the lower bowel, Dr. Visek suggests that it may be related to the high incidence of bowel cancer that occurs in America and other countries consuming large amounts of meat.

Americans eat far more protein than they need. According to the Food and Nutrition Board, the average male (23-50 years, 154 lbs.) should get 56 grams of moderately high quality protein and the average female (23-50 years, 128 lbs.) should get 46 grams. These allowances include a generous 30 per cent cushion to allow for individual variation. Typical meat menus consumed by Americans provide 100 or more grams of usable protein per day or twice the allowance.

It should be emphasized that most scientists do not accept the theory that excess protein as such is carcinogenic. Many, however, warn against the possibility that meat may contain known or suspected carcinogens, such as nitrites, hormones, and pesticides. Some researchers claim that to the extent nonfibrous foods such as meat replace plant foods (generally high in fiber) the possibility of colon cancer and other diseases is enhanced. (See Chapter XI, pages 316-322.)

Charcoal Broiled Steak and Cancer

The charred outer layer of charcoal broiled steak contains high levels of the carcinogenic hydrocarbon, benzo(a)pyrene. An average 4 ounce portion of well-done steak (8 ounces raw) contains the quantity of benzo(a)pyrene present in the smoke of 135 cigarettes. It appears that substances in the melted fat are decomposed as it drips onto the hot coals, producing the carcinogens which are then deposited on the meat as the smoke rises. In other methods of cooking such as gas or electric oven broiling or roasting, the decomposition does not occur and hence no carcinogenic hydrocarbons are produced.

According to Drs. William Lijinsky and A. E. Ross, of the Chicago Medical School, the harmful effect of charcoal broiling may be lessened (but not eliminated) if the meat is not allowed to contact the cooking flames, if the steaks are cooked for a longer period at lower temperatures, and if meat with a minimum of fat is used.

An even greater hazard than eating the steak may be inhaling of the smoke during the charcoal grilling, and hence those who work as grill cooks may be at risk from lung cancer.

Meat, Poultry and Fish —A Listing

CHICKEN

Before 1930, poultry-raising was generally a small-scale enterprise. Farmers' wives customarily earned pin money by keeping a flock of chickens and selling them to the local poultry buyer when cash was needed. All chickens then were raised "organically." Today, almost all chickens are raised in factories holding ten thousand or more. Concentration indoors permits breeders to control closely the chickens' rate of growth through the optimum combination of feeding, heating, lighting, and other environmental conditions. The crowded conditions cause stress, which is conducive to disease, including chicken leukemia. In order to reduce stress and consequent infection, the chickens are heavily doused with antibiotics and tranquilizers. Those with chicken leukemia cannot be sold but an undetermined number may find their way to the retail refrigerated cases because of inadequate inspection. A clear relationship between chicken leukemia and human disease has not been established.

Feeding of antibiotics at a low level is necessary in the crowded and sometimes unsanitary environment of the factory, but is a questionable practice in terms of human health. Despite all the medicine, chicken is a carrier of bacteria, most particularly of salmonella, which causes nausea, vomiting, chills, fever, and may be fatal to infants and the elderly. Salmonella poisoning is extremely widespread and is often incorrectly diagnosed as "flu" or as some other virus-caused disease. About half of all chicken contain salmonella bacteria. (The FDA traced one hundred deaths to foodborne salmonella poisoning in 1970.) Fortunately, salmonella bacteria are destroyed in normal home cooking, but the real problem occurs when salmonella bacteria contaminate raw food such as salad vegetables. Separate cutting boards for salad vegetables are recommended.

Chickens are prone to develop coccidiosis, an ulceration of the intestinal lining caused by protozoa which breed in the chicken excrement. The disease is apparently not a threat to humans but the coccidiostats, which are chemical agents used to suppress the protozoa, may be harmful. The FDA requires that coccidostats be removed from feed several days before slaughter, but there is, of course, no assurance that this is always done.

Chicken will keep without spoilage for about eighteen days at 32°, about eleven days at 37°, and only two days at 68°. Supermarkets can, with the unlikely combination of good management and good intentions, deliver all chicken to retail customers without spoilage. However, optimum quality is incompatible with the supermarket type of distribution because chicken should be eaten within eight to twenty-four hours of slaughter for maximum flavor. The water in which most chicken carcasses are soaked during processing also contributes to poor flavor. The chickens are frozen and when thawed, the water leaches out, taking much of the flavor and some nutrients with it.

All poultry moving in interstate commerce must be federally inspected for wholesomeness, and the plants processing such poultry must be inspected for sanitation. The retail customer will not often find the USA inspection label on the outside of the chicken package, but in the paper in which the eviscera are wrapped. Often, the federal inspection stamp is missing altogether from the retail package but appears only on the shipping container. Because of the many opportunities for deterioration in transit and in the store, federal inspection does not guarantee wholesomeness but is preferable to state inspection of chicken.

In addition to federal inspection for wholesomeness, there is also a federal grading system on the health of the bird and the absence of defects, but it is not always used by the industry. U.S. Grade A chicken, the highest grade, is usually worth the price premium not only because it is likely to have better flavor but also because the grade is indicative of more conscientious processing.

Chickens in supermarkets are usually classified as broilers, which weigh about 2½ pounds, fryers, which weigh 2½ to 3 pounds, roasters which weigh 3½ to 5 pounds, fowls, which are older and tougher chickens suitable for stewing, and capons (castrated males), which weigh 6 to 8 pounds. Capons are usually roasted.

Many people are confused by the terms "broiler" and "fryer." The terms are indicative primarily of size and age. Broilers are usually slaughtered at six weeks, fryers at eleven weeks, roasters at twelve weeks or more while capons are kept for eighteen weeks or more. There is more meat per pound on a fryer than on a broiler. Both can be used for frying, broiling, roasting, or barbecuing. Roasting chickens, which have relatively more meat, are supposed to be higher priced than fryers and hence some butchers take advantage of this by trying to sell fryers as roasters.

FISH, CANNED

Canned fish is a more reliable product than fresh or frozen fish which are more susceptible to deterioration in handling and storage. In the processing of canned fish, fairly high temperatures—up to 254° F—are used in the sterilization phase in order to destroy *clostridium botulinum*. Except for substantial loss of thiamine, the vitamins are virtually unaffected by this heat processing. Protein loss in processing is insignificant. Very few additives are permitted in canned fish and none, with the possible exception of M.S.G., which is rarely used, are inimical to health.

Canned Tuna

For consistently good quality at reasonable prices, canned tuna is far ahead of other widely available fish products. It is a better protein source than steak, and, moreover, contains twice as much niacin and 25 per cent more vitamin B_{12}. Canned tuna is regulated by a federal standard of identity which specifies that only meat from certain types of fish may be labelled as "Tuna." All tuna is classified as either solid pack, chunk style, flaked or grated, according to the degree to which the muscle is retained intact. Color designations permitted are white, light, dark, and blended. Nutritionally, the differences among the various types are not important: the solid type has slightly more protein than chunk while chunk has slightly more than grated or flaked. Tuna comes packed in oil or water. Water packed tuna has about 16 per cent more protein per can than the oil packed. MSG and various flavoring ingredients may be used but must be listed on the label.

Canned Salmon

Canned salmon, like canned tuna, is a highly nutritious product. Salmon comes in five grades which are, in order of decreasing price, Chinook (also called Spring or King), Red (also called Sockeye or Blueback), Medium Red (also called Silver, Silverside or Cohoe), Pink (also called Humpback), and Chum (also called Keta or Dog). The only additives permitted in salmon are salt and salmon oil, both of which must be noted on the label.

Mercury in Fish

Mercury levels in fish became a serious environmental concern in late 1970 when more than twelve million cans of tuna were removed from the market after samples were found to contain more than the 0.5 ppm level specified by FDA guidelines.

The original shock spurred considerable research on mercury and led to the startling discovery that samples of sixty to ninety-year-old fish taken from museums had levels of mercury comparable to those found in current catches. The obvious conclusion— that man had lived for many years with significant mercury in seafood—helped to allay some of the fear.

There has been no outbreak of mercury poisoning in North America. The toxic level is apparently lower for pregnant women, small children and persons with abnormal metabolism and hence there is still a possible hazard for these groups. Also, dietary deficiencies will enhance the adverse effects of toxic substances. The best course that potentially susceptible individuals can follow may be to switch brands frequently in order to minimize the possibility of ingesting large amounts from a high level lot. Non-pregnant adults in good health apparently need not worry about the toxic effect from either tuna or other fish.

FISH, FRESH AND FROZEN

One of the meanings of "fishy" according to Webster's Third International is "inspiring doubt or suspicion: dubious, questionable, unconvincing." This definition, which undoubtedly has an ancient origin, aptly describes much of the frozen or so-called "fresh" fish available today. Fish are caught by large trawlers which stay at sea for ten days or more. They are then stored in the hold with layers of ice, the fish at the bottom often being crushed under great pressure. The lack of air in the tightly packed mass of fish may hasten decomposition through bacterial action.

The characteristic "fishy" taste, which turns so many people into fish haters, may develop at this point through bacterial action. During the process of distribution many other opportunities for deterioration arise: for example, when the unloaded fish are left on the dock for extended periods, or conveyed in trucks with inadequate refrigeration.

The odor of fresh fish should be mild, the eyes should be bright, clear and bulging, the scales closely attached and iridescent, the gills red and free from slime, and the flesh should not separate from the bones but should be firm and elastic. Except for some seacoast towns where small commerical boats bring in the catch daily, fish like this is difficult to find. Fresh fish from inland lake catches used to be widely abundant but have declined substantially because of contaminated waters.

Today, frozen fish is considerably more important in tonnage than refrigerated fish. The process of freezing toughens fish muscle to a greater extent than it does in terrestrial animals; while drying out, which occurs in the frozen state, may result in loss of flavor and color and contribute to rancidity. Careful handling procedures, including thorough washing before freezing, prevents or reduces bacterial growth. For convenience in the processing cycle, some fish are thawed and refrozen, a process that may result in loss of quality.

Frozen fish are generally cellophane wrapped. A tight moisture proof wrap with no entrapped air provides maximum protection. Breaded fish usually comes in a box with no inner wrap and, therefore, is less well-protected. Unlike plain fillets, breaded fish are precooked, usually in an oil such as corn oil. The batter and breading material provide a good medium for the growth of bacteria. The process of producing and marketing frozen fish, which begins with the catch and ends with the retail purchase, may extend over a year or more and provides many opportunities for deterioration in quality. Temperatures may rise above 0° F during transport from the trawler to the processing plant, from processing plant to wholesale distribution point or retail outlet, and in the retail freezer case where temperatures are often above 0° F. Even at 0° F, flavor will deteriorate after five to six months.

Federal grading of frozen fish is optional with the result that few processors use the grading system. The lack of standards, together with opportunities for deterioration of this highly perishable type of product, account for the generally low and uncertain quality of frozen fish. Consumers Union has conducted several studies of fish. Of 41 frozen fillet products, it graded 25 as either "poor" or "not acceptable." Of 20 fish stick products, it rated 5 as "sub-standard" or "not acceptable." Of 32 breaded fish products, 16 were "not acceptable." Of three brands of frozen salmon steak, all were rated not acceptable because of rancidity. Examination of the Consumers Union reports shows that there is no one brand that consistently gets high marks for quality. Frozen fish, if properly processed, can be a very flavorsome food, as is evidenced by the high ratings given by Consumers Union to some retail brands. Good freezing practice results in virtually no loss of vitamins or protein value.

FROZEN DINNERS, POT PIES, ETC.

Frozen dinners, pot pies, breakfasts and meat entrees are made by quick freezing, a mild process which under proper handling results in little nutrient loss. Significant losses can, however, occur if products are thawed and refrozen.

The advantage of frozen meat products such as TV dinners is, of course, their convenience, but the price is fairly high as compared to home cooked meals with the same quality ingredients. Depending on the brand name, the cost premium may range from 25 per cent to 500 percent for some of the fancier items. One disadvantage shared by nearly all these products is that the user has no control over such additives as salt (sometimes added at the 1 per cent level or greater) and MSG.

Frozen dinners are partially precooked to halt enzyme activity. If the packages are thawed and refrozen, bacteria can multiply at a rapid rate. Consumers Union found evidence of high bacterial counts in several frozen dinners checked in a study done in 1967. CU concluded that the products probably left the plant in wholesome condition but were mishandled in distribution.

The federal government has recently established standards for protein, vitamins and iron in frozen heat-and-serve dinners. An analysis of twelve typical dinners from two manufacturers showed that all the dinners were significantly below the FDA standard for one or more of the nutrients. Federal standards for chicken and turkey dinners require 18 per cent poultry by weight but legally the processor can put as little as 12 per cent into the dinner if the poultry is breaded. Frozen beef dinners, on the other hand must contain at least 25 per cent meat.

Processors of frozen dinners are not required to state on the package the amount of meat and other ingredients and can, within the USDA labeling requirements, manipulate the proportions. According to Consumers Union the processors have, over the years, reduced the amount of meat and compensated by substituting more gravy, potatoes and other inexpensive components.

Frozen entrees, which are composed of frozen sliced meat or poultry with gravy or sauce, are sold under several labels including Banquet, On-Cor, Freezer

Queen, and Stouffer's. The USDA Standards for labelling prescribe the following minimum amounts of meat:

Beef with gravy	50%	Gravy with Swiss	
Swiss Steak with		Steak	35%
gravy	50%	Gravy with	
Poultry with gravy	35%	poultry	15%

The "gravy with" products as shown in the table predominate in the supermarket.

Hamburger

The USDA defines two classifications, "hamburger" and "chopped beef," both of which must be made from fresh ground beef with no meat by-products (such as snout or ears) and with no nonmeat extenders such as soy isolate. Fat content must be no more than 30 per cent. Loose beef fat and seasoning may be added to "hamburger," but nothing may be added to "chopped beef." It is not mandatory for butchers to use the USDA terminology for ground meat. Common names that are widely used are "ground round," "ground chuck," and "ground beef." Round steak before grinding has less than 10 per cent fat while unground chuck has about 15 per cent fat, and the meat from which ground beef is made averages about 25 per cent fat. Added fat is apparently mixed in on a routine basis in many stores. Consumers Union, in a check of Philadelphia stores, found fat content ranging from 5 to 27 per cent in ground beef and 8 to 22 per cent for ground sirloin.

The grinding of hamburger releases fluid from broken tissues and thus provides an opportunity for accelerated bacterial growth. Consumers Union, in its Philadelphia study, found unacceptable levels of coliform bacteria in 73 per cent of samples checked. A seven-city survey reported by the publication *Media and Consumer* showed uncomfortably high levels of coliform bacteria in 9 per cent of all samples checked. Coliform bacteria usually indicate fecal contamination and hence the possibility of disease-carrying organisms. In thorough cooking, the coliform bacteria are largely destroyed, but what happens to those who eat their hamburger rare?

Hamburger presents the unscrupulous meat seller with the opportunity to adulterate in several ways. A study done by the *Buffalo Evening News* revealed illegal additives (mostly dry milk) in seven out thirteen stores checked. A long-standing custom is the adulteration of hamburger with pork. Pork, if not adequately cooked, may cause trichinosis and toxoplasmosis, both of which are threats to those who like their hamburgers rare. Although most butchers probably do not allow this practice, it is unwise to eat store ground hamburger without cooking through to the center. One way to avoid possible contamination is to have chuck or round portions ground in the store before your eyes or, better still, grind it at home, thus avoiding possible trichinosis and toxoplasmosis contamination from store grinders that may have been used for pork.

MEAT ANALOGS

For many years, processors such as Worthington and Loma Linda have been selling canned meat analogs including imitation frankfurters, hamburger and sausage based on soy protein or wheat protein. More recently, several processors have offered frozen meat analogs. Among the most heavily promoted of these are Morningstar Farms (Miles Laboratories) and Betty Crocker Country Cuts (General Mills).

These products contain less saturated fat than their meat counterparts, but some such as the Morningstar Farm Breakfast Links, Breakfast Patties and Breakfast Slices, contain partially hydrogenated fat. The taste of the analogs is often surprisingly good but is achieved with the aid of artificial flavors. Some analogs, such as Betty Crocker Country Cuts, contain artificial color.

MEAT, CANNED

Most canned meat products, such as hash or luncheon meat, are processed at 240 to 250° F for up to two hours. This comparatively severe heat treatment causes substantial loss in flavor, texture, color and nutrient value. Reduction in protein value varies with ingredients, temperature and processing time but probably is moderate in most commercial processing operations and probably little more than would occur in home processing. The combined effect of processing and prolonged storage can result in sizable losses in protein and vitamin values.

Meat content of most packaged meat products is regulated by the USDA but is rarely shown on the label. Lack of informative labeling can be quite confusing: who else but an expert would know that spaghetti and meat balls has a minimum of 35 per cent meat, while spaghetti sauce with meat balls has only 6 per cent meat? The minimum percentages for the most popular types of canned meat and poultry are shown in Table I.

Table I

CANNED MEAT AND POULTRY MINIMUM PERCENTAGE OF MEAT REQUIRED BY USDA

Barbecue sauce with meat	35%
Beans with bacon in sauce	12
Beans with frankfurters in sauce	20
Beans with meatballs in sauce	20
Beef sauce with beef and mushrooms	25
Beef with gravy	50
Gravy with beef	35
Chili con carne	40
Chili con carne with beans	25
Chop Suey (Amer. Style) with macaroni and meat	25
Chop suey vegetables with meat	12
Chow mein vegetables with meat	12
Chipped beef	18
Egg foo young with meat	12
Goulash	25
Ham spread	50
Hash (incl. corned beef hash)	35
Liver spread and liver sausage	30(1)
Meatballs in sauce	50
Meat ravioli	10
Spaghetti sauce and meatballs	35
Spaghetti sauce with meat	6
Spaghetti with meatballs and sauce	12
Beef Stew	25
Corned beef hash	35

Boned solid-pack chicken or turkey	95(2)
Boned chicken or turkey	90(2)
Boned chicken or turkey with broth	80(2)
Chopped chicken or turkey with broth	43
Chicken barbecue	40
Sliced chicken or turkey with gravy	35
Sliced chicken or turkey with gravy and dressing	25
Chicken a la King	20
Chicken fricassee	20
Chicken cacciatore	20
Creamed chicken or turkey	20
Chicken chop suey	4
Chop suey with chicken	2

(1) Per cent liver
(2) Per cent meat, skin and fat.

MEAT, REGULAR CUTS

The dedicated meat eater can, with a little effort, probably get a more wholesome product by purchasing regular cuts of fresh meat rather than by buying processed products such as sausage, bologna or canned meats. Regular cuts are preferable to meat that has been processed in the store such as hamburger, cube steak or anything from the delicatessen section of the supermarket. Processed meats, whether from the factory or the store, may contain highly objectionable ingredients introduced by design or through unsanitary conditions. Regular cuts of meat are more difficult for the unscrupulous to adulterate and, moreover, the inside of the cut, unlike that of processed meat, will be virtually sterile.

Unfortunately, the retailer has splendid opportunities

for petty larceny in selling regular cuts. One of his techniques is to use nonstandard terms, a practice which can make identification and hence price comparison difficult for the consumer. One way to beat the butcher in this game is to learn the standard cuts by name and appearance. The National Livestock and Meat Board, in an effort to help consumers, has encouraged the use of standard terminology through the dissemination of well-designed charts showing the various cuts. The idea is for butchers to display these prominently. Those who do not have access to the charts can get a set by writing to The National Livestock and Meats Board, 36 S. Wabash Avenue, Room 700, Chicago, Illinois, 60603. Ask for "retail meat charts."

Another useful guide to buying is the grade system. The grade system is primarily designed to measure flavor, juiciness and tenderness for oven cooking or pan frying. The first three grades, "prime," "choice" and "good" are generally acceptable for oven cooking or frying, while the next two grades, "standard" and "commercial," usually must be prepared with moist heat (steaming or stewing) or tenderized with papain to be acceptable. The fat in prime and choice grades is what lends them flavor, but skilled cooks can make highly platable dishes from the standard and commercial grades. The "good" and "standard" grades have higher protein value and are more acceptable nutritionally to anyone wishing to cut down on saturated fat. Some commercial grade cattle bypass the feedlot with its unnatural stresses and hence may be healthier animals than their more expensive cousins. Herewith are the official descriptions of the five retail grades as applied to beef, veal and lamb. Pork is not graded.

Prime: The most juicy, tender and flavorsome. Has abundant marbling (flecks of fat within the lean) which enhance flavor and juiciness. Sold primarily to high-priced restaurants. Not sold in most retail stores.

Choice: Only slightly less juicy, tender and flavorsome. Slightly less marbling—less fat. Most popular retail grade.

Good: Less juicy, tender and flavorsome, leaner and less marbling than choice.

Standard: More lean than good grade, mild flavor (applies to beef and veal only).

Commercial: Has abundant marbling but unlike top four grades, comes from mature animals and hence is tougher (applies to beef only).

Because of the laxity of most state inspection and the filthy conditions found in many plants, shoppers who want the best available protection would be wise to avoid meat which is not federally inspected. A grade label or other federal stamp on meat, however, does not protect against adulteration or unsanitary conditions in retail cutting rooms for it indicates federal supervision only in slaughterhouses and packing houses.

The federal program itself has come under attack by the highly respected American Public Health Association. In 1972, the Association sued the government to force dropping of the inspection seal and force substitution of a warning that meat might contain disease germs.

MEAT, SMOKED AND CURED

Man's most ancient method of food preservation is curing; that is, the use of salt to inhibit bacterial growth and hence, spoilage. Because salt alone imparts a harsh dry flavor, sugar or some other sweetener such as corn syrup is added to soften the flavor. The levels of salt in cured products are usually in the 2 to 3 per cent range while sugar is about 0.3 per cent. Other ingredients, including spices and MSG, are used while phosphate is added to increase water retention.

Smoked Meat and Cancer

In the last two decades scientists have been studying the diet of certain countries with a high incidence of stomach cancer, such as Iceland and the Baltic states, in order to find out if some carcinogenic substance in the diet is responsible.

A study reported in 1958 suggested that the high incidence of stomach cancer in Iceland may be related to a high intake of smoked meat and fish. This conclusion was based on the discovery that such smoked foods often contained extremely high levels of a group of cancer-causing substances known as polycyclic aromatic hydrocarbons, of which the most potent is benzo-(a)pyrene. Benzo(a)pyrene readily causes tumors in test animals and, because it occurs in the tar of cigarette smoke, it is implicated in lung cancer as well.

Some smoked fish used in Iceland and certain European countries contained levels of benzo(a)pyrene as high as 60 parts per billion (ppb). A pound of this fish would contain the same amount of benzo(a)-

pyrene found in the smoke of over 4,000 cigarettes! Other studies have indicated that most smoked fish and smoked meat have much lower levels of the carcinogens than this, but their presence in any amount is, of course, potentially hazardous.

An analysis of fifty-six assorted foods by the USDA Meat Inspection Division and the FDA found benzo-(a)pyrene in 32 of the samples, with eleven of these containing amounts from 1 to 7 ppb. A pound of these foods would contain the same amount of the benzo-(a)pyrene found in the smoke of 35 to 245 cigarettes. Smoked whiting, cod, whitefish and barbecued pork were particularly high while smoked sausage and ham had lesser levels.

Any wood-smoked food can be expected to have some traces of the carcinogenic hydrocarbons because these chemicals are a normal component of wood smoke and will become deposited on the food being smoked, especially on the outer surfaces.

Because the carcinogens are fat-soluble, substantial amounts tend to be lost in the fat drippings from bacon. Thus, by discarding the fat, the amount of benzo(a)-pyrene ingested from smoked bacon can be reduced by at least half.

Perhaps the safest alternate is to choose products that have been artificially smoked with a "liquid smoke" additive. These smoke flavors are prepared by absorbing the vaporous components of wood smoke in water and removing all of the insoluble particles, a process which appears to effectively remove the carcinogens as well. Two cancer experts from the Chicago Medical School, Drs. William Lijinsky and Philippe Shubik, analyzed two brands of liquid smoke and found a total absence of benzo(a)pyrene and, hence, recommended products made with liquid smoke as a means of avoiding the potential hazard from even small amounts of carcinogens in conventionally smoked foods. Liquid smoke is often noted on the retail labels.

Sodium Nitrate/Nitrite

By far the most controversial additives in cured meat products are sodium nitrate and sodium nitrite. The function of these ingredients is to give the characteristic red color to meat, to add flavor, to retard rancidity and, most important of all, to inhibit toxin-producing microorganisms, particularly the deadly *clostridium botulinum* organism. Nit*rite* is the active ingredient; nit*rate* serves as a source of nitrite. Nitrite breaks down to nitrous acid which can react with a class of chemicals known as secondary amines to form *nitrosamines*. These are known as powerful carcinogens in animals and have been found in cured products including sausage, pork, bacon and dried beef.

Critics of nitrite emphasize that the additive is probably not necessary in the prevention of botulism except in the case of canned hams where the oxygen-free environment permits growth of the spores. In other products, including sausage and bacon, the additives serve primarily a coloring function.

Processors must list nitrite and nitrate on the label. Any ham or bacon that has the characteristic red color has been treated. Most cured and canned meat products with the exception of the precooked or brown-and-serve type and fresh pork sausage, are treated with these additives.

The industry claims that, without nitrite, products such as frankfurters would have an unappealing gray-brown color, a bitter taste, and pose a botulism risk. Yet frankfurters without nitrite such as those sold by Shiloh Farms, have been successfully produced without a botulism problem.

In an unusual joint statement on August 12, 1978, the FDA and USDA announced that "the use of nitrite as a deliberate additive to food may pose a hazard to human health." The announcement came with the release of a three-year MIT study ordered by the FDA, which "strongly suggests that nitrite produces cancer of the lymphatic system in test animals." According to the joint statement the study "leads us to the concern that nitrite may increase the incidence of human cancer." Despite the concern, neither agency ordered a ban on the use of nitrite as a food additive.

Sausage

The term sausage is generally used to denote any meat that is ground, chipped or emulsified and then stuffed into a casing. Sausages may contain discrete particles as in head cheese or blood tongue sausage or may be emulsified as in bologna, liverwurst or frankfurter. Sausage may range in size from the small cocktail type less than ½ inch in diameter to bolognas that are 6 inches or more in diameter and weigh over 20 pounds. Sausage may include chunks, hams, loins, shoulders and other parts ordinarily bought as regular cuts. Most of the meat, however, is from regular cut trimmings and from such parts as the cheeks, heart, tripe, liver, tongue, lips, giblet, esophagus, snout and navel. Most of these parts, although unacceptable to the squeamish in their original form, are highly esteemed as sausage. Protein and vitamin value of these animal parts are comparable to that of regular cuts but fat content of some types may be very high (up to 40%). Sausages containing liver such as liverwurst and braunschweiger have higher amounts of niacin and particularly of vitamin A than regular cuts of meat.

Sausage meat may be extended with cracker meal, flour and water, powdered milk and soy protein. These extenders, which are ordinarily used for emulsion stability, for improving flavor or texture, and for improving slicing characteristics, must by law constitute no more than 3½ per cent of the weight. Soy protein is permitted up to the 2½ per cent level. Sausage which exceeds these limits must be labeled as "imitation." Sausage with added pimento, cheese and olive in excess of these limits need not be labelled "imitation."

Frankfurters and bologna have 55 per cent or more water, semidry types such as thuringer have about 48 per cent while dry types such as salami have about 30 per cent. The dry types keep better and are considered more a delicacy by connoisseurs.

For many, the important question about sausage products is, "What's *really* in it?" The industry has been less than forthright in its labeling while the FDA has been backward about promoting full disclosure. Consumer Reports pointed out that the typical frankfurter in 1937 was about 20 per cent protein and 19 per cent fat as compared to 12 per cent protein and 28 per cent fat in 1972.

The frankfurter processors, instead of improving their product, reacted by defending the present composition of their current product.

Ham

Hams come from the upper part of the hog's hind leg. The principal method of preserving hams is by arterial pumping, a method which was, appropriately enough, said to be invented by a New Zealand embalmer. The cure liquid or pickle, as it is usually called, is sometimes held in the ham for as little as two to three hours but most often for one to three days. Nitrite and nitrate, which are used in the pickle, prevent growth of botulinum spores in canned ham but serve primarily as a coloring agent in hams which are not canned. All reddish-colored hams have been processed with these additives. (Fresh ham is grayish in color.)

Country hams, which are the most highly prized of all cured meat products, are not cooked but rendered safe to eat by prolonged curing, usually thirty to forty days at smokehouse temperatures of no more than 100°. The hams are then aged six to nine months at 70° to 85° F, a process which encourages the enzymatic activity responsible for the flavor. Smithfield hams, produced exclusively in Smithfield, Virginia, are the best known of the country hams. Many canned meat products, such as canned hams, are also cured and smoked. Canned hams are classified as perishable or nonperishable according to the degree of temperature treatment. Those which are processed between 140° and 147° F (internal temperature) are labelled perishable and must be cooked further in the home. Those which are processed at 148° F or higher are variously labeled either as cooked, thoroughly cooked, fully cooked, ready-to-serve, or ready-to-eat. Both types are free from trichina which is killed by temperatures of 137° F.

Since no federal standards for canned ham have been established, quality is quite variable. A 1970 study by Consumers Union found wide variations in flavor, while protein content ranged from 11 per cent to 20 per cent. CU concluded that the small perishable hams (3 pounds and under) tend to have more flavor and better texture because less heat is used in processing. Canned hams deteriorate with age; the deterioration is faster in the perishable type. The pasteurization process controls bacteria and enzymes for six to nine months in perishable hams, but those which are not refrigerated deteriorate faster. The consumer usually has no way of knowing about deterioration before tasting. Canned ham contains sodium nitrite or sodium nitrate but some brands also contain sodium ascorbate or sodium erythorbate which may inhibit or prevent the formation of nitrosamines.

Bacon

Bacon, which is made from the belly of the hog, is usually cured for ten to fourteen days under refrigeration and then cooked and smoked. Internal temperatures during cooking and smoking are kept at 140° or less.

Among the traditional foods, bacon is by far the worst bargain because of its extremely high fat content, but then most people probably buy it for its unique flavor. Raw bacon contains only 8.4 per cent protein as to compared to 17.9 per cent for raw hamburger. At best, bacon loses half of its weight during cooking and may lose up to 85 per cent. Bacon costs more per pound than hamburger, which ordinarily loses only 10 to 20 per cent of its weight in cooking. There is no federal grading system to guide the retail customer in determining the fat content, and furthermore, it is often deceptively packed with the meat part shown and the fat hidden.

Bacon is ordinarily not dated which is unfortunate

because it loses much of its flavor after a week or so in the supermarket refrigerator case. Like other cured pork products, bacon contains sodium nitrite and sodium nitrate.

MEAT STRETCHERS

In the past few years meat stretchers have proliferated, marketed under such names as Hunt's Skillet, General Mill's Hamburger Helper, Kraft's Chef Surprise and Pillsbury's Busy Day.

Typically, these contain several packets of ingredients. For instance, Hunt's Skillet Stroganoff has a 12.75 ounce can of "Beefy Sauce with Mushrooms" (which contains no beef), a 2 ounce packet of sour cream and seasoning mix, and a 2½ ounce packet of enriched egg noodles. With most of these products you supply the protein, usually in the form of hamburger, tuna, or chicken.

The concept behind these meals-in-a-box is to provide easy-to-make gourmet meals. The *Buffalo Evening News* evaluated four of these products against homemade equivalents and concluded that the flavor of the homemade meals was better in three cases and about equal to the packaged product in the fourth. More significantly, not one of the homemade dinners took more than three minutes longer to prepare while one took three minutes *less* than its packaged counterpart. Since the extra utensils required for the completely homemade meals were also minimal, it is difficult to think of these products as convenience foods. Homemade dinners are, of course, cheaper than dinners made with the packaged products.

Generally, the packaged products include enriched pasta or white rice (products of marginal nutritional value) in addition to several questionable additives such as MSG, hydrogenated vegetable oil and artificial color.

ORGANIC BEEF AND POULTRY

Organic meat comes from cattle allowed to graze freely in pastures uncontaminated by pesticide and herbicide residues. The cattle are not subjected to the unnatural practices of the feedlot, such as routine use of antibiotics and hormones. In other words, organic cattle-raising methods are similar to those practiced for millennia before hormones, antibiotics, pesticides and herbicides were invented.

Organic meat is available in both regular cuts and processed form and in most areas is found exclusively in health food stores or a few co-op stores. It is possible to buy organic meat directly from the farm, usually in bulk. Ordinarily, organic meat producers are not in the Yellow Pages but you might locate one through a state or regional organic farming organization.

The meats found in health food stores are almost always frozen. None, including the processed meats, contain sodium nitrite or sidium nitrate. Prices are usually higher than for comparable products in the supermarket. Shiloh Farms, which is one of the biggest producers of processed organic meat, offers a fairly wide variety, including hot dogs, beef sausage roll, brown-and-serve sausage links, ground beef and luncheon meat, all bearing the USDA inspection label.

Quality of the meat in health food stores varies considerably; the stock in many stores apparently suffers from inadequate freezing to judge by the misshapen packages and freezer burn. As with organic produce, one cannot be sure the products are truly organic. However, because organic meat, unlike most fresh produce, is usually sold under a brand name, the producers have an interest in building and protecting their reputation.

SHELLFISH

Shellfish, such as lobster, shrimp, and crab, are as nutritious as they are expensive. All contain substantial amounts of excellent quality protein, shrimp is very high in iron (a 100-calorie, three-ounce portion has three times the RDA for iron), and crab is a good source of both iron and calcium.

Although lobster and oysters have three times the cholesterol of beef, this is balanced by their extremely low fat—averaging only one-sixth the fat of lean ground beef.

Also classed as shellfish are clams, mussels, oysters, and scallops. These are very low in fat, calories, and sodium, and high in protein, thiamine, riboflavin, niacin, and iron (100-calorie portions of clams or oysters have eight times the RDA for iron).

Unfortunately, these nutritious foods are associated with several diseases ranging from mild gastrointestinal upset to botulism, but in recent years the two diseases of greatest concern have been infectious hepatitis and paralytic shellfish poisoning.

Hepatitis

Most commercially important species of mollusks grow only in estuaries, which are subject to varying degrees of sewerage pollution. The mollusks feed on plankton and in order to get sufficient amounts of these tiny organisms, they pump in large amounts of water. The eastern oyster, for example, pumps up to 25 gallons per day. The gill system acts as a filter, not only removing the plankton from the water, but also bacteria and hepatitis viruses. Thus, the mollusks act as machines for concentrating viruses and other objectionable material, much of which is deposited in the stomach and gastrointestinal tract of the creatures.

Hepatitis is characterized by loss of appetite, fatigue, nausea, vomiting, diarrhea, gastric discomfort, flu, cough, upper respiratory infection, inflammation of the pharynx, jaundice, pains in muscles and joints, and a need to avoid light. The disease runs its course in several months and is seldom fatal.

Unlike other shellfish, oysters, clams and other mollusks are eaten raw or only partially cooked, and the gastrointestinal tract, with its potentially heavy load of bacteria and viruses, is not discarded. There is a myth that steaming until the clams open will insure safety. This is not correct: many bacteria may be killed by steaming clams for 5 to 6 minutes but even then the clams cannot be considered safe. The Center for Disease Control notes that the hepatitis virus is killed by boiling in water for twenty minutes, a procedure that gourmets may deplore. Those who insist upon raw or lightly steamed mollusks must hope that the Public

Health Service does an adequate job in policing the clam diggers. Fried clams are apparently safe. Canned clams and clams used in such products as clam chowder have been treated with sufficient heat to kill any virus that may be present.

Paralytic Shellfish Poisoning

Paralytic shellfish poisoning is associated with the "red tide," a phenomenon caused by reddish microorganisms. These organisms, one of a group known as dinoflagellates, live in shore areas, but are ordinarily not a hazard unless special conditions such as reduced salinity and higher temperatures lead to their proliferation. The mollusks concentrate the organisms but are not themselves adversely affected.

Humans who take in contaminated shellfish may experience initially a slight tingling, burning sensation or numbness in the tongue, gums, lips, and face followed by muscle weakness, spreading of the sensations to the neck, arms and legs, and progressing to complete paralysis of the extremities and, in extreme cases, to respiratory paralysis and death. There is no antidote to the disease. Shellfish which are affected appear normal in every way, and the toxin is not destroyed by heating. The only protection is an alert public health service. In the most recent outbreak, which occurred on the New England coast in 1972, there were at least thirty-three cases of disease but no recorded deaths.

TURKEY

At one time, turkey was sold strictly as a commodity item with no brand name and with virtually no processing other than defeathering and devisceration. Like most other food, it is now mainly a branded item marked by such corporate giants as Swift, Greyhound (Armour) and Ralston Purina.

You'll have difficulty finding a plain turkey that is neither self-basting nor prestuffed. The self-basting type cost up to ten cents or more per pound over regular turkeys. Thus, for a fifteen pound bird, you may pay an additional $1.50 for this feature.

Self-basting turkeys are injected with a basting fluid. Armour Gold Seal Turkeys have real butter in this fluid, but Checkerboards and Butterballs do not. (The name of the latter implies "butter" but the small print on the label states, "no butter added.") The basting fluid in some brands contain sugar in the form of corn syrup solids, while the fluid in several, such as Butterball and Checkerboard, contains unspecified artificial flavor. The Butterball turkeys also contain unspecified artificial color. Sodium phosphate is injected to enhance water retention with the effect of increasing the legal weight of the bird. Salt is usually added.

Turkey, like chicken, beef, pork and other animal foods has high quality protein, but of all these, turkey is highest in the amino acid lysine. Grains are deficient in lysine and hence turkey with grain is a particularly good combination in terms of enhanced protein value. A turkey sandwich with either white or dark meat will supply more usable protein than either turkey or the bread alone. Although the egg has the most complete protein of all food, turkey is actually more effective in supplementing the protein in wheat because it has a greater excess of lysine than egg.

CHAPTER VI

Fats and Oils

If you believe the television commercials, heart disease can be avoided simply by using the margarine "recommended by doctors every fifteen minutes," or the salad oil "highest in polyunsaturates." The remedy for heart disease is, of course, not that simple. The role of fats and oils in the diet is certainly the most controversial subject in nutrition today. The heated arguments between the experts added to the distortions of the advertisers result in confusion for the consumer.

Nutritional Value

In terms of calories, fats and oils are the single most important component of the typical American diet, supplying 40 to 50 per cent of the total intake. Fat is a concentrated source of energy, supplying 9 calories per gram as compared to only 4 calories per gram of sugar. Fat is also a carrier of certain important vitamins. Butterfat, for example, has substantial amounts of vitamin A, cod liver oil has vitamin D, while nut oils contain considerable vitamin E. Fats and oils contribute palatability to other foods, a point which anyone who has had to eliminate butter, margarine, mayonnaise, and cream will appreciate. Meals that contain fats and oils have more satiety value than those low in fat because the fat is digested more slowly, thus delaying hunger.

Fats and oils are composed of fatty acids and these are classified into three broad groups: polyunsaturated, monounsaturated and saturated. The arrangement of the atoms of the three elements found in all fats and oils—carbon, hydrogen, and oxygen—determines in which of these three groups each substance is classified. The polyunsaturated fatty acids, which are essential for well-being, are found in high concentrations in many plant foods such as corn, cottonseed, soybeans and peanuts, but are also available in smaller but nutritionally significant amounts in animal foods including lard, chicken fat, and eggs. There is no dietary need for saturated or monounsaturated fatty acids.

A deficiency of polyunsaturated fat can result in stunted growth, poor reproductive performance, dermatitis, decreased resistance to stress, and other disorders. Polyunsaturated fats play a role in the regulation of cholesterol (a high intake reduces the serum cholesterol level) and are important in synthesizing prostaglandins, hormone-like compounds which are apparently involved in many physiological functions including blood pressure regulation.

The Food and Nutrition Board of the National Academy of Sciences has set no specific recommended dietary allowance for polyunsaturated fat, apparently because deficiencies are unlikely. It notes that the need is satisfied if polyunsaturates account for 1 to 2 per cent of total calories. This means the need is satisfied by as little as one or two teaspoons of corn oil or its equivalent. Ordinarily, this amount is supplied in any well-balanced diet without any supplementation. Weight watchers, who sometimes try to eliminate all salad oil, mayonnaise and margarine, are the only groups who might be deficient.

The Processing of Vegetable Oils

Extraction, which is the first step in the processing of vegetable oils, is accomplished either by pressure or by use of solvents.

Pressure extraction, which is simply a method of squeezing the oil out of the seeds, is commonly classified into two basic types, cold pressing and hot pressing. This difference has caught the fancy of some in the health food movement who fervently champion the virtues of "cold pressed" oils, claiming that they are richer in vitamin E.

Cold pressing goes back to antiquity. High oil content seeds, such as sesame and the oily pulp of olives, yield oil under relatively low pressure. Other oil seeds, however, are processed under greater pressure and for this, the more efficient expeller press, which operates on the meat grinder principle, is used. The expeller press generates temperatures of at least 160° F but little or no vitamin E is lost as a result of this process. Such oils are called "cold pressed" by some marketers despite the heat treatment. Furthermore, much of these so-called "cold pressed" oils are filtered to remove impurities that make them unsuitable for high-temperature frying. In this respect, they are more or less similar to the widely advertised brands found in supermarkets, with the significant difference that many of the latter are solvent extracted. "Cold pressed" oils are generally much more expensive than the brands found in supermarkets.

In Europe, there is a considerable amount of oil, including peanut, sesame, and safflower oil, which is actually made by true cold pressing methods, but with the exception of a very limited amount of olive oil, true cold pressed oil is virtually unobtainable on this side of the Atlantic.

In America, a more meaningful label designation is the term "crude" (or "virgin," in the case of olive oil), which indicates that no further processing has been done after pressure extraction. All other oils undergo further processing. This includes the heavily advertised oils used in vegetable shortening such as Crisco.

Solvent extraction is a relatively new process which removes a slightly higher percentage of oil from the seeds than would be possible through pressing. In the U.S., it is mostly soybean oil that is solvent extracted, but corn oil and some other oils are partially extracted in this way. Soybean oil is by far the most widely used oil and is found in most margarines, and many cooking oils. Hexane, the solvent most commonly used, has not been adequately tested for its carcinogenic potential.

The refining stage removes "impurities" by mixing with a strong caustic solution, usually sodium hydroxide. Although refining does not substantially affect the color or flavor of oil, it removes up to a fifth of the vitamin E content, a loss which may be nutritionally important because of the marginal amounts of this vitamin in many oils. To make up for losses of vitamin

E, synthetic antioxidants (such as BHA and BHT) are added to protect the oil from oxidation. Removal of lecithin and other compounds by caustic refining is especially important in producing oils for high-temperature frying as these substances smoke and char at high temperatures.

The safety of refined vegetable oils has been questioned because analysis by FDA researchers of samples of corn, soybean, cottonseed, olive and peanut oils obtained from local retail markets has revealed small amounts of the carcinogen benzo(a)pyrene in some samples. Originally it was thought that this carcinogen originated in the solvent but subsequent research showed that some crude oils also contained the carcinogen. It is not clear to what extent carcinogens in oils are a hazard. One course for the wary oil-user to follow is to keep switching among brands and types and thus minimize the possibility of ingesting benzo-(a)pyrene on a steady basis.

Bleaching is the process used for the removal of color pigments from the oil, producing the uniform pale-to-bright yellow color consumers have come to expect from their oils. A chemical bleach is not used; the oil is instead mixed with activated charcoal or bleaching clay. Vitamin E is unaffected by this procedure, but manufacturers may use bleaching as a way to salvage improperly stored oils which have become rancid (and thus lost their vitamin E content), since bleaching removes the products of rancidity. The resulting oil appears "fresh," but is devoid of vitamin E and is very susceptible to further oxidation unless synthetic anti-oxidants (BHA, BHT) are added.

Most oils undergo a final stage, deodorization, a process in which odors and flavors are removed to provide a uniformly bland finished product. During this process, a thick sludge containing substantial amounts of vitamin E floats to the surface of the oil. Perhaps because the sludge is so rich in vitamin E (it may reach levels of almost 10 per cent, one hundred times greater than the concentration in the original oil) some advocates of unrefined oils have claimed that refined oils are virtually devoid of the vitamin. This claim has not been verified. The available information, which is based on an analysis of cottonseed oil, shows that over 95 per cent of the vitamin E remains in the oil.

Some oil products go through two further steps, winterizing and partial hydrogenation. The only major vegetable oil to be winterized is cottonseed oil. The oil is simply chilled, either in outdoor storage tanks in the cool southern winter or in tanks inside a cooled room. Partial hydrogenation, however, changes the nature of the fat in a way that may have adverse consequences.

Hydrogenated Fats and Oils

Many processed food products, such as potato chips or frozen fish sticks, contain a certain amount of oil after cooking. During storage this oil can become rancid (oxidize) and develop an unacceptably bitter taste. To combat this the food industry often chemically alters the oil through hydrogenation.

In this process hydrogen gas is bubbled through hot oil which changes the molecular structure of the oil. Depending upon the amount of hydrogen combining with the oil, the result may be solid fat at room temperature (as in shortening or margarine), or, if only lightly hydrogenated, may be a solid at lower temperatures but "melt" back to a liquid oil when warmed. Completely hydrogenated fats are most often used where long storage life is required.

The melting point is important because fats with melting points much above body temperature (98.6° F) are less digestible than those which can be melted easily by the body. In order to avoid a greasy taste, margarine processors use hydrogenated fat that melts near 98.6° F. Some vegetable shortenings are said to be "digestible," but this is not strictly true, since they combine some fats which melt near body temperature with other hydrogenated fats that have high melting points and are not digestible.

When an oil is only partially hydrogenated it may remain high in polyunsaturates (and still be susceptible to oxidation), but the process is used here primarily to make a solid fat from a liquid oil (as in margarine manufacture).

Normally for a fat to be a solid at room temperature it must be saturated, yet hydrogenation can produce solidified fats which are high in polyunsaturates and low in saturates. This bit of chemical trickery results from the creation, during hydrogenation, of an unnatural, "upside down" molecular structure called a *trans*-isomer. Although rare in natural oils, *trans*-isomers are produced in 50 to 60 per cent of the polyunsaturated components in soybean oil during hydrogenation.

Trans-isomers are what make a polyunsaturated margarine solid at room temperature, but they are also the cause for concern about the safety of hydrogenated fats.

Because these *trans*-isomers are extremely rare in nature, some nutritionists have speculated that they may be harmful. One of the chief critics of hydrogenated fat is Dr. F. A. Kummerow of the University of Illinois, who found that rats fed a basic diet, 20 per cent of which was hydrogenated soybean oil (in which 50 to 60 per cent of the polyunsaturated fatty acids are converted to *trans*-isomers during hydrogenation), had significantly more lipids (fatty edible substances like fats and oils) deposited in their heart tissues than those fed 20 per cent beef tallow, a highly saturated fat.

Dr. Kummerow also found that swine, whose physiology is remarkably similar to humans, tended to develop atherosclerotic lesions when fed *trans*-fatty acids. The fat used in his study contained 40 per cent *trans*-fatty acids, an amount found in some commercial margarines.

Dr. Kummerow says that his studies also suggest that eating hydrogenated fats may modify the body's formation of adrenal harmones, which in turn could have important effects upon the metabolism of carbohydrates, protein and fat. He recommends that *trans*-fatty acids be eliminated from margarine and other foods.

Numerous studies exploring the relationship between hydrogenated fat and serum cholesterol tend to support Dr. Kummerow. In one study, human subjects given hydrogenated oil suffered from increased serum cholesterol and also "remarkably high levels of trigycerides in the serum." A high level of triglycerides, like a high level of cholesterol, is considered to be risk factor in heart disease.

On the other hand, a very extensive study published in 1975 by a leading expert on fats, Dr. Roslyn B. Alfin-Slater, head of The Environmental and Nutritional Sciences Division of the University of California,

Los Angeles, School of Public Health, does not support Dr. Kummerow's findings. In her study, forty-six generations of rats were given a diet with about 10 per cent hydrogenated vegetable oil (half the level used in Kummerow's rat studies). Compared to untreated oils, she found the hydrogenated fats nutritionally adequate as measured by weight gain, reproduction and lactation, longevity, and other criteria, and produced no toxic effects. The animals consumed many times the amount of *trans*-isomers that would normally be consumed by humans.

Obviously, hydrogenated fats are a controversial topic. Those who do not want to risk the possible dangerous effects would have to avoid vegetable shortenings, margarine, liquid oils which state on the label that they have been "specially processed," "partially hydrogenated," or "partially hardened" and all processed foods made with hydrogenated fat. There may be, as we will see, other reasons for avoiding the more highly refined oil products.

Synthetic Antioxidants

Antioxidants such as BHT (butylated hydroxytoluene), BHA (butylated hydroxyanisole), and propyl gallate are added to oils and a large variety of other foods.

Questions about the safety of these antioxidants go back to 1959 when a group of Australian researchers found that BHT fed to rats caused their hair loss and birth defects. In many subsequent studies, however, no birth defects were seen even when massive amounts of BHT were given frequently to pregnant animals.

Surprisingly, several researchers found that the mutagenicity and carcinogenicity of numerous toxic chemicals was *decreased* when BHT was added to the diet, while both BHA and BHT were reported to markedly reduce the incidence of stomach cancer in mice exposed to potent carcinogens. One expert, Dr. Raymond J. Shamburger, of the Cleveland Clinic, has even suggested that the declining incidence of stomach cancer in America during the past forty years may be due in part to the widespread consumption of breakfast cereals containing BHA and BHT. This view is not widely accepted.

BHA and BHT are not yet in the clear as definitive testing for carcinogenic effects still needs to be done. A few studies have indicated that large quantities resulted in certain cellular changes of a type that precede the development of cancer, but the additives have yet to be shown to actually cause cancer. In the meantime, the Food and Agriculture Organization of the U.N. has given BHA and BHT a "temporary acceptance" for use in foods.

Propyl gallate is also given a "temporary acceptance" although one study published in 1965 raised questions about possible liver damage on exposure to high doses. The FAO says that studies on reproduction of mixtures of BHA, BHT and propyl gallate are required to evaluate their combined effect.

The synthetic additives have a minor effect in retarding rancidity in vegetable oils and generally are not even necessary. Some oils, for example, Crisco Oil, have BHA and BHT while others, such as Fleischmann's Corn Oil, have no antioxidant and no apparent problem with rancidity.

The adequacy of vitamin E in oils and foods preserved with synthetic antioxidants has been questioned. According to Dr. Robert S. Harris of the Massachusetts Institute of Technology, "An oil stabilized with BHA, for instance, may be protected against rancidity, but its tocopherol content may be destroyed. This BHA-rich, tocopherol-poor oil may then provoke vitamin E deficiency in those who habitually consume it, for this oil is deficient in vitamin E."

Polyunsaturated Oil and Vitamin E

The vitamin E content of fats and oils is very important because the body's need for the vitamin is directly related to the amount of polyunsaturated fat consumed. Vitamin E apparently protects polyunsaturates in the body tissues from oxidation and thus prevents the formation of substances called free radicals, which seem to destabilize cell membranes and may accelerate the aging process.

Heating at frying temperatures results in significant losses of vitamin E while reuse of the cooking oils compounds the effect. Fried foods, such as potato chips, lose most of their vitamin E in storage. Freezing apparently does not retard the loss for frozen french fried potatoes suffer just as great a loss.

According to the National Research Council, diets that have a ratio of 0.5 milligrams vitamin E to one gram polyunsaturated fatty acids are satisfactory. This ratio, which is known as the E:PUFA ratio (*PolyUn*saturated *Fatty Acid*) has been calculated at 0.60 for soybean oil, 0.49 for corn oil, 0.35 for safflower oil, and 0.83 for hydrogenated shortening made predominantly from soybean oil. The authors of the study in which these figures are reported suggest that safflower oil, as the only dietary fat "is inadequate after prolonged periods, but more extensive studies are necessary to confirm this." In 1971 consumption of safflower oil was not significant and thus the potential problem was not considered serious. However, subsequent introduction and extensive promotion of Promise, a safflower-based margarine, may result in a greater per capita consumption of this oil. Promise is not supplemented with vitamin E. At least until the matter is thoroughly examined, it would be prudent not to rely exclusively on safflower-based margarine, such as Promise or safflower cooking oils.

Vitamin E can be conserved by not storing the oil for too long, particularly at high temeperatures, and by not exposing it to air and light for longer than necessary. Unheated oils are likely to supply more vitamin E than those that are heated.

Polyunsaturates and Cancer

The possibility that substantial consumption of polyunsaturates over an extended period may cause cancer was raised by an eight year long controlled study conducted in a Los Angeles veterans' home. In this study a control group of 422 veterans received specially prepared meals intended to represent a conventional American diet, while another group of 424 received meals which looked and tasted very similar to the control diet, but had nearly four times the polyunsaturated fat and half as much saturated fat and cholesterol. The control group received only 4 per cent of their total calories in the form of polyunsaturates while the experimental group received about 15 per cent of their calories as polyunsaturates.

The most striking fact in the report was the higher death rate from cancer among those receiving the high polyunsaturate diet: thirty-one from the experimental group died from cancer compared with seventeen in the control group. The difference is not as significant as it would appear, however, because those in the experimental group were less inclined to follow the diet. When those who adhered to either diet less than 30 per cent of the time are excluded, the difference in cancer mortality between the two groups became thirteen vs sixteen—interesting, but not very dramatic.

The conclusion of most authorities regarding a link between human cancer and a diet high in polyunsaturates is that the evidence, which includes other studies as well, so far indicates little risk. However, the number of animal studies that *do* show a correlation suggests that individuals should be cautious about radically increasing their polyunsaturate intake without the close supervision of their physician. Women should be especially cautious because a number of the animal studies have showed an increase in mammary cancer, and the experiments indicating safety with humans have involved men only.

Are Heated Oils Harmful?

Numerous studies have shown the toxic effects of fats and oils heated to high temperatures in the laboratory, but fats used by commercial bakeries, restaurants, potato chip processors and doughnut processors are apparently non-toxic. There is evidence, however, that heated fat may be co-carcinogenic, that is, it may stimulate the effect of some other carcinogenic substance. Used corn oil from potato chip frying was found to cause a high incidence of mammary and liver tumors and early death among test animals when the animals were also given low levels of a chemical called AAF (2-acetylamino-fluorine). When the animals were given AAF with fresh corn oil, no tumors were formed and no deaths occurred during the test period.

The co-carcinogenicity of heated oil combined with AAF is generally accepted but whether a similar effect occurs when oil is combined with other chemicals as in commercial or home frying has not yet been established.

Heated Oils and Atherosclerosis

Heated polyunsaturated oil prepared under conditions similar to those in home frying (for example, 400° F for fifteen minutes) have been shown to promote atherosclerotic deposits in test animals. Dr. David Kritchevsky, Wistar Professor of Biochemistry at the University of Pennsylvania, says that this action is due to substances called free fatty acids which are present in oils and particularly unrefined oils. Other authorities do not agree with Dr. Kritchevsky.

Whatever the reason for this phenomenon, it raises, at least tentatively, questions regarding the safety of heated oils and particularly those which are high in polyunsaturates. In animal experiments heated corn oil was found to have a much greater effect than heated olive oil which has far less polyunsaturates.

Saturation of Heated Oil

Health food advocates have claimed that cooking causes polyunsaturated fats to become saturated. Consumers Union tested this theory by heating and reheating oils at 375° F five times over and found an insignificant increase in the degree of saturation.

The Consumers Union report does not agree with an earlier study in which potatoes, chicken and corn fritters were cooked in fat. This study showed that the polyunsaturates in corn oil were decreased by 10 per cent and the saturated fat increased by 82 per cent when the oil was used to fry potatoes for fifteen minutes at 400° F. Reuse of the oil increases the degree of saturation.

The use of heated polyunsaturated oils is a controversial subject and the research to date provides no clearcut guide to consumers. Those who engage in home-frying should consider using low-temperature methods which will conserve nutrients better than higher temperatures and may also result in less saturation.

Low-temperature Frying

There is a myth that the best way to fry food in oil is at very high temperatures, often twice as hot as boiling water. Yet it is unnecessary to fry at such temperatures in order to make food palatable and indeed, low-temperature frying may result in more palatable food. Furthermore, high-temperature frying destroys nutrients and may have adverse consequences. (See preceding section.) Foods can be successfully fried at surprisingly low temperatures. A sunny-side-up egg, for example, can be fried at 185° F or 27 degrees below the temperature used to make soft boiled eggs.

A much wider selection of oils is available to those who adopt low-temperature frying. In high-temperature frying, only highly refined oils can be used, because refining removes substances such as lecithin and naturally occurring mono- and diglycerides which can char and cause the oil to smoke at temperatures above 300 degrees. The standard criterion of cooking oil quality is the smoke point or the temperature at which thin wisps of bluish smoke begin to rise from the surface. However, for those who adopt low-temperature frying (between 150° and 250° F) the smoke point becomes irrelevant because even crude oils do not smoke until they reach temperatures of over 275 degrees.

When water is heated it will never reach a temperature above 212° F (except in a pressure cooker) no matter how high the flame is turned up. Oil, on the other hand, continues to absorb heat and can become extremely hot very quickly. For this reason anyone wishing to adopt the low-temperature method of frying must have a thermometer made especially for cooking. An electric frying pan with a thermostatic control is also useful, since range-top burners are difficult to regulate. Unfortunately, electric frypans with controls that accurately measure temperatures as low as 150 degrees are hard to find; usually there is only the vague term "warm" for setting below 250° F.

The lecithin in crude oils provides an added benefit for the low-temperature cook because it is an excellent "antistick" compound, and it also causes beneficial "foaming" of the oil, thus preventing spattering during frying. In high-temperature frying, foaming is considered a bad quality and a synthetic "antifoam agent" is often added in the form of methyl silicone, and apparently safe substance.

To avoid making the food greasy, the experts recommend warming it quickly in the oven to about 185° F, or on a rack in a pan (with no added water) on the stove. The preheating prevents the oil from penetrating the food. Another secret of successful low-temperature frying of starchy food is to remove the food from the oil when half done for one or two minutes before returning it to the oil. This allows the gases to escape and improves the flavor and texture.

Storage of Fats and Oils

Fats and oils become rancid more quickly when exposed to high temperatures, light, certain metals, and oxygen (except when antioxidants are present). Therefore, to prevent deterioration of fats and oils (and also preserve the vitamin E content), they should be refrigerated, kept away from light (ideally in brown or opaque glass bottles), and kept tightly closed in containers which do not leave a lot of empty air space above the oil. When buying oil in bulk, transfer the oil to several smaller brown bottles than can be filled to the top. These can be stored at room temperature, while the bottle for daily use should be refrigerated. Cloudiness which may occur in any oils on refrigeration does not affect the qualities of the oil.

The Big Controversy over Fats and Oils

Most authorities agree that saturated fat, cholesterol and polyunsaturates in the diet are in some way involved in heart disease.

Those who have high blood pressure, high serum cholesterol or other danger signals are usually advised by their doctors to limit intake of saturated fat and cholesterol. There is little disagreement on this, but there is vigorous disagreement as to whether such advice applies to people with no signs of disease.

The American Heart Association advises the public to cut down on dietary saturated fat and cholesterol. On the other hand, Mark Altschule, M.D., Clinical Professor of Medicine at the Harvard Medical School and Editor-in-chief of the journal *Medical Counterpoint,* deplores agencies such as the American Heart Association which try to convince the general public that there is a definite link between diet and heart disease. "The role of diet remains unproved," declares Dr. Altschule, "despite the efforts of various agencies to consider it established."

Others, like Dr. Ancel Keys, the noted diet researcher from the University of Minnesota, claim that saturated fat but not cholesterol is a causative factor. Raymond Reiser, Ph.D., Distinguished Professor of

Biochemistry and Biophysics at Texas A and M University, emphatically denies the adverse effect of saturated fat and claims that dietary cholesterol is the arch villain.

Despite the disagreement, there probably are benefits to cutting down on fat, at least for those on typical American diets in which 40 to 45 per cent of the calories are from fat. It would be particularly beneficial to replace the fat with a variety of cereals, fruits, vegetables, and legumes.

Polyunsaturates

Most experts agree that a high serum cholesterol level is associated with heart disease although not all agree that high serum cholesterol is a causative factor. The experts also concur that polyunsaturates lower the serum cholesterol level, but they strongly disagree as to why this occurs. Some say that the polyunsaturates are effective simply because they replace saturated fats while others feel there is an active ingredient in the polyunsaturates such as phytosterols which lowers the cholesterol. The long-term biological effects of consuming large amounts of polyunsaturates are unknown, and there is no strongly convincing evidence that large amounts actually reduce the risk of heart disease.

Despite the lack of proof that increased polyunsaturates will reduce the risk of heart disease, manufacturers of margarine and vegetable oils have spent millions of dollars every year since the early 1960's to convince the public that their products do indeed prevent the disease.

In 1973, the Federal Trade Commission ordered Standard Brands, makers of Fleischmann's Margarine to "cease and desist" advertising claims "that the use of Fleischmann's Margarine or other food fats or oils will prevent or mitigate heart and artery disease." The FTC called such advertisements "false, misleading and deceptive," and was especially critical of ads showing pictures of children with captions such as "should an 8-year-old worry about cholesterol?" and "Is there a heart attack in his future?" because, in the words of the FTC, "It has not been established by competent and reliable scientific evidence that premature heart and artery disease during adult life is causally related to diet during childhood."

Since then, Standard Brands has attempted to *imply* that their product prevents heart disease by using headlines such as "Every 15 seconds a doctor recommends Fleischmann's Margarine." The small type copy below makes no claim for disease prevention but notes the role of Fleischmann's Margarine in reducing serum cholesterol as "part of a total dietary program" that also includes less fat, fewer eggs, and skim milk.

Other products, such as Kraft Safflower Oil and Mazola Corn Oil vie with each other to convince the consumer that their level of polyunsaturates is highest. Such advertising must imply to many readers that polyunsaturates are synonymous with heart disease prevention.

Dr. Edward R. Pinckney, a former editor of *The Journal of The American Medical Association* and at one time in charge of preventive medicine teaching at Northwestern University College of Medicine, states that, "There is now considerable sound evidence that more and more people are eating more and more polyunsaturates strictly for health purposes. However, this deliberate dietary alteration is based on the completely *un*proven hypothesis that such foods will prevent, and even cure, heart disease." Dr. Pinckney notes one survey which shows that nine out of ten patients who increased their consumption of polyunsaturates did so as a result of advertising or news media publicity and not on the advice of their physician.

If there are good reasons for avoiding too much fat, equally good ones suggest an avoidance of an imbalance of saturated and unsaturated fat.

The Ratio of Polyunsaturates to Saturates

For many years, medical researchers have talked in terms of the polyunsaturated/saturated ratio or P/S ratio. According to the theory, there is a beneficial effect on serum cholesterol (a reduction of more than 10 per cent) when the P/S ratio is at least 1.5, that is, when the amount of polyunsaturates is one and one-half times that of saturated fat.

It is obviously difficult to determine the P/S ratio for an entire day's intake of food because of the influence of "invisible" fats in the diet, in meat, nuts, eggs, milk, etc. The basic concept is nevertheless important for studies have shown that to significantly reduce serum cholesterol levels, the relative quantity of polyunsaturates to saturates is critical.

Within the frame work of an overall low-fat diet, a moderate reorientation from saturates to polyunsaturates and monounsaturates should have no adverse consequences for the normally healthy person.

The Total Fat Content of the Diet

The Dietary Goals for the U.S. (see Appendix IV, page 343), call for a reduction in fat consumption from approximately 40 per cent of total calories to about 30 per cent. This 30 per cent should be split evenly with 10 per cent of energy intake coming from saturated fat, 10 per cent from polyunsaturates and 10 per cent from monounsaturated. Others, such as Dr. William Conner of the University of Iowa College of Medicine, suggest restricting fat to 20 to 25 per cent of calories, keeping saturated fat to a maximum of 5 to 6 per cent and polyunsaturated fat to a maximum of 10 per cent.

In practice, it is quite difficult to keep track of total fat and the different types of fat in the diet. One approach is to use prepared menus such as those found in the books by Payne and Callahan and by Stead and Warren listed in the bibliography.

More simply, just emphasize low fat foods over

those high in fat. Limit your use of sausage, pork, beef, cheese, whole milk, butter, margarine, nuts and even salad oil. Replace these with poultry, fish, skim milk, cottage cheese, fruits, vegetables, or bread and other cereal products.

Cholesterol

Many experiments with both animals and humans have shown that added cholesterol in the diet raises the serum cholesterol level. High serum cholesterol is associated with heart disease. For this reason, some researchers such as Raymond Reiser insist that dietary cholesterol is the arch-villain in the genesis of heart disease.

Harvard's Jean Mayer also places strong emphasis on the effects of dietary cholesterol. He suggests that men should restrict their intake of eggs to just two a week "as a Sunday treat."

On the other hand, Dr. William Kannel, Director of the Framingham Heart Study, believes it unlikely that cholesterol is essential in the genesis of atherosclerosis but says that it becomes involved in the atherosclerotic process simply because it is present. However, he considers elevated serum cholesterol levels as only one among many risk factors. Its importance, he says, is dependent upon the other factors present.

Dr. Ancel Keys and his associates at the University of Minnesota, who are among the foremost researchers on dietary fat in the U.S., say that the many studies which do show a significant increase in serum cholesterol resulting from increases in dietary cholesterol involve "formula diets" rather than diets of natural foods. They note that normal diets of natural foods containing cholesterol have virtually no effect on blood cholesterol.

Most authorities agree on one aspect of the cholesterol controversy, that above a certain level—about 600 mg. per day—the amount of dietary cholesterol does not have a significant effect on the levels in the blood. Thus, those who eat four eggs a day (about 1000 mg. of cholesterol) may be no more at risk than those who eat only two. The real disagreement is over whether dietary cholesterol below about 600 mg. or so per day is relevant. Even among those who believe it is relevant, there is disagreement as to whether only those who are known to be at risk from heart disease should reduce dietary cholesterol or whether every male above puberty should reduce intake.

The concern about cholesterol centers on adult males. Healthy women and children can eat eggs without worry and indeed eggs are an excellent food for these groups as they contain substantial iron, a nutrient which is deficient in many diets.

If you, as a layman, are confused by the disagreement of the experts, you are not alone. The late Dr. Paul Dudley White, who was considered by many to be America's leading heart specialist, once said, "I must admit I'm thoroughly confused about cholesterol."

Cholesterol is composed of several different substances which should be measured separately. The two most important components are made of fat and protein and are called *lipoproteins*; one is called "high density lipoprotein" (or HDL), and the other is "low density lipoprotein" (LDL). About one-fifth of the total blood cholesterol is in the HDL form and appears to be beneficial. HDL apparently travels throughout the body picking up "bad" cholesterol (the LDL form) from the arteries and delivering it to the liver, where is is removed from the blood and excreted. High levels of LDL may be acceptable if HDL is also high. Researchers with the Framingham Heart Study suggest an LDL to HDL ratio of 3.5 to 1.

Diet seems to have a greater influence on LDL than on HDL. Eating red meat, eggs, cheese and butter will raise HDL levels but raise LDL levels even more, cancelling out the positive impact of the HDL. Vegetarians have high HDL, especially if they "cheat" and eat fish.

Women normally have 25 per cent higher HDL levels than men (this may be one reason women generally have less heart disease). Genetics may play a role, as longevity runs in families with high HDL levels. Exercise increases HDL; losing weight will raise HDL while gaining weight will lower it. Even drinking moderately—two drinks a day—will raise HDL.

All this is not proof, of course, that a high HDL level will afford protection from heart disease, but the "circumstantial evidence" looks promising.

Fats and Oils—A Listing

ANTISTICK PAN SPRAYS

The lecithin that is removed from crude oils in the refining process has many valuable qualities. This naturally occurring lecithin in unrefined oils, when used for low-temperature frying, acts as an excellent "antistick" agent. This property of lecithin is the basis for a relatively new type of product, the antistick spray in an aerosol can. Among the leading brands are Pam and Golden Touch. These sprays are effective and even prevent baked-on foods from sticking to the pan, but are expensive (more than a dollar for a small 10 oz. can).

Artificial flavors are used in most of these products, while Golden Touch even has artificial color. Pam is one of the few that has no additives except for the propellant.

A lecithin spray is of minor value, of course, with Teflon-coated pans or with a well-seasoned cast iron fry pan.

BUTTER AND MARGARINE

Butter

Butter, unlike margarine, is a very simple product. It is made from milkfat, buttermilk and water, usually has salt added and may contain a coloring agent. The fat content is about 80 per cent. Grade AA, which is made from high-quality fresh sweet cream, is the best while Grade A is made from fresh cream and is supposed to be of only slightly lower quality. Grade B is made from sour cream. Much of the butter sold in supermarkets is not graded because participation in the program is optional. In most supermarkets, retail customers find that their choice is restricted to Grade AA and the ungraded product.

If you wish consistently high quality, buy Grade AA. Butter is often stored at below freezing temperatures for nine months or more but good quality butter does not undergo significant flavor changes under extended storage whereas the flavor of poor quality butter may be considerably affected.

Butter made in the winter is ordinarily light in color and deep yellow in early summer. The difference in color is caused by variance in the amount of carotene available to the cows. The amount of carotene is related to the vitamin A content which may vary from 9,500 I.U. per pound in late winter to 18,000 I.U. in the summer. Because of the color variation, the USDA permits butter to be colored with either annatto, beta carotene, or one of the coal tar dyes, Yellow No. 5 or Yellow No. 6. Use of color additives need not be noted on the package. Annato is a natural food color extracted from plant seeds and has been used for years without apparent harm, but nevertheless The Joint FAO/WHO Expert Committee on Food Additives believes that testing for possible adverse effects is needed. Beta carotene is approved by the Expert Committee and indeed is a source of vitamin A. Use of the two coal tar dyes in butter is highly questionable but fortunately most butter processors either do not add color or use one of the more acceptable ones. Land O' Lakes, for example, uses annatto in their winter butter.

Whipped butter, which has its volume increased through the addition of air or an inert gas such as nitrogen, has the same value per pound as hard butter but per pat or spoonful, the value is lower. Sweet butter contains about .01 per cent salt as compared with 2 per cent for salted butter. Salt is used as a preservative, but if you use butter fairly fast there should ordinarily be no problem with the keeping quality of the unsalted variety. For longer storage, unsalted butter may be frozen.

Butter supplies vitamin A and fat but little else. The fat is over 60 per cent saturated and for this reason butter, like other dairy products, has come under attack.

Margarine

All margarine, regardless of brand name or whether solid, soft or liquid, is composed of oil and fat, aqueous liquids (water and/or milk), emulsifiers, preservatives, artificial butter flavoring, coloring agents and added vitamins. Most have salt added (1½ to 3 per cent). All these additives are safe with the possible exceptions of the artificial butter flavoring and the artificial colors.

Margarine today is almost always composed of vegetable oils. The fat or oil content must, by law, be 80 per cent while the aqueous liquid content must be 16 per cent. The degree of hardness is achieved in part by varying the proportions of fat (a solid) to oil (a liquid). Thus, soft margarines usually contain a greater proportion of oil than regular margarine while liquid margarine contains even more oil. (Whipped margarines are usually solid margarines that have been given a softer consistency by blending with air.)

All fats and oils are mixtures of saturates, monounsaturates and polyunsaturates. If a fat is high in saturates, it is usually solid at room temperature; if it is high in polyunsaturates, it is usually liquid at room temperature. Using special manufacturing techniques, solid fats and liquid oils can be blended together with water to produce almost any consistency desired, although only three consistencies are commonly produced (solid, soft, and liquid). Ordinarily, most of the fat is in the form of oil which is liquid at room temparature and must be made into a solid through hydrogenation.

Diet imitation margarine is usually similar to regular solid margarine except that it contains half as much fat, the balance being made up with water. Despite this, diet imitation margarines actually sell for several cents more than regular margarines.

Regular or solid, margarine is by no means a uniform product even though color and texture of the various brands may appear similar. Some brands have a hydrogenated oil as their leading ingredient while in others the leading ingredient is liquid oil. Some are based primarily on safflower or corn oil while others are based on oils with lower polyunsaturate levels. There is a wide variation in the type of fat even among brands which are based on the same kind of oil. One analysis of two brands of corn oil margarine showed that one had 38 per cent and the other 54 per cent polyunsaturates. In general, soft margarines that have liquid oil as the first listed ingredient contain more polyunsaturates and less hydrogenated oil than other types.

Like butter, margarine has virtually no protein and no carbohydrates and therefore its only contribution to the diet nutritionally is in the form of fat and certain vitamins. Today all margarines sold at retail in America are fortified with vitamin A at 15,000 IU units per pound. In this respect, margarine is a more reliable source of vitamin A than butter which normally fluctuates from 9,500 IU for winter production to 18,000 in spring and summer. Some margarines are also fortified with 2,000 IU of vitamin D per pound, a fact which must be noted on the label. Margarine contains a limited amount of vitamin E, which probably varies by brand.

Which Should You Use?

Should you use butter or margarine? Butter is high in saturated fat (46 per cent by weight) a substance which most, but not all authorities believe is related in some way to heart disease. (See "The Big Controversy Over Fats And Oils," page 191.) On the other hand, margarine contains hydrogenated fat (18 to 40 per cent), a substance which several researchers believe may also be a cause of heart disease. (See "Hydrogenated Fats And Oils," pages 178-181.) Margarine has been sold largely on the basis that its polyunsaturated content prevents heart disease but this is highly questionable. Excessive use of polyunsaturates has been linked at least tentatively, to cancer in humans. (See "Polyunsaturates and Cancer," page 184.)

If you decide to take the advice of certain nutritionists who advocate a drastic reduction in fat intake for every healthy person, the problem might be simplified by eating neither.

LARD

Almost all experienced cooks prefer lard for baking pie crusts, crackers, and pastries because it contributes an exceptional flakiness; on the other hand, it gives poor results in cake baking. Some lard is altered chemically by a process called "intersterification" which rearranges the molecular structure, making it suitable for a wider range of functions, although its flaking ability is somewhat reduced. Animal studies have shown no difference in the health effects of inter-esterified fats as compared to regular fats.

Contrary to popular belief, unhydrogenated lard is relatively low in saturated fat compared to other animal fats such as butter or tallow, for it has only slightly more saturated fatty acids than cotton-seed oil (33 vs 27 per cent). The ratio of saturates to unsaturates in lard is extremely variable and is dependent upon the type of diet fed to the hogs. Hydrogenated lard is widely available, but nonhydrogenated lard is difficult to find in many areas.

Lard is an animal product and therefore contains cholesterol but the amount is small (about 16 mg. per tablespoon).

MAYONNAISE AND ITS IMITATORS

By law, mayonnaise consists of vegetable oil, an acid (such as vinegar or lemon juice), egg yolk (as an emulsifier), and spices and flavorings. Also permitted are oxystearin (inhibits crystallization), calcium diso-dium EDTA (traps metal impurities and acts as an antioxidant) and the flavor enhancer MSG. Oxystearin and EDTA are safe. MSG need not be noted on the label. The processors of Hellman's and Kraft say that they do not contain MSG.

Some gourmet style mayonnaise contains virgin olive oil, but most mayonnaise is based on refined soybean oil or a combination of refined soybean and cottonseed oils. The oils are usually not hydrogenated. Most brands supply high levels of polyunsaturated fatty acids. Hellman's, for example, contains 51.5 per cent polyunsaturates, 30 per cent monounsaturates, and 18:5 per cent saturates.

Although mayonnaise contains cholesterol (because it contains egg yolk), the amount of egg yolk used in the commercial product is so low (less than one yolk per pint of mayonnaise) that a tablespoon contains only about 6 milligrams compared to 16 mg in a pat of butter, or 250 mg in a whole egg. Mayonnaise is usually about 80 per cent fat (although legally it can can be as low as 65 per cent) and therefore is high in calories (about 100 per tablespoonful).

A lower cost alternative to mayonnaise is mayonnaise type salad dressing such as Kraft Miracle Whip. Its tart and tangy taste (mayonnaise is relatively bland with a more subtle flavor) is actually preferred in the Midwest and other parts of the country where it often commands as high a price as mayonnaise itself. These products contain less oil and more water than regular mayonnaise.

In some store brands, sugar is the second most plentiful ingredient. Legally, a portion of the emulsifiers used must be egg yolk. MSG may be added as a flavor enhancer but does not have to be listed on the label.

Imitation mayonnaise is an inferior substitute for real mayonnaise and mayonnaise type salad dressings, as it contains hydrogenated oil, artificial color and artificial flavor. Imitation mayonnaise has been promoted as a low-calorie product on the basis of its high water content and low oil content.

OILS, REFINED

Refined oils lose some vitamin E during processing. Refined soybean oils are usually partially hydrogenated but refined corn oil, peanut oil and safflower oil are not. With the exception of Wesson Buttery Flavor soybean oil, which contains unspecified artificial color and flavor, most oils are made without questionable additives. The additives commonly found in refined oils, including isoproyl citrate and citric acid (antioxidants), dimethylpolysiloxine and methyl silicone (antispattering agents), and oxystearin (anticlouding agent), are considered safe.

In addition to being less expensive, refined oils have high smoke points which permit high-temperature cooking (375° to 500°). However, at such temperatures much of the nutrient value of the food may be lost. Unless there is a very special reason to cook at such high temperatures, low-temperature cooking (150° to 250°) is highly preferable. At the low temperatures, the crude or unrefined oils can be used with suitable temperature controls.

If you intend to fry the high-temperature way, you need an oil with a high smoke point. The maximum temperature for this method should be at least 35 degrees below the actual smoke point for the oil deteriorates at that point.

Often the label of a refined oil states that it is good "for frying, salads and baking." This is misleading, because oils with characteristics that are good for conventional high-temperature frying (such as having a high smoke point or being free of emulsifiers like lecithin), are not ideal as a shortening in baking, which requires the presence of emulsifiers. Products which claim to be good for all three purposes are a compromise at best. The exception is an unrefined oil which can be used in salads, for low-temperature frying, and even for baking (because it contains naturally-occurring lecithin and other compounds that act as emulsifiers).

The use of cottonseed oil as a food has been questioned because of potentially high residues of pesticides that may be present. Cotton is the most heavily-sprayed crop in America because it is technically not considered a food crop but refined cotton seed oil has no residues. This was clearly demonstrated in a study in which 14 different pesticides (including aldrin, dieldrin, lindane and DDT) were added to various crude vegetable oils at levels three times the tolerance level permitted in seeds from which oil is extracted. Following alkali-refining, bleaching and deodorization, no residue from any of the 14 pesticides could be detected. Thus, as far as pesticide residues are concerned, refined cottonseed oil is preferable to crude cottonseed oil.

OILS, UNREFINED

If an oil is marketed without any further processing after extraction, it is called "unrefined" or "crude." So-called "cold pressed" oils are not necessarily crude. (See "Processing of Vegetable Oils," this chapter.) Crude oils have rich colors, and are slightly cloudy in appearance due to the presence of various nonoily substances, and have stronger flavors and aroma than refined oils. The types generally available are soybean, sesame, peanut, corn, safflower, sunflower and olive oil. These are available under various labels including Hain, Arrowhead and Erewhon. They can be found in health food stores and in health food sections of a few supermarkets.

Unrefined oils may seem too strong in flavor to many who have grown accustomed to pale-yellow or crystal-clear refined oils with a uniformly bland taste, but users claim that they add a new flavor dimension to salads and other foods. Unrefined oils are quite expensive compared to refined oils apparently because the market volume is lower.

Unrefined oils are usually thought of as salad oils, but they can also be used for low-temperature frying (150° to 250°). High-temperature frying (375° to 500) is not practical with unrefined oils because the lecithin and other materials in the oils smoke or decompose.

Olive Oil

Olive oil, most widely-used of the unrefined oils, is made in three basic forms: virgin, pure and blended. Virgin olive oil, which is the most highly prized because of its rich flavor, is cold pressed, often with small hand presses and is made from the fruit of the finest ripe olives. It is not refined any further, because deodorization would destroy much of its characteristic rich flavor, and bleaching would remove its desirable green color.

Virgin olive oil is often hard to find in the U.S., even in specialty shops, and when it is available it may sell for as much as ten dollars or more a gallon (compared to about five dollars per gallon for the standard domestic types such as Wesson Oil or Crisco Oil).

When shopping for virgin olive oil, keep in mind the following grading system: (1) *Extra:* Olive oil of perfect flavor, with a maximum acidity of 1 per cent; (2) *Fine:* Same flavor as "Extra" but with 1.5 per cent acidity; (3) *Unnamed grade:* Slightly off-flavor, maximum acidity of 3 per cent. This is the grade of virgin olive oil commonly sold in the U.S.; (4) *Lampante:* Off-flavor with over 3.3 per cent acidity (very poor quality oil).

So-called "pure" olive oil, the most widely-sold variety in the U.S., is made from highly-processed oil pulp residues, along with lower-grade olives, ground-up pit kernels, and the pulp residues left over from the pressing of virgin oil. This material is solvent extracted and goes through other processing steps similar to most supermarket oils. The resulting oil is very bland in flavor compared to virgin olive oil.

In blends, only 10 per cent is olive oil and the remaining 90 per cent of the oil is usually a refined oil such as soybean or cottonseed. Cost is about the same as that of most refined oils such as Wesson or Mazola and well below that of "pure" olive oil. Those made with virgin oil are considered superior to those made with pure olive oil but are not widely available.

Olive oil will deteriorate less readily than most oils, but in time will go rancid. Opened containers of olive oil kept for any length of time should be refrigerated despite label instructions to the contrary. The labels advise against refrigeration because olive oil becomes solid in cold temperatures and the manufacturers are concerned that the consumer will view this as a sign of inferior quality. Solidification is not a sign of inferiority for the oil returns to liquid upon warming at room temperature. Olive oil is unique among oils in having little saturated or polyunsaturated fatty acids. It is primarily composed of monounsaturates which do not seem to affect serum cholesterol levels one way or the other.

SALAD DRESSINGS, PREPARED

Although salad dressings are extremely easy to make, many people today prefer to buy their dressing ready-made in the familiar "banjo" bottle. The basic forms are French, Italian, Russian and Blue Cheese, but most manufacturers use more exotic names to call attention to their products, such as "Green Goddess," "Caesar," and "Viva Italian!" These dressings usually have an oil content of 40 to 50 per cent, the balance is water, vinegar, sugar, spices, emulsifiers and other synthetic additives.

Most brands enhance their "thick and creamy" texture with a variety of emulsifiers and natural and modified vegetable gum thickeners. At least one of these additives, gum tragacanth, has not been adequately tested.

These products are clearly not made for those on sodium-restricted diets for on the average they have about twice the sodium levels of mayonnaiselike salad dressing and three to four times as much as real mayonnaise. The Italian dressings are usually highest in salt.

Salad Dressing Mixes

While low cost may be the most attractive feature of these mixtures of spices and additives, many people prefer them because of the option of using their own choice of oil and vinegar. Dressings made from mixes cost up to one-third less than comparable prepared dressings in the banjo bottles, even when the cost of the added oil and vinegar is included. Unfortunately, most of the available mixes contain artificial color while some also contain MSG.

VEGETABLE SHORTENINGS

The introduction of solid vegetable shortening was a real boon to the cook back in the days of the ice box. It would keep for long periods at room temperature, unlike lard which deteriorated rapidly, even when kept cool.

Although vegetable shortening is no match for lard in making flaky pie crusts and pastries, it is superior for cakes and can also be used for frying as well. Vegetable shortening is a compromise between the qualities of lard and those of a cooking oil, but its long-term stability and convenience have made it about three times more popular.

Vegetable shortening is usually composed of a partially hydrogenated oil mixed with a relatively small amount of very hard hydrogenated fat in crystal form. These hard crystals are dispersed evenly throughout the oil, giving it a solid appearance. Most shortenings are "fluffed" by whipping in nitrogen (an inert gas). Fluffing improves the shortening's baking properties as well as making it easier to use, since less beating is required to entrap air prior to adding other ingredients to the batter. When the batter is baked in the oven the shortening melts and releases the air bubbles which contribute to the lightness of the finished baked goods.

Shortenings vary markedly in their degree of saturation. The proportion of polyunsaturated fatty acids varies from 10 to 42 per cent while saturated fat varies from 15 to 35 per cent. Crisco, the leading shortening, has 26 per cent saturates.

Crisco does not contain any preservatives, and the only additive listed is methyl silicone, an antifoaming agent for high-temperature frying, considered to be completely safe. Proctor and Gamble, the makers of Crisco, also make an artificially-colored fluffed yellow shortening called "Golden Fluffo" which imparts a yellow color to baked goods. The coloring used in this product is carotene, a beneficial additive that is a precurser of vitamin A.

The cook who wants to avoid hydrogenated fats could use unhydrogenated lard instead of vegetable shortening, but if the former is not available, a second-best alternative would be a crude vegetable oil, although such oils may not impart the flaky texture provided by vegetable shortening or lard.

CHAPTER VII

Beverages

Water, mother of all beverages, is the most essential of nutrients. Death comes more surely and more swiftly from lack of water than from lack of any other nutrient. In high temperatures, football players have died on the field when denied it. When deprived of any other essential nutrient, normally healthy people survive for weeks or even months.

Many people satisfy virtually all of their requirements for water by drinking coffee, tea, cocoa, fruit juice, soft drinks or other beverages. This practice may have its healthy aspects in view of the many disclosures regarding industrial pollutants and possible carcinogens in tap water. Common beverages, however, have their drawbacks, including unwanted stimulative effects, tooth decay and possibly even lead poisoning.

Stimulative Effects of Coffee, Tea, Cocoa and Cola

Coffee, tea, cocoa and cola have such powerful stimulative effects that, if they had just been invented, the Food and Drug Administration might well permit them to be sold only with a prescription. It is, of course, the stimulative effects that make them popular. Many advocates of natural foods scorn these beverages for just these effects despite their derivation from natural sources: coffee beans, tea leaves, cocoa beans and cola nuts.

Caffeine, theophylline, and theobromine belong to a class of stimulative chemicals called *xanthines*. Caffeine is predominant in the xanthine-containing beverages, but tea is also rich in theophylline, while cocoa also contains theobromine.

Caffeine, theophylline, and theobromine share in common a number of effects on the body, although each has more or less effect depending upon the specific area of action.

Table I

RELATIVE EFFECT OF XANTHINES

	Central Nervous System & Respiratory Stimulation	Skeletal Muscle Relaxation	Diuresis (increased urine flow)	Cardiac stimulation	Coronary Dilation
Caffeine	XXX	XXX	X	X	X
Theophylline	XX	XX	XXX	XXX	XXX
Theobromine	X	X	XX	XX	XX

Source: J. M. Ritchie, "Central nervous system stimulants II, The Xanthines," in *Pharmacological Basis of Therapeutics*, L. S. Goodman and A. Gillman, eds. (New York: Macmillan, 1970) p. 355. Copyright © 1970, Macmillan Publishing Co.

The xanthines stimulate the central nervous system, especially the brain, which is the effect most people seek from these beverages. Caffeine is especially effective in this action, producing a more rapid and clearer flow of thought and allaying drowiness and fatigue. Activity is increased, but tasks involving delicate muscular coordination and accurate timing may be adversely affected. There is also an increased sensitivity to sensory stimuli which can become unpleasant when too much coffee is consumed. Nervousness and irritability also result from large amounts. This excitation of the central nervous system by large amounts of caffeine is followed later by a depression of all these functions. The theophylline in tea is less powerful as a central nervous system stimulant, while the theobromine in cocoa is virtually inactive in this respect.

All parts of the circulatory system are affected by the xanthines, particularly by the theophylline in tea. One of the primary effects is excessively rapid beating of the heart. After large amounts of xanthines are consumed, this stimulation can be extreme enough to cause irregularities in the heartbeat. The xanthines cause the coronary arteries to dilate thus increasing the blood flow. In the parts of the body farthest from the heart the opposite effect occurs, with the blood vessels becoming constricted, especially in the brain, causing a decrease in cerebral blood flow. This effect is thought to be a factor in caffeine's ability to alleviate headache (caffeine is often included with aspirin in pain relievers) while "withdrawal headache" is a symptom in heavy coffee drinkers who give up the beverage. Effects of caffeine on blood cholesterol levels are variable, with both higher and lower levels being reported in experiments on animals and humans.

Man's capicity for muscular work is increased by caffeine, which appears to render muscle less susceptible to fatigue. This effect, however, is short-lived.

All the xanthines are diuretics; that is they increase the production of urine. Theophylline is the most effective diuretic of the group. Theobromine is less active, but its effect is more sustained, and caffeine is the least diuretic in effect.

While the effect of any single ingestion is undoubtedly minor, some researchers are concerned with the long-term effects of the lifelong use of these substances. The addicting capacity of xanthine-containing beverages indicates that serious metabolic changes may be taking place. Studies have shown that heavy consumers of these beverages (five or more cups daily) experience "withdrawal" symptoms, including irritability, an inability to work effectively, nervousness, lethargy and headache if they do not drink coffee in the morning. Noncoffee drinkers who try the beverage are apt to experience such unwanted consequences as sleeplessness or diuresis, but regular coffee drinkers apparently build up a tolerance of caffeine and do not experience these symptoms. Little work has been done on the cumulative lifelong effect of xanthines on the central nervous system.

The high consumption of xanthines by children in the form of cola beverages and chocolate has concerned nutritionists for many years. Many parents deny their children coffee yet allow virtually open access to cola and chocolate. Children are more strongly affected than adults by caffeine, which can readily cause hyperactivity and nervousness, insomnia and excessively rapid beating of the heart. A twelve ounce bottle of cola contains between one-third and one-half the caffeine of a cup of brewed coffee, while a cup of cocoa has one-fifth to one-third the caffeine. Soda beverages other than colas usually do not contain caffeine, Dr. Pepper being the chief exception. Although the cola nut naturally contains caffeine, it is largely lost in the processing, and cola manufactureres actually add caffeine back to the beverages in order to give them that extra "zing." (Its source is the caffeine which is removed from decaffeinated coffee!)

Because of its chocolatelike taste, carob (powdered St. John's bread) has been suggested as a caffeine-free substitute for chocolate and cocoa. However, carob is not without some hazards of its own, especially for growing children. (See "Tannins," pages 219-220.)

Caffeine and Heart Disease

Over the years, several studies have suggested that heavy coffee-drinking is a risk factor in heart disease. All of these studies have been discredited either because the sample was too small, or it failed to incorporate an adequate control group of noncoffee drinkers for comparison, or for failure to control for other relevant risk factors such as cigarette-smoking.

In 1973, however, researchers from the Kaiser-Permanente Medical Center in Oakland, California, published a large-scale, well-controlled study. They concluded that "Coffee drinking is not an established risk for myocardial infarction." This conclusion was subsequently corroborated by re-evaluation of data from the Framingham study, the long-term study of heart disease conducted in Framingham, Massachusetts.

Although most studies have failed to link coffee or tea drinking with heart disease, a 1979 study found that caffeine (at a level equivalent to that in two to three cups of coffee), raised blood pressure substantially for several hours. More research is needed to determine the long term signʾficance of this temporary rise in blood pressure, but it does suggest moderation for those susceptible to hypertension.

Caffeine and Other Diseases

Although early studies indicated that caffeine caused mutations in mice, these studies were later shown to be based on faulty data, and subsequent studies have given negative results. However, while caffeine does not cause mutations, it does cause birth defects, at least in animals. According to Michael F. Jacobson, Co-Director of The Center for Science in the Public Interest, the small amount of caffeine in one or two cups of coffee a day may lead to birth defects. He warns expectant mothers in the first three months of pregnancy to reduce or totally eliminate beverages, foods and drugs containing caffeine.

A number of hormonal effects are produced by xanthines, especially the release of epinephrine (adrenaline) and norepinephrine. This results in changes in blood sugar metabolism, including increased insulin secretion. Such effects have been linked to the occurrence of hypoglycemia (low blood sugar).

Many normal people experience stomach upset from drinking coffee. This effect is usually attributed to certain essential oils in coffee rather than the caffeine.

Thus, even decaffeinated coffee can stimulate gastric secretions.

Tannins in Coffee, Tea, Cocoa and Carob

Another important group of naturally-occurring components in coffee, tea, cocoa and carob are the tannins. These substances are used industrially in the tanning of leather, but also contribute certain characteristics to beverages. The dark red color of tea is largely due to tannin, which also contributes to the taste. The tannins are valued in these beverages because they possess astringency which influences flavor and contributes body to these as well as to wine, cider, and beer. Excessive astringency causes a puckery sensation in the mouth, also produced when tea becomes high in tannins from overbrewing.

Questions regarding the safety of tannins have been raised recently. Experiments have shown that tannin-containing food can depress the growth rate of young animals. These effects are so pronounced that the editors of the journal, *Food and Cosmetic Toxicology,* believe that there may be a strong case against the use of carobs in animal feeds. Tannins bind with protein to form indigestible compounds, and it was at first thought that this was the cause of growth depression. Later work indicated that tannic acid might instead reduce absorption of protein through the intestinal wall. The substitution of carob for chocolate in the diets of children is recommended by advocates of health-foods, yet the scientific evidence indicates that carob, while free from caffeine, should be used in moderation especially in the diet of the young.

Acidic Beverages and Tooth Decay

Virtually every beverage consumed by humans, except for water and milk, contains acids strong enough to dissolve tooth enamel. Many believe that carbonated soda beverages are acidic enough to "eat the rust off of car bumpers," but few realize that natural fruit drinks also contain high levels of erosive acids. Health-food advocate are quick to point out the hazards of cola drinks yet fail to mention that some natural juices, such as lemon juice, can be even more destructive of tooth enamel than the colas.

The protective enamel on the surface of teeth is the hardest substance in the body and is virtually impervious to destruction except by strong acids. Ordinarily, such acids are produced by bacteria which thrive on sugars that cling to the teeth, and this is usually considered the primary cause of dental caries. However, the erosive properties of acids present in beverages also dissolve the tooth enamel thus magnifying the effect of acids produced by bacteria. In this process, the acids in beverages appear to be much more important than their sugar content.

Fruit Juices

Acidity is measured by pH, lower values indicating high acidity. In common beverages pH varies from an average of 5.0 for coffee and tea to 2.0 or less for lemon juice. Research on dental enamel suggests that a pH of 3.5 or less is a potential source of damage to the teeth. Pineapple and tomato juice have a pH above 3.5, apple, grape, orange, and prune juice range from moderately below to moderately above 3.5, while grapefruit, lemon, and lime have a pH below 3.5. The latter two are particularly acidic.

The most common acid in fruits and fruit juices and drinks, citric acid, has been shown to be more than twice as destructive as hydrochloric or nitric acid in dental erosion. Lemon juice appears to be extremely destructive of tooth enamel (in both animals and humans) perhaps due to its high acidity (pH 1.9 to 2.1) and also its high levels of citric acid. Numerous other studies indicate similar effects of lemon juice. Fortunately, most fruit juices, unlike lemon juice, do not erode the enamel very much unless taken in excessive quantities.

Whole fruits may have less effect on enamel than the

juice. A study done at the University of Hawaii using laboratory rats shows that eating the fruit instead of the juice results in a definite protective effect. The beneficial effects of eating whole fruit instead of drinking juice do not hold for lemons.

Soft Drinks

The widely held belief that cola beverages can erode tooth enamel is verified by many experimental studies. Perhaps the most well-known of all were those conducted by Dr. C. M. McCay of Cornell University in the late 1940's. Dr. McCay was alarmed by the tremendous increase in consumption of carbonated beverages which occurred during World War II, especially by servicemen. To observe the effects on tooth enamel, Dr. McCay and his colleagues immersed extracted human teeth in a common cola beverage and found that they gradually lost calcium over a two week period. They also found severe enamel destruction in the teeth of rats who drank cola for as little as five days.

Although the effects of carbonated beverages have not yet been substantiated in carefully-controlled studies with humans, the extensive animal studies are generally accepted as valid evidence of the adverse effect on humans. Furthermore, clinical reports show that people who drink large amounts of carbonated beverages tend to have enamel erosion.

The Position of the American Dental Association

The American Dental Association in an official policy statement takes the view that because a number of soft drinks and fruit juices are acidic, decalcification occurs when they are consumed in large amounts or at frequent intervals, but that decalcification should not be significant unless abnormal amounts are consumed.

What is "abnormal" consumption? Although orange juice and cola beverages are both acidic and both can dissolve tooth enamel, the relative amount of acid activity is substantially different. With a pH of 2.5, cola beverages have ten times the activity of orange juice with a pH of 3.5. Theoretically at least, one would get the same effect from twenty 6-ounce glasses of orange juice as from one can of a cola beverage. Many people, especially children, may drink five cans of cola a day, resulting in an acid intake roughly the same as from one hundred glasses of orange juice, yet the juice consumption would appear "excessive" while the cola might be considered "normal." Each 12 ounce can of cola and other soda beverage contains the equivalent of almost 8 teaspoonsful of sugar, which may enhance the cariogenic effect.

Lead Poisoning from Glazed Pottery

A further hazard from the acids in beverages is their tendency to leach toxic metals from glazed pottery in which they are stored or consumed. The hazard, which comes from lead, cadmium and antimony, can occur not only with highly acidic beverages such as juice and soft drinks, but also with the less acidic beverages, such as coffee and tea, more commonly used in glazed containers. Lead can produce liver, kidney and brain damage, and deterioration of the central nervous and reproductive systems. Children are especially susceptible to the effects of lead poisoning, which include mental retardation and other signs of central nervous system involvement. Even sub-toxic amounts of lead at very low levels can have chronic effects such as reduction in the activity of enzymes essential for synthesis of hemoglobin (a protein pigment in red blood cells). Lead can also destroy existing red blood cells.

During firing of pottery, the complex mixture of ingredients that make up the glaze melt and fuse together to form an insoluble glass. If the temperature is not high enough or the time not long enough, or the air flow within the kiln is imperfect, or if copper-based colors (generally greens and blues) are present, the finished glaze is partly soluble in acidic foods and beverages. The most acute hazard occurs when acid beverages, especially fruit juices, are stored in glazed containers for more than a few hours. Many potters now have a card saying, "This piece was fired at 2300° F. No lead was used in the glaze."

The American pottery industry has recently begun testing and certifying dishes produced by voluntarily participating manufacturers. Glazes that release less than the FDA minimum standards may use a stamp on the dish which says "Glaze Tested Approved; U.S. Potters Association." However, a large proportion of the decorative mugs are imported from foreign countries, and are only spotchecked by the FDA.

To protect yourself from effects of toxic metal poisoning follow these precautions: never store food in anything except glass, stainless steel, Pyrex, Corelle, or polyethylene containers. Acid foods (such as tomato dishes) should never be cooked in ceramic or enamel containers unless these are known to be free of lead. Acid beverages, including coffee, tea, beer, wine, orange, apple and other juices, and carbonated beverages, should never be served in anything except a glass, polyethylene or certified safe ceramic container. Children should always be given juices or soda in a glass, or, if they prefer a cup, it should be made of plastic. Coffee and tea drinkers should especially avoid decorative or handmade mugs and cups, unless safety has been certified. A significant exception is stoneware (also called ironstone) because it is fired at higher temperatures (2300-2400° F) than earthenware (fired at 1000-2200° F). If the label does not say "stoneware" or "ironstone" assume that it is earthenware.

The highest levels of lead occur in green or blue glazes, and if you have mugs which are of either color on the inside surface, they should be removed from the kitchen and recycled as pencil holders, planters, or any other nonfood use. Cadmium and antimony, other extremely hazardous metals, are used only to produce bright red and yellow colors. Ceramics with these color glazes should also not be used for foods or beverages. There is also a hazard of lead poisoning from silver plated cups according to the FDA.

Beverages—A Listing

CAROB

Carob powder, also known as powdered St. John's Bread, is highly esteemed by health-food advocates as a completely safe chocolate substitute for children. Because carob contains no caffeine or other stimulants, it may be better for children than cocoa or cola, but because of its high tannin content, it is not without potential hazard. (See "Tannins in Coffee, Tea, Cocoa and Carob" in this chapter.)

Carob powder is not as soluble as cocoa and, therefore, has a slightly "gritty" feel in the mouth, and it also settles rather quickly to the bottom of a cup of the beverage. Unlike cocoa, carob is naturally sweet and thus requires much smaller amounts of sugar to produce a palatable beverage. Some chocolate enthusiasts claim that considerable imagination is required to consider carob a substitute for real chocolate flavor, but with the addition of a little vanilla extract, carob beverages can be quite tasy. Carob appears to be less allergenic than cocoa.

COCOA

Cocoa is available in a variety of forms ranging from plain powder which must be cooked with milk and sugar to instant mixes which contain everything—cocoa, sugar, even milk powder—and require only water to make a hot or cold beverage.

Cocoa beverages are stimulants because they contain theobromine and caffeine—a cup of cocoa contains about one-fourth the caffeine of a cup of coffee. Cocoa is also high in tannins, which may inhibit growth, as well as oxalic acid, which can prevent the absorption of calcium by the body. Cocoa (and chocolate as well) are therefore of questionable value in the diet of children. Many people, especially children, are very allergic to cocoa or chocolate. On the positive side, cocoa is an excellent source of certain essential trace minerals. Among all foods, cocoa is one of the best sources of copper and magnesium and is a fair source of iron and potassium.

Powdered Cocoa

The amount of fat (cocoa butter) in cocoa is regulated by law: breakfast cocoa must contain a minimum of 22 per cent cocoa fat, plain cocoa must contain between 10 and 22 per cent fat, while products containing less than 10 per cent fat must be labelled low-fat cocoa. Since cocoa butter consists of about 60 per cent saturated fat, 38 per cent monounsaturated and only 2 per cent polyunsaturates, those on a low saturated fat diet may wish to select the plain or low-fat cocoas. Most supermarkets, however, carry only the plain cocoa.

Powdered cocoa is usually prepared by cooking in a mixture of two-thirds milk and one-third water, along with sugar. Cocoa has quite a bitter taste and substantial amounts of sugar are needed to make the beverage palatable. (Usually equal amounts of cocoa and sugar are used.) Plain powdered cocoa will not mix with cold milk and thus is not as popular today as the instant cocoa mixes (see below).

Dutch Process Cocoa

Often cocoa is treated with an alkali to darken its color and modify its flavor. This is called "Dutch Process" cocoa because the process originated in the Netherlands, but the product does not have any other connection with that country. Although the alkali treatment is not considered harmful, Dutch Process cocoa is less desirable than regular cocoa because more sugar must be added to attain the same level of sweetness. Most Dutch Process cocoa is not sold in plain form but is used in cocoa mixes.

Cocoa Mixes

Chocolate-flavored products which mix easily with milk (such as Nestle's Quik and Hershey's Instant) feature sugar as the most prominent ingredient and contain unspecified artificial flavors. These ingredients, combined with the naturally-occurring caffeine, theobromine, theophylline and tannin, make such cocoa products of dubious value for children.

Even less desirable are the "complete" mixes such as Swiss Miss or Hershey's Hot Cocoa Mix, which only require water to be added. At least insofar as children are concerned, the powdered milk they contain is an inferior substitute for the whole milk added to the other products.

COFFEE

There are only two types of coffee important in world commerce: Arabica and Robusta. About one-fourth of the world's coffee is Robusta which comes from Africa. The harsh Robusta flavor is not very acceptable to the consumer and hence sells for about half the price of milder coffees. Because of its low price it is usually mixed with better coffees to produce a more palatable blend, and is used especially in instant coffee production because its harsh flavor is tempered by the processing.

Arabica can either be of high or low quality, depending primarily upon the altitude at which it is grown. Although Arabica originated in the Middle East, it is now virtually the only coffee grown in the Americas. The finest quality Arabica coffee is mild, aromatic and flavorful, and comes from the mountainous countries of Central America and, in particular, Colombia. Brazil, which produces almost half the world's coffee, grows primarily a lower quality Arabica.

The coffee bean starts out as a nutritious product but during processing where temperatures of 500° F are sustained for five minutes, virtually all the nutrients with the exception of a small amount of niacin, are lost. Caffeine occurs at about 1 per cent in Arabica and about 2 per cent in Robusta. Thus the corresponding cups of coffee have 100 and 200 mg. caffeine.

The method of brewing affects the amount of caffeine in a cup. A six-ounce cup of coffee made in an automatic drip coffeemaker contains about 180 mg. of caffeine, while a cup from an electric percolator has only 124 mg.

Instant Coffee

Instant coffee is made by taking ground coffee and percolating it. The percolated liquid is then converted to a powder through a spray drying process after aromatic oils salvaged from previous processing stages are added.

In the freeze drying process, the percolated liquid, instead of being spray dried, is converted directly to a solid at 32° F or lower under a vacuum. The process results in a better flavor because it avoids the heating of the spray drying process.

Coffee made from both regular instant powder and freeze dried granules has about one-half the caffeine of regular coffee (79 mg. in a six-ounce cup). Per cup, instant is about half the cost of brewed coffee while freeze dried is about the same as brewed.

Decaffeinated Coffee

Being "97 per cent caffeine free" should mean that these products are far safer to consume than regular coffee. Certainly as far as caffeine is concerned this is true, but questions have been raised as to the safety of chemical residues which may remain in the product as a result of the decaffeination process. Decaffeination involves use of solvents such as trichloroethylene, chloroform or benzene. Because coffee-making procedures are jealously guarded industry secrets, it is not always possible for the outsider to determine whether or not a particular brand has been processed by methods which leave residues of these chemicals.

One of these solvents, trichloroethylene, is a possible cause of liver cancer and has been used in General Foods' decaffeinated products, Sanka and Brim. Following publicity about the possible toxicity of trichloroethylene by the Ralph Nader affiliated Health Research Group, General Foods discontinued use of the solvent in 1975 and instead is now using methylene chloride.

This chemical is also questionable. According to a CBS news report broadcast June 22, 1976, the National Cancer Institute is suspicious of methylene chloride because it is related to other known cancer-causing chemicals. CBS also says that no one has tested it yet for cancer. When interviewed by CBS, Food and Drug Administration Commissioner Dr. Alexander Schmidt conceded that "in moving from trichloroethylene to methylene chloride we may have gone from one fire to another or the pan to the fire. We simply don't know."

COFFEE SUBSTITUTES

Roasted cereals, ground and brewed in water to make a hot caffeine-free beverage, were very popular in the early part of this century but their consumption diminished with the advent of decaffeinated coffee. The two brands still enjoying modest sales are General Foods' "Instant Postum" and the imported "Pero." Postum is prepared from roasted whole wheat, roasted bran, and molasses, which are ground and mixed together.

These beverages have somewhat more nutrients than coffee. Three cups of Postum, for example, supply eight per cent of the iron requirement for an adult woman.

FRUIT DRINKS

Packaged fruit drinks are one of those minor rip-offs which everyone recognizes but which go on and on because children love them. When you buy such products as Hi-C or Hawaiian Punch, you pay mostly for water. The juice content in such products may cost up to seven times as much as a comparable amount of whole juice. Both products contain sugar and unspecified artificial color.

The Food and Drug Administration regulations for juice drinks are, one suspects, designed to confuse the consumer: who would think that "orange juice drink" must, by law, have five times as much juice as "orange drink?"

Table II

FDA CLASSIFICATION— ORANGE JUICES AND DRINKS

	% Juice
Orange Juice	100%
Orange Juice Drink	50%
Orangeade	25%
Orange drink	10%
Orange soda	No juice requirement but must be true fruit flavor.
Imitation Orange	No juice required, artificial flavor permitted.

Plain fruit juices—those with no added sugar, artificial color or other objectionable additives—are less expensive. Plain unadulterated fruit drinks are not ordinarily found in the supermarket, but you can achieve the same result by simply diluting full-strength juice.

FRUIT JUICES

Fruit juices, particularly the citrus juices, are nutritious because they are natural sources of vitamin C and other nutrients. Tomato and vegetable juices such as V-8 are also valuable because they are good sources of vitamins A and C. Prune juice is a source of iron. Apricot nectar is a good source of vitamin A. Fruit juices, unlike the original fruit, have very little fiber.

Several widely-advertised juices are relatively less valuable and considerably more expensive than others. Grape juice, for example, commonly costs approximately more than twice as much as orange juice but has less nutrients. Measured in terms of juice content, cranberry juice cocktail costs approximately eight times as much as orange juice.

The quality of frozen concentrated citrus juices varies depending upon composition and storage. In orange juice, excessive orange oil pulp or skin can cause off-flavors while quality will decline if the product is stored above 0° F. Many brands have the USDA Grade A label but this does not insure high quality. Consumers Union did a study on orange juice in 1967 in which it found that 31 per cent of all the brands tested were below the standards established by the

Florida Citrus Commission. Despite these disadvantages, frozen concentrated is generally the best form in which to buy juice. Freshly-squeezed juice, of course, is somewhat better in nutrient quality if the fruit is in good condition. Canned and refrigerated orange juice is usually of lower quality than the frozen concentrate.

Bottle refrigerated full-strength orange juices are highly susceptible to deterioration unless kept at a constant low temperature and consumed within a short time (about a week) of processing. The only good reason for buying refrigerated orange juice is to get the flavor of freshly-squeezed oranges. However, bottled freshly-squeezed orange juice is virtually unavailable in most parts of the country. Most refrigerated juice is made from concentrated and ordinarily costs more than juice made at home from concentrate.

Canned fruit juices present a special problem because they are highly acidic and, therefore, can leach lead from the can's soldered seams. Unless the can is aluminum and hence has no lead seams, it would be wise to buy the juices in bottled form. There is no danger from frozen concentrated juices because these are always in aluminum or fiber cans.

Flatulence from Juices

Studies indicate that apple juice produces 90 per cent as much gas as canned beans while raisins produce 60 per cent as much and grapes about 35 per cent. Orange juice and apricot nectar produce no gas.

FRUIT JUICES, SYNTHETIC

The introduction of Tang by General Foods in 1959 was a milestone in the evolution of American food. Until then, junk foods and nutritious, staple foods were thought of as different by most people. Everyone knew that soda pop was just sugared and flavored water and therefore was all right as a snack but obviously not as a replacement for staple foods in the diet. One such staple food was orange juice, which many people drank in a conscious effort to obtain vitamin C and other nutrients.

Because of massive advertising, many people have apparently come to accept Tang as a substitute for real orange juice. In switching to Tang, they give up many valuable nutrients and substitute several substances of dubious value. Tang is primarily sugar plus additives including such questionable ones as artificial color, artificial flavor, hydrogenated coconut oil and BHA. The competitive orange drinks Start and Awake (also made by General Foods) are of equally dubious value. What little nutrient value these imitation products have is contributed entirely by a limited number of synthetic vitamins and minerals. Natural orange juice contains small but possibly nutritionally significant amounts of at least a dozen nutrients not present in synthetic juices. The manufacturers of synthetic juices claim that in addition to vitamin C and A they also contain calcium, phosphorous and potassium but these substances are present in the products only incidentally for they happen to be components of such artificial additives as potassium citrate and calcium phosphate.

Frozen concentrated orange juice actually has a cost advantage over some of the synthetic products. As compared to Minute Maid, the biggest selling premium priced frozen concentrate, Tang is slightly more expensive on a per serving basis. Awake, which might be termed Tang in frozen concentrate form, costs about the same as the lowest priced frozen orange juice on a per serving basis.

A product similar to the synthetic juices but one that claims to contain "no less than 50 per cent orange juice" is Birds Eye "Orange Plus." At one dollar for a 12 ounce can, Orange Plus is more expensive than many brands of 100 per cent orange juice, and for the extra money you receive in addition to one-third the orange juice, some sugar syrup, corn syrup, orange pulp, and a host of additives including artificial flavor and artificial color.

HERBAL TEAS

To a botanist, the term "tea" refers specifically to a water infusion made from the leaves of the plant *Camellia sinensis*. Anything else is not "tea" but falls into the category usually called "herbal teas."

The sources of herbal teas are bound only by the imagination. Virtually any leaf, twig, seed, or flower can be (and probably has been) soaked in hot water to produce a beverage and over the years most have been endowed with "medicinal" virtues by those who consume them.

Advocates of herbal teas emphasize that these beverages are much safer than regular teas because they contain no caffeine. Some herbal teas, however, may be more hazardous than caffeine teas. For example, in 1960 safrole was banned as a potent carcinogen after use for many years as a flavoring for root beer. Safrole is the primary flavor component of the bark of the root of the sassafras tree. The root beerlike flavor of "sassafras tea" has long been a favorite among herbal tea fanciers, yet the evidence suggests that this beverage is questionable.

Another example is a tea made from the flowers of the chamomile plant. Chamomile tea contains at least three very potent drugs: chamazulene, en-yn-dicycloether, and apigenin-7-D-glucoside. These substances have anti-inflammatory, antiallergenic and other druglike properties. Although they are present in small quantities in each cup of chamomile tea, they may exhibit cumulative effects, and this beverage should therefore be consumed only in small quantities, especially by children.

A tea made from rhubarb or sorrel leaves is extremely high in oxalic acid, which combines with many minerals (especially calcium) to form insoluble salts which cannot be utilized by the body. Frequent consumption of such a tea could result in various mineral deficiences, and in children, could produce retarded growth.

On the other hand, many herbal medicines have been found to contain pharmacological active substances which are indeed beneficial in treating illness. Advocates of herbs are quick to point out that such modern medicines as quinine for malaria, digitalis for heart conditions, ephedrine for asthma and many more were originally "folk" remedies, but for every herb that has been found to contain beneficial ingredients, perhaps a hundred others have proved to be without effect.

It may be risky to use herbal teas for their medicinal values because the effects can be variable depending on the concentration of the drug in the plant. Health food enthusiasts have recently shown interest in a cyanide-containing substance known as amygdalin which is said to be beneficial in the treatment and prevention of cancer. Amygdalin is found in the seeds of many fruits including apricot kernels, cherry pits, bitter almonds and seeds of other fruits. This may possibly prove to be beneficial in treating cancer but, as in most other forms of cancer chemotherapy, there is probably a thin line between the amount that will kill the cancer and the amount that will kill the patient. Because the amount of the key ingredient in various seeds and leaves varies substantially, a brew may be tolerated one time yet be toxic the next. Commercially prepared drugs, on the other hand, are of consistently known dosage.

Most herbal teas, such as peppermint tea, are, of course, simply pleasant-tasting, warm, comforting beverages which offer a refreshing change from regular tea or coffee.

SOFT DRINKS

Are soft drinks as bad as they say? The answer is yes. Most soft drinks contain substantial amounts of artificial flavors and colors. Some, such as the colas and Dr. Pepper, contain caffeine, a substance which should not be given to children. For most parents, the worst thing about soft drinks is the sugar. Colas, for example, have the equivalent of eight level teaspoons in every 12 ounce can. The acidity of these beverages may, however, be even more deleterious for high acidity is as likely to promote dental problems as sugar.

Soft drinks may be flavored with synthetic compounds, natural flavor extracts, fruit juice concentrates, or any combination of these. Synthetic fruit flavor compounds may have over two dozen different chemical constituents. (See Appendix I.) Cola flavors are even more complex and their formulation is such a closely-guarded secret that they are even formulated with ingredients which are used only to make analysis and duplication by competitors difficult. When fruit derivatives are used that contain flavor oil, it is necessary to use an emulsifying agent to keep the oils from separating out in the beverage.

Virtually all colors used in soft drinks are synthetic and are primarily coal tar dyes. Even when natural fruit extracts or concentrates are used, synthetic colors are added because of their greater coloring power and color stability.

Cola beverages are the most acidic of all soft drinks with a pH of 2.6, and, therefore, are potentially the most likely to promote dental problems.

Diet Soft Drinks

Diet soft drinks became a billion-dollar-a-year business by the late 1960's through the use of the nonnutritive sweetener, cyclamate. When that chemical was finally banned in 1969 as a possible carcinogen, the industry quickly capitalized on what first appeared to be a disaster by substituting saccharin (another nonnutritive sweetener) and adding back some sugar (which was needed to counter saccharin's bitter aftertaste), and then prominently displaying labels which reassuringly proclaimed "NO CYCLAMATES." Since then saccharin too has come under fire as a possible carcinogen. The FDA removed saccharin from the "Generally Recognized as Safe" list early in 1972, and some consumer groups claim that enough evidence has been accumulated to show that saccharin is even more dangerous than cyclamate, but that the government refuses to ban it because this time industry does not have anything to take its place. The National Institute of Health advises people who use products containing saccharin to withdraw them from their diet completely for about three days each month to prevent toxic levels of saccharin building up in the liver.

Some nutritionists, such as Dr. John Yudkin, feel that the harmful effects of sugar are so great and the risks of saccharin so minor in comparison, that they recommend diet beverages over regular soft drinks. Other experts point out that unless the overall diet is carefully regulated and an exercise program started, "diet" beverages are of no use in weight reduction.

TEA

There are basically three classes of teas: green, black and oolong; all of them can be made from the same tea leaves, but with varied processing. The significant processing step that teas go through is called fermentation, but is actually enzymatic oxidation. The enzymes naturally present darken the tea leaves in the same way that a cut apple darkens. If the enzymes in the tea leaf are destroyed by blanching, the leaves will remain green. If the blanching is delayed, the leaf will be slightly darkened and oolong tea is produced: complete fermentation produces black tea. They are distinguished by subtle flavor differences but all have similar levels of caffeine.

Teas are graded according to the age of the leaves used. Orange pekoe is the best grade, made from terminal buds and the youngest leaves. Buds and young leaves are highest in caffeine. Lower grades are pekoe, pekoe souchong and souchong, in that order. Like coffee, the highest quality teas are grown at the highest altitudes.

Commerical teas are further distinguished by other names. Some are named after the province or area where they are grown (such as the Indian provinces of Assam and Darjeeling). Others, which are blends of teas and spices, are given commercial names such as Constant Comment (a mixture of black tea, spices and pieces of orange rind).

Analysis of different brands of six-ounce cups of bagged tea brewed according to package instructions showed significant differences in caffeine content. Red Rose was the highest of the domestic brands with 46 mg. caffeine per cup. Salada contained 40 mg., Lipton had 38 mg., and Tetley contained only 25 mg. of caffeine. Imported tea brands were consistently higher in caffeine. Twinings English Breakfast Tea (bagged) had 52 mg., and Twinings Darjeeling tea had 65 mg. caffeine.

Loose tea brewed in a pot releases more caffeine than bagged tea (a cup of tea made from loose Twinings English Breakfast had 77 mg.). Loose domestic tea made in a "Mr. Coffee" appliance was also high in caffeine (Tetley produced 71 mg. per cup). Mixed according to instructions, Lipton Instant Tea contained 62 mg., and Nestea Instant had 48 mg. caffeine.

The strength of the brew also affects the amount of caffeine. For example, while a weak cup (tea bag soaked 1 minute) of Red Rose had 45 mg. of caffeine, a strong brew (5-minute soak) resulted in 90 mg. per cup. Tetley ranged from 18 mg. in a weak brew, to 48 mg. at medium strength (3-minute soak), to 70 mg. caffeine in a strong (5-minute) cup.

The distinctive red color of black tea infusions is due mainly to tannins, but green tea also is high in tannins (in forms which have not been oxidized to a darker color). Tannin content of tea varies between 5 and 20 per cent, depending on geographical place of origin, genetic strain, length of brewing time, and other factors. The problems associated with tannins relate mostly to children since growth retardation seems to be the primary hazard. In this sense carob and cocoa are of more concern than tea, which is infrequently consumed by children in America. (See page 219.)

Tea is about as acid as coffee, and heavy tea drinkers should be wary of toxic metals leaching from cups and mugs. There is no evidence that tea drinking is linked with cardiovascular disease.

Instant Tea

Instant tea is made in much the same way as instant coffee but the process is not as advanced technologically. Instant tea begins with extraction in hot water of black tea types chosen for their reddish color. The infusion is then concentrated by partial dehydration and the extract is spray dried. Aromatic chemicals which escape during the processing are captured, concentrated, and added back to the extract just before drying.

Some manufacturers also supplement the tea concentrate with a form of starch called dextrin which protects some of the flavor and makes the instant products dissolve faster in cold water. Some brands of orange and lemon flavored instant tea contain chemical additives of doubtful value. Salada lemon-flavored tea, for example, has artificial color, while Nestea lemon does not. Sugar is the leading ingredient in some iced tea mixes.

WATER, BOTTLED

Many are concerned about the safety of the public water supply because of industrial pollutants or because of fears that the chlorination process may result in carcinogenic substances in the water. Others are concerned about the widespread reports linking soft water and atherosclerosis. Still others may object to the fluoridation of public water. For any of these reasons, and also because they may not like the taste of tap water, an increasing number of people are turning to bottled water.

Unfortunately, bottled water varies in quality from brand to brand and sometimes from season to season. The FDA has issued standards for bacterial content of bottled water shipped in interstate commerce but these set no limits on pesticides or organic compounds in the water. Bottlers can deviate from the standard if the deviation is noted on the label.

Bottled water may be spring water, purified tap water, distilled tap water, or what is called spring-type water. In distillation, the impurities, including minerals, are lost through vaporization. As the water condenses, it does not carry the impurities back into solution. Purified water is water from which the minerals have been removed to a level of less than 10 ppm by distillation or other means. Spring-type water is distilled water to which minerals have been added. Unless the bottler lists the mineral content, there is no way for the retail customer to know what is inside.

During the sixties and seventies considerable research was done on the possible protective effect of the minerals in water against cardiovascular disease. Many studies have shown that cardiovascular disease is lower in areas with hard water supply than in areas with soft water. Although a clear-cut cause-and-effect relationship has not yet been proven, the presence of a protective but as yet unidentified factor in hard water is accepted by many scientists.

Those who live in hard or moderately hard water areas would, by switching to bottled water, be giving up the possible protective effect of minerals in their tap water. In exchange, they will not always get a pure product. There have been reports of bacteria counts in well-known brands of bottled water 70 times greater than in the local tap water. The FDA has declared that 8 per cent of all bottled water—spring and purified —sold in the United States contains too many bacteria to meet national health standards. Although high bacteria counts are not necessarily harmful, they are indicative of careless processing procedures. In addition to less than perfect quality, a certain amount of outright fraud exists. In one well-publicized case, the Sierra Spring Company was fined $10,000 for advertising bottled Sacramento city water as "Spring Water."

The safety of bottled water is the responsibility of the FDA, which sets limits on the levels of chloride, copper, iron, manganese, phenols, sulfate, zinc, total solids, and several chemicals. The Environmental Protection Agency (EPA) sets limits for arsenic, barium, cadmium, lead, selenium and silver. Bottled water coming from other than municipal water systems must be analyzed for bacterial contamination at least once a week, but sample testing for minerals need be done only once a year.

Distilled water has been advocated by Paul Bragg, an elderly physical fitness enthusiast from Hawaii. In his book, *The Shocking Truth About Water* (Burbank, Cal., Health Science, 1970), he claims that chlorine, alum, calcium carbonate, magnesium carbonate, potassium carbonate and other minerals in water are injurious to health. Bragg may be correct about the chlorine in view of disclosures by the Environmental Defense Fund of its possible toxic effect, but there is no reason to believe that health would be improved by the absence of minerals. Indeed the scientific evidence strongly suggests that some of the minerals play a protective role.

The problem for most consumers is a choice between unknowns: on the one hand, a tap water which may provide possibly protective minerals but which also may contain carcinogenic substances; on the other hand plain bottled water which ordinarily is not labeled with the mineral content and which may not be as pure as the local tap water.

Increased popularity of bottled water is due largely to a multi-million dollar advertising campaign by Perrier, a naturally effervescent (sparkling) mineral water imported from France. Perrier sales soared from about $1 million in 1975 to an estimated $130 million in 1979.

In Europe, mineral water is thought to provide health benefits, and European medical journals regularly carry reports of its healing powers. American researchers have largely ignored its possible health aspects, and mineral water seems to be popular here because it is "chic," rather than for any curative effects. Those on a sodium-restricted diet should avoid the mineral waters (and club soda), because of the high sodium content.

While the mineral content of mineral water may prove beneficial, we consider the real value of sparkling water to be its increasing use by consumers as a replacement for soda beverages, especially diet soda. A glass of sparkling mineral water with a twist of lime is a refreshing drink that contains no sugar, no calories, and no saccharin, artificial flavors or colors.

CHAPTER VIII

Sweets

The Varieties of Sugar

If you look closely at food package labels you may be confused by the variety of sugars listed. Sucrose, dextrose, corn syrup, invert sugar and lactose are often seen on ingredient listings. They are derived from three basic sugars: *Glucose* (also called dextrose) is found in most fruits, is an important constituent of the bloodstream, and is the chief source of energy in the body. *Fructose* (also called levulose) is one of the principal types of sugar in fruit. *Galactose* does not occur in nature except as a constituent of more complex sugars such as lactose.

These three basic sugars form the basis for several other widely available sugars classified as disaccharides, or sugars that can be broken down into monosaccharides:

Glucose + Fructose = Sucrose
Glucose + Galactose = Lactose
Glucose + Glucose = Maltose

Sucrose, of course, is common table sugar or confectionery sugar. Lactose is derived from milk. Maltose is present in germinating grain but is not abundant in nature. One of the most common food additives is invert sugar which is sucrose that has been broken down into its constituent monosaccharides—that is glucose and fructose—by using a catalyst. Invert sugar is used by food processors because it resists crystalization and retains moisture. Corn syrup is increasingly used in food products because it sweetens like sucrose but costs far less to manufacture. Dextrose is a purified form of corn syrup.

Sugar and Disease

There are many unanswered questions and much conflicting evidence regarding the relationship of sugar to disease. The evidence available indicates that sucrose affects the body in different ways from other types of carbohydrates such as starch or glucose. Very few harmful effects have been attributed to glucose, even in relatively large quantities, and this is especially true of glucose in the form of starch. (Starch is composed of many glucose molecules linked together in long chains.) Since sucrose is half glucose and half fructose, it is thus assumed that its harmful effects result from the fructose portion. Experiments comparing the effects of sucrose, glucose, fructose and starch generally show similar harmful effects from both fructose and sucrose, which tends to confirm speculation that fructose is the real troublemaker. Because fructose is a natural component of most fruit, and fruit seems to be beneficial, it is generally assumed that fructose is not harmful in itself, but only when consumed in excessively large quantities. Thus, if problems such as diabetes, hypertension, and atherosclerotic heart disease can be linked to too much fructose, replacing white sugar with such high fructose products as brown sugar, "raw" sugar or honey will not eliminate the hazard. Pure corn syrup (but not the modified supermarket variety) may, on the other hand present less of a hazard. (See "Corn Syrup" in this chapter.)

Sugar and Dental Caries

Although several factors are involved in the formation of dental caries, sucrose stands out above all others as being the primary cause. Today, the only experts who deny this relationship are industry spokesmen such as Dr. Gary E. Costley, director of nutrition for the Kellogg Company who says: "In my opinion sugar is unrelated to dental caries."

Dental caries can be virtually eliminated by avoiding all refined sugar including all the processed foods such as carbonated beverages or cereals that have sugar as a leading ingredient. Short of such heroic self-denial, other measures can be salutory.

Experts from Harvard's School of Dental Medicine suggest the following:

1. Eat a well balanced diet where "as many of the

foods as possible are purchased in their natural state without excessive refining,"

2. Include foods that require vigorous chewing to stimulate teeth and gums,

3. Avoid sticky, sugary foods,

4. Eat fresh fruits, vegetables, fruit juices or milk and dairy products as between meal snacks,

5. Drink fluoridated water,

6. Clean your teeth thoroughly, especially after eating foods that cling to your teeth. Follow your dentist's directions for brushing and flossing.

Unrefined Sugars and Tooth Decay

Many health food advocates, among others, believe that "raw sugar" and other unrefined forms do not cause dental caries as much as similar amounts of refined white sugar. A number of scientific investigations have explored the possibility that unrefined sugars contain certain protective factors which might reduce the detrimental effect on teeth, but with conflicting results.

It has long been known that dental caries are absent in some primitive people (for example, Eskimos who pursue the traditional hunting economy) but become rampant when these people adopt a Western diet (for example, trading post Eskimos). Two South African researchers who studied the problem among the Bantus before World War II proposed the theory that unrefined foods contain protective factors.

Since then, a number of studies have been done in an attempt to discover what these factors might be, or even if they exist at all. Although many of the studies indicate that there may be protective factors in sugar cane juice and molasses, none have conclusively proven the case. One of the studies showed that "raw sugar" and brown sugar are not significantly different in their effects from plain white sugar, while another study showed that honey apparently causes more caries than plain sucrose.

Foods Which Protect Against Caries

Several foods apparently have a protective effect against caries. In an elaborate study done at the National Institute of Dental Research (part of the U.S. Dept. of Health, Education and Welfare), laboratory animals were given dozens of different commonly consumed human foods. In order to determine whether the foods had a protective effect, they were fed both with and without sucrose.

Of the foods tested, popcorn, peanuts and whole milk were found to have a protective effect while six other foods were found to have no effect on caries. (See Table I.) Among the foods found to be highly cariogenic were cola, milk chocolate, white bread with jelly, and orange drink. Seven of the foods tested also produced dental erosion apparently because they are highly acidic. (For more on acidity and dental erosion, see "Acidic Beverages and Tooth Decay," page 220.)

Some may question whether studies of laboratory animals such as this are applicable to humans. Animals are, however, probably better suited for the experimental study of caries than any other disease because animals and humans have similar tooth composition while differences in digestion and assimilation, which must be taken into account in studies of other diseases, can be largely ignored in caries studies.

Table I

FOODS GROUPED BY ABILITY TO CAUSE CARIES IN TEST ANIMALS
(Within groups, the listing is in order of cariogenic activity.)

A. Anticariogenic (protective effect)

popcorn	whole milk
peanuts	

B. Neither cariogenic nor anticariogenic

lemons*	lettuce
corn chips	dried apricots*
cabbage	oranges*

C. Slightly cariogenic

soda crackers	cracked wheat bread
spinach	potato chips

D. Moderately cariogenic

whole wheat bread	graham crackers
carrots	raisin bread
cornstarch	melba toast
white bread and butter	white bread
white bread and peanut butter	

E. Moderately to highly cariogenic

white bread with raspberry jam
figs
rye bread
chewing gum
caramels
chocolate graham crackers
baby cookies
honey graham crackers
apples*
vanilla wafers
bananas
chocolate sandwich cookies

grapes*
candy mints
teething biscuits
cola*
marshmallows
dextrose
raisins
dates
milk chocolate
white bread and jelly
confectioners' sugar
orange drink*
sucrose

* Produced dental erosion

SOURCE: Adapted from R. M. Stephan, "Effects of different types of human foods on dental health in experimental animals," *Journal of Dental Research*, 45:1551 (1966).

Sugar and Obesity

For many years the Sugar Information Bureau, Inc., a trade organization representing the processors, claimed that sugar consumption before a meal, would suppress the hunger mechanism and thus curb the appetite during the meal. In 1972 the Federal Trade Commission brought Sugar Information Bureau, Inc. to court, charging that there was no reasonable basis for the claim.

Not only does this claim lack supporting evidence, but studies indicate that sugar consumption actually leads to more rapid accumulation of fat than an equal amount of calories from other foods such as starches or fats. Although authorities are not in agreement on the causes of obesity, a number of well-known experts suggest that dietary sugar plays an important role in the production of excess fat tissue. They claim that sugar is much more rapidly absorbed than calories from less digestible starches and fats and that its rapid absorption disrupts a number of the body's mechanisms which regulate fat accumulation. Furthermore, sugar is so rapidly absorbed that it evades the normal satiety mechanisms, resulting in a feeling of hunger even when large amounts are consumed.

Sugar, especially sucrose, appears to promote not only fat storage but also seems to inhibit the breakdown of stored fat, placing the obese sugar-eater in double jeopardy. These effects of sugar on fat storage and fat reduction may be in part responsible for the frequent finding of doctors that simply eliminating sugar and sugar-containing foods from the diet of the obese will often result in the prompt loss of excess weight.

Sugar and Hypoglycemia

A certain amount of sugar, in the form of glucose, must constantly be present in the blood stream to provide energy for a wide variety of bodily activities and especially for normal functioning of the brain. Unlike the rest of the body, which uses both glucose and fats for energy, brain cells use glucose almost exclusively. If the level of glucose in the blood stream drops too low, normal brain function is impaired. The body utilizes a complex but extremely efficient system to keep the blood glucose at an optimal level.

After a high carbohydrate meal, glucose pours into the blood stream following digestion of starch or sugar. To reduce the resulting elevated blood glucose content, the body secretes the hormone insulin into the blood as it passes through the pancreas. The function of insulin appears to be the reduction of glucose in the blood by facilitating its temporary storage in the tissues, especially the liver. Glucose is stored as glycogen, a form similar to starch.

Abnormally low blood sugar is known as hypoglycemia. The condition is characterized by such overt symptoms as fast heart action, sweating, shaking, trembling, anxiety, headache, sensations of hunger, brief feelings of weakness, and occasional seizure or coma, symptoms which obviously may be due to a variety of causes. Although everyone experiences mild hypoglycemia occasionally, chronic hypoglycemia is thought to be the result of overproduction of insulin. A diet which contains large amounts of sugar requires in turn a high production of insulin by the pancreas in order to keep the blood glucose at normal levels. To meet this demand, the insulin producing glands increase in size and produce large quantities of insulin. This is considered to be an abnormal condition if it continues for long periods and seems to result in a much less accurate response by the body to sugar. The overproduction of insulin (known as hyperinsulinism) has also been linked to heart disease.

Until a few years ago most medical textbooks considered hypoglycemia to be an extremely rare condition which resulted primarily from tumors on the pancreas, but this viewpoint has been increasingly attacked. One expert, R.D. McCracken, of UCLA's School of Public Health, told a convention of the American Anthropological Association that hypoglycemia may affect upwards of forty million Americans.

There have also been a number of popular books and magazine articles on the evils of hypoglycemia. The late J.I. Rodale, who perhaps took the most extreme position on the subject, claimed that excessive sugar consumption results in hypoglycemia and that this is the cause of much of the world's crime, mental illness, juvenile delinquency, and drug addiction. Excessive sugar consumption, however, is only one of many possible causes of hypoglycemia. One authority lists twenty-two distinct causes ranging from pancreatic tumors to alcoholism. Most authorities agree that hypoglycemia is a condition affecting substantial numbers of individuals, but there is disagreement as to whether nutrition plays a major role in its occurrence. Some people react adversely to sugar but others, even those with severe hypoglycemia, are little affected.

Sugar and Diabetes

Diabetes is characterized by too much glucose in the blood and urine, leading to problems such as increased susceptibility to infection and eye disorders.

Although injection of insulin will relieve the symptoms, many patients do not need insulin injections if they follow a diet that is low in carbohydrates, especially sugar. For this reason a popular belief asserts that diabetes is originally caused by eating too much sugar. Although some medical authorities also claim that excess sugar consumption leads to diabetes, the weight of medical opinion is that the causes of diabetes are not known, except heredity seems to play an important role and obesity frequently results in symptoms of the disease.

Sugar and Heart Disease

The noted British nutritionist, Dr. John Yudkin, is the chief proponent of a theory which links large amounts of sugar in the diet to heart disease. He notes that there has been a twenty-fold rise in the amount of dietary sucrose during the last two centuries in England and America, countries that have experienced the greatest increase in coronary heart disease. He also cites studies which show a correlation between sugar intake and serum cholesterol level. Yet Ancel Keys, a leading authority on atherosclerosis, cites many studies which contradict Yudkin's hypothesis. Most researchers say that sucrose has little or no effect on cholesterol levels. On the other hand, there is little dispute that sucrose increases levels of serum triglycerides, one of the main fatty substances in metabolism. There is evidence that serum triglyceride measurement should be considered, along with serum cholesterol, as a primary risk factor in coronary heart disease.

Despite the evidence that excess sugar consumption can cause certain abnormalities in blood components, (such as elevated triglycerides, hyper-insulinism and impaired glucose tolerance) there is nevertheless heated debate over the role of sugar as a cause of heart disease. Until the experts can agree on this role, those who want to cut down on sugar may find other reasons for doing so, such as its adverse effect on dental health and its role in obesity.

Effect of Sugar on Nutritional Balance of Diet

Experimental studies have shown that when solutions of sugar in water are given to animals on otherwise adequate diets, the animals favor it over other foods, become malnourished and die.

Malnourishment through overuse of sugar may also affect humans as well. Americans eat, on the average, 110 pounds of sugar per year, or about two pounds per week. Calorically, two pounds of sugar are equivalent to thirty half-pound T-bone steaks or eighty-six grapefruits or sixty-two slices of whole wheat bread or eighty-two large carrots or 160 tomatoes or 43 stalks of celery or one thousand large strawberries.

To the extent that such wholesome foods are displaced by sugar, malnutrition is a danger. If sugar is added to an adequate diet, there is danger of obesity.

Sugar and Chromium

In recent years, attention has been directed toward the role of the trace mineral chromium in human and animal nutrition. It is now clear that chromium is linked to the body's mechanism for utilizing sugar and seems to function as a glucose tolerance factor needed for optimum insulin function. Some diabetics have improved when given chromium supplements and chromium supplements were shown to reduce blood cholesterol levels in experimental animals. This evidence, although inconclusive, has led some researchers to suggest that the absence of chromium from refined sugar may be linked to refined sugar's role in elevating levels of fats in the blood, but this effect is not yet proven. The refining of sugar eliminates virtually all of the chromium originally present in the natural cane juice. Whether this loss has adverse consequences may depend upon the amount of sugar consumed and the amount of chromium in the balance of the diet. By substituting equivalent amounts of brown sugar for white sugar, chromium intake would increase by 250 per cent. (Chromium appears to be the only nutrient of significance in brown sugar.)

Table II

CHROMIUM CONTENT OF SUGAR	
Raw sugar (Philippines)	240 ppb
Raw sugar (Columbia)	350 ppb
Molasses	1210 ppb
Dark brown sugar	200 ppb
Maple syrup	290 ppb
Corn syrup	150 ppb
White sugar	80 ppb
White superfine sugar	20 ppb

SOURCE: Principal source is R. A. Ahrens, "Sucrose, Hypertension and Heart Disease," *American Journal of Clinical Nutrition,* 27:403 (1974).

Sugar in Fruits

In most fruits, sugar is the main caloric element. (Avocados, which are high in fat, are the major exception.) Sugar content of fruits (like virtually all other components) may vary considerably even within the same species depending on the variety, soil conditions, and climate.

The average sugar content of fruits is usually in the range of 5 to 10 per cent, but there are notable exceptions. At one end of the scale, the juice of the lime may contain no more than traces of sugar, while at the other extreme, 61 per cent of the weight of fresh dates consists of sugar and the concentration is even greater in the more commonly available dried dates. In general, fruits prepared for preservation by drying (dates, figs, raisins), those used in the production of alcoholic drinks (grapes, cider apples), and a few tropical fruits (pineapple, bananas), contains the highest amount of sugar.

There exists a popular misconception that the sugar in fruits is mainly fructose, commonly called "fruit sugar." Actually glucose and not fructose is the predominant sugar in most fruits.

Another misconception is that fruits, being "natural" sources of sugar, do not contain sucrose, the form of sugar considered by some to be harmful to health. Sucrose is the predominant sugar in the apricot, banana, cantaloupe, peach, and pineapple. On the other hand, some fruits, including the cherry, fig, grape, lemon and tomato, contain little or no sucrose.

Because they contain "natural" sugars, dried fruits, such as dates, figs, prunes, and raisins, are often suggested by health food advocates as alternatives to such "unnatural" sweets as candy bars. Considering the high level of sugar (up to 64 per cent by weight in dates), the presence of up to 10 per cent sucrose, and their stick-to-the-teeth consistency, these foods are of dubious value as safe replacements for other sweets. Dentists classify prunes, dates, and figs in the same category as candy bars, taffy, caramels and other adhesive, sugar-containing foods.

Raw fruits in quantity supply substantial amounts of sugar. For example, five medium apples are equivalent in sugar value to a half cup of granulated sugar while six medium bananas are equivalent to a full cup. Does it, therefore, follow that large amounts of fruit will have the same adverse consequences as large amounts of refined white sugar? The question has not been systematically investigated, but a substantial case may be made for the existence of protective factors in fruit not present in white sugar. Fruit, of course, contains fiber, the absence of which may contribute to bowel cancer. Most fruits also have somewhat less fructose, the most suspect of the sugars. The ancestors of man, it is believed, lived on a largely raw fruit and vegetable diet for much of their history and did so presumably without adverse health consequences. Primates in the wild state today subsist on largely plant diets including substantial amounts of fruit.

Many raw fruits and vegetables are composed of fibrous tissues which can help cleanse the teeth, and thus apples, carrots, celery and other plant foods have long been recommended for caries prevention. (It is doubtful, however, whether such roughage aids in cleaning in the areas between the teeth for which dental floss is required.)

The acid content of fruit may counter the protective role of fiber. One researcher suggests that apples may cause enamel to erode since they are somewhat acid and acid is erosive. Whole fruits, however, are less apt to erode enamel than fruit juice. Vegetables such as carrots and celery are far less acidic and hence may be more beneficial to teeth than fruit.

Sweets—A Listing

ARTIFICIAL SWEETENERS

The chief artificial sweetener permitted by The Food and Drug Administration is saccharin, a product which has been used since its discovery in 1879. For many years, saccharin was felt to be safe, but in 1957 a report was published showing that it caused bladder cancer in laboratory mice. In 1977, the FDA proposed a ban on saccharin after further research indicated the substance also caused bladder cancer in rats. Congress, however, has delayed the ban pending further research.

Two major studies released early in 1980 indicate that human bladder cancer occurs no more frequently in diabetics or obese individuals than in the general population. Since diabetics and the obese tend to be heavy users of saccharin, supporters of the sweetener claim the new studies show it is safe to use. Other experts are still critical and call for further research.

CANDY

As everyone knows, candy is the most delectable of the things we are not supposed to eat because it contains sugar, usually about 50 to 60 per cent. Those who seek other reasons for abstinence need only look at the ingredient labels for virtually all of the products contain additives of questionable safety.

Of thirty-six best selling candies, including all of the most heavily advertised, thirty-four contain questionable additives: thirty-three have unspecified artificial flavor while eleven have unspecified artificial color. The only two without these additives are Peppermint Lifesavers and Reese's Peanut Butter Cup. Pure chocolate bars are almost impossible to find at candy counters. If you want the real thing, go to the baking ingredients section and get a bar of German's Sweet Chocolate, which contains sugar, chocolate and coca butter only.

Several experiments in which chocolate products were fed to young laboratory animals have been conducted over the years to determine whether there was any adverse effect. One study showed the large amounts of cocoa fed to rats on a low-calcium diet resulted in lower retention of calcium. Another study with rats showed that the digestibility of milk protein was reduced moderately when large amounts of cocoa were given. A third study found that mice given low levels of Dutch process cocoa or tannic acid and theobromine (which are components of cocoa), suffered somewhat from stunted growth. Whether large amounts of chocolate stunt the growth of humans is not clear but nutritionists are concerned that children may be affected by the stimulant properties of theobromine, a substance which is related to caffeine.

One report noted a correlation between excessive eating of chocolate bars in childhood and coronary artery disease in later life but did not present evidence of a cause and effect relationship. Cocoa butter, the fatty part of chocolate, has been under suspicion, because it has a higher saturated fat content than most animal fat. Researchers found, however, that, unlike other highly saturated fats such as butter fat or beef fat, cocoa butter does not affect serum cholesterol levels, because much of its saturated fat is in stearic acid rather than in lauric, myristic and palmitic acids, the only forms which raised serum cholesterol. The evidence accumulated thus far does not seem to implicate chocolate as a cause of heart disease.

As one time it was thought that chocolate was harmful in cases of common acne but this is no longer accepted by most dermatologists, A study published in 1969 showed that subjects with mild acne who ate large amounts of chocolate bars over a four week period had no more acne lesions than a control group who ate no chocolate.

A hazard which parents should be aware of is lead from the colored inks on candy wrappers, chewing gum, bakery confections and frozen ice cream bars. One report shows the lead content ranging from 8 ppm up to 10,000 ppm. Such wrappers could be a hazard if children lick or chew them to get at any remaining edible part.

Hard Candy

Hard candies are particularly destructive of tooth enamel because they contain citric acid, the most erosive of all acids found in foods. Occasional use of hard candies probably has little effect, but anyone who makes a daily habit of sucking on these confections is in serious danger of extensive enamel erosion.

Breath Fresheners

The chief ingredient in breath fresheners, such as Chlorets, Certs, Dynamints and Tic Tacs is, of course, sugar. Chlorets contain artificial color, while Dynamints have both artificial color and flavor. All of these products contain either magnesium stearate or stearic acid, both of which are harmless. Many undoubtedly use these products as candy, but at up to eight dollars a pound, this can be an expensive habit.

CHEWING GUM

Chewing gum usually consists of 60 per cent sugar, 15 per cent syrup plus flavorings in a gum base. Most dentists consider this confection to have adverse effects on dental health. However, one study done with Greek children indicates that this may not always be true. The children, aged twelve to fifteen years, were given five sticks of a popular chewing gum per day for a period of three years and, as a group, they developed no more caries or other signs of dental disease than a control group which was not given chewing gum. Critics point out, however, that if the children have a high incidence of caries from a diet already high in sugar, the effect of the chewing gum would not be observable.

CORN SYRUP

Corn syrup, which is chemically derived from corn starch, is known as "commercial glucose."

Corn syrup is used by manufacturers to thicken as well as sweeten foods and beverages. It also helps prevent the crystallization of sucrose in candy, icings, and fillings, and prevents moisture loss in cookies, cakes, whipped food. When dried it is called corn syrup solids and is used in powdered products such as nondairy coffee whiteners. Corn syrup is about half as sweet as sucrose.

The absence of sucrose in corn syrup makes this

product of potential value in the diet as a replacement for a white sugar. Animal studies have shown that both glucose and maltose are far less cariogenic than sucrose while starches, such as dextrin (the major nonsugar component of corn syrup), also have a very low potential for producing caries. (It should be noted that while glucose and maltose are less cariogenic than sucrose, they will still cause caries if taken in large amounts.) It is difficult to obtain plain corn syrup. Most brands on the market (such as Karo) contain added sugar (sucrose) syrup.

HONEY

Honey, unlike refined sugar, is a very lightly processed product. The key stage in honey-processing is heating which is done after removal of the comb from the hive in order to destroy yeast and thus prevent fermentation. Following this, the honey is strained to remove wax particles and pollen grains, and then is cooled rapidly and packaged. Honey is mostly invert sugar but also contains some sucrose, maltose and other sugars.

Honey and refined white sugar are virtually identical nutritionally. Honey tends to have less fructose, the form of sugar which may have the most adverse effect on health. (See "Sugar and Disease," page 247.) The proportion of fructose varies; some honey has about as much as refined sugar while other honey may have half as much.

Honey, like sugar, has been indicated as a cause of caries and indeed one study showed that more caries were produced among animals fed honey than those fed an equivalent amount of sucrose. While the stickiness of honey may be the villain, one researcher suggests that because honey is somewhat richer in vitamins and trace minerals than refined sugar, it provides a better environment within the mouth for caries-producing bacteria!

Some health food stores promote "organic" honey, the implication being that the supermarket product contains pesticide residues. Back in 1972, Consumers Union checked for chlorinated hydrocarbons, the most likely pesticide residue, in both "organic" and supermarket honey and found no detectable trace in either type. Organic honey, of course, sells for a premium over supermarket honey.

Maple Syrup and Maple Sugar

The most expensive and highly prized sweetener is maple syrup or maple sugar. The sugar in maple syrup is about 98 percent sucrose, making it almost identical chemically to regular white table sugar. The unique taste of maple syrup and maple sugar comes from trace amounts of other sugars, acids, calcium, potassium and other matter.

Because the tap hole in the maple tree often becomes clogged, some producers have begun using a pellet composed of paraformaldehyde which is placed in the tap hole to keep it open longer. The Canadian government has refused to sanction use of the pellets, and maple syrup from that country will be free from any paraformaldehyde residues. Vermont producers reportedly do not use the pellet either.

There is reason for concern regarding the contamination of maple syrup with very high levels of lead, a toxic metal. This contamination comes from the soldered joints and patched holes in the homemade evaporating pans used by most maple sugar producers. In the past it also leached from the lead paint used on wooden buckets, although today it can come from metal buckets which have been patched with lead solder. The metal also enters the syrup from the lead seams in the metal cans in which it is commonly marketed. The high levels of lead which can occur in maple syrup make it a very questionable product, especially for children.

The lead content in maple syrup imported from Canada must be below levels specified by the FDA, and can be considered safe, especially if it is packaged in glass bottles. The only good way to find out about lead in American produced syrup is to visit the supplier and check on whether he uses stainless steel buckets, evaporating pans, and storage tanks. Few producers today have such safe, but expensive equipment.

That maple syrup can cause lead poisoning was apparently known for many years to farm families for a "folk remedy" has evolved to remove much of the lead. This consists of boiling the syrup with 15 per cent added skim milk for five minutes, then skimming and filtering the curd that forms. A scientific study done some years ago indicated that this method removed up to seven-eighths of the lead present in the syrup.

PANCAKE SYRUPS

Because maple syrup may be contaminated with lead, the inexpensive pancake syrups found in supermarkets may be less risky to use. Typically, these products are based on sugar syrup (sucrose) and glucose with a very small amount of maple sugar, usually 3 per cent. Most contain an unspecified artificial color but Heartland Natural Syrup, does not. Heartland is somewhat more nutritious than most other widely distributed supermarket brands because it contains some molasses and less sucrose.

SUGAR AND ITS DERIVATIVES

White Sugar

White sugar, which is 100 percent sucrose, is made from either sugar cane or sugar beets. The product made from cane and beets is identical. Other than 15 calories per teaspoon, it has no nutritional value.

Molasses

In the refining of white sugar most of the nutrients are removed in the form of molasses. There are usually three states of refining in which molasses is produced and these stages correspond to the three common grades: light, medium and blackstrap.

Advocates of molasses have emphasized its mineral content. Actually, the mineral content of molasses is extremely variable as it depends upon sugar cane growing conditions. Sugar cane leaches large amounts of minerals, depleting the soil, and hence the mineral content of molasses from this source gradually declines. Adequate fertilizer, including trace elements, is required to maintain high level of nutrients in the molasses. The consumer, of course, has no way of knowing whether his particular jar of molasses comes from adequately fertilized soil.

Brown Sugar

Brown sugar is composed of white sugar crystals covered with a molasses flavored syrup. It may be made by adding a molasses syrup to plain white sugar although the bigger processors usually produce it by boiling an unrefined sugar syrup down into crystals. The difference in processing makes little difference in the end product, and other than its chromium content, brown sugar is not appreciably more nutritious than white. Brown sugar is available in several degrees of darkness depending on the molasses content.

Raw Sugar

Raw sugar, the product of the first crystalline stage in processing, is brown or tan, and is not to be confused with brown sugar. Raw sugar, because it contains such contaminants as soil, molds, fibers, lint and waxes, is banned for food use by the FDA. Turbinado sugar is partially refined raw sugar and is closer to fully refined white sugar in nutritive value. It is actually less nutritious than brown sugar.

"Sugar in the Raw" is a light tan processed sugar marketed by the Cumberland Packing Corporation. In the past, advertisements claimed that the product was not bleached or processed, was organically grown, and was not stripped of nutrients. The Federal Trade Commission claimed that none of this was true and the company agreed in a consent order to desist from further advertising of this sort. "Sugar in the Raw" is more expensive than plain white granulated sugar and hence there would seem to be little reason to buy it or any other "raw" or "unrefined" sugar. Real raw sugar cannot legally be sold.

"SUGARLESS" PRODUCTS

Increasing public concern over the adverse effects of sugar in the diet led to the marketing of many "sugar-free" products during the 1970's. Saccharin continued to be the principal alternative sweetener, but studies implicating it as a possible carcinogen led to its replacement in some products by sorbitol and manitol, naturally-derived substances called "sugar alcohols." Studies indicate sorbitol and manitol do not promote dental caries like sucrose, although they do supply a similar level of calories.

Chewing gums such as Care-Free and Trident were among the first products to use alternate sweeteners. Going one step further, Wrigley introduced Orbit chewing gum, the first product in the U.S. to use another sugar alcohol called xylitol.

Found in small amounts in fruits, such as raspberries and strawberries, xylitol has a sweetness and energy value similar to sucrose. Extensive studies in Scandinavia found xylitol-containing chewing gum actually decreased plaque and inhibited dental caries. It also does not require insulin to be utilized by the body and could prove useful for diabetics. Enthusiasm for the sweetener soured in 1979 when studies suggested that xylitol might cause cancer, and Wrigley quickly removed it as an ingredient in Orbit. The future of xylitol as a "miracle" sweetener will depend on the results of further cancer studies.

CHAPTER IX

Other Foods

The old advice to eat something from each of the four basic food groups—cereals, vegetables and fruits, dairy products, and meat, fish and poultry—is sometimes difficult to follow when foods do not fit very neatly into these categories. Soup, for example, straddles at least two of thse categories while pizza is in all four. These foods, together with nuts, baby foods, seaweed products and a variety of condiments and cooking ingredients are discussed in this chapter.

BABY FOODS

Prepared baby foods were first marketed in 1928 and since then have become a staple of the American infant diet. These foods can be prepared quickly and make it easy for the parent to introduce a wide variety of tastes and textures to the infant. They are blander than most adult fare and hence more suitable to the infant palate.

The foods generally come in two textures: the strained types are for infants less than a year old while the junior types, which have more texture, are designed to bridge the gap between strained food and normal adult food. In addition to these, Gerber, the leading processor in the field, offers "Toddler Meals," which can be used to ease the transition from junior to regular food. Packaged baby foods, when used in conjunction with milk or formula, can provide the recommended dietary allowance of all nutrients. Two generations of Americans have been weaned on packaged baby foods with no apparent ill-effect. There is little question about the microbial safety of the products for they are sterilized and furthermore come with an excellent device that warns the parent if the jar seal has been broken. (The top is concave before the seal is broken but convex when reclosed.)

Why then have these foods been increasingly criticized? The most common charge against prepared baby food is the inclusion of additives, specifically salt, sugar, nitrates, and synthetic antioxidants.

Infants cannot distinguish between salted and unsalted food until at least seven months of age, but it is added to most baby foods apparently to make them more palatable to adults. Added salt serves no useful purpose in infant nutrition but, on the other hand, could be a cause of hypertension, a condition that could lead to heart disease. In one experiment, a group of rats genetically disposed to hypertension were fed commercial baby foods containing salt. All developed hypertension, and half died within eight months. Despite such experiments, some researchers see no conclusive evidence that salt in baby foods leads to hypertension in adult life, but in view of the potential for harm and the total lack of benefit, its use in baby foods should be considered highly questionable.

Baby foods contain other questionable additives including sugar, and unspecified artificial flavors.

Those who wish to reduce the risk to their infants by avoiding questionable ingredients will find that virtually every product has such ingredients with the exception of some of the plain dry cereals. Infant cereals, however, may be inferior nutritionally; one researcher has found that these cereals have extremely high levels of phytate, a substance which can bind zinc, calcium, and other minerals, making them unavailable to the body. (See pages 100-103.)

The easy availability of packaged baby foods has probably influenced the trend toward earlier introduction of solid foods. At least one study suggests that early consumption of solid foods and use of formulas rather than breast feeding encourages obesity which continues into adult life.

By most standards, baby foods are expensive in relation to the alternatives available in the supermarket. Canned baby orange juice, for example, costs up to four times as much as regular frozen concentrated orange juice and is, moreover, an inferior product because it contains added sugar. The plain cereals are the least overpriced of the baby foods.

There could also be important differences in trace mineral content between commercial formulas and breast milk. As Dr. Charles Lowe, Scientific Director of the National Institute of Child Health and Human Development has noted, such products could lose trace minerals in processing which future research may show to be of importance.

An even more important difference may be in cholesterol content. The three most widely used formulas have about 1.5 to 3.3 mg. per 100 ml. while human milk has 20 mg. per 200 ml. In one study, infant rats given a cholesterol free diet developed elevated blood cholesterol levels when older. This and other studies suggest that cholesterol-free formulas for infants may eventually lead to atherosclerosis in later life which is quite the opposite effect that cholesterol may have when taken by adults.

Two of the leading prepared formulas, Similac and Enfamil, contain carrageenan. This additive, which is used as a stabilizer and preservative, has been removed from the "Generally Recognized as Safe" list because it was suspected of causing ulcerative colitis (inflammation and ulceration of the colon), but its use is still permitted. Although definitive testing may well prove this additive harmless, it does not seem wise to expose infants to an unnecessary risk. At least one prepared formula, Similac Advance, which is designed for older infants, contains an unspecified artificial flavor. Few artificial flavors have been adequately tested for safety.

Many packaged formulas contain sucrose rather than lactose, which is the natural sugar in breast milk. The wisdom of using sucrose, a cause of dental caries and possibly other diseases, is questionable. Also questionable is the high salt level found in many packaged formulas.

Those who make formula at home using evaporated milk may be exposing their infants to toxic levels of lead from the metal containers (see "Lead in Canned Milk," page 31). Lead is not confined to evaporated milk or infant formulas for in 1973 the New York City Bureau of Lead Poisoning Control found significant levels in canned juice products put out by several baby food manufacturers. According to Dr. Sidney Wolfe, Director of the Ralph Nader affiliated Health Research Group, an infant drinking canned juices and evaporated milk could get more than two times the safe amount of lead. Cans used for frozen concentrate are safe as they do not contain lead.

There are strong arguments for rejecting formulas, whether store bought or homemade, and breast feeding the baby instead. One authoritative pediatric textbook notes that breast fed babies have less feeding difficulties, colic and allergic reactions, somewhat less eczema and respiratory conditions than bottlefed babies and, in addition, enjoy the psychological benefits of close contact with the mother.

There is evidence that breast feeding may inhibit obesity, malocclusion (failure of upper and lower teeth to meet properly when jaws are closed), gastroenteritis, and may possibly protect against sudden infant death syndrome. According to Harvard Medical School experts, women who nursed for less than three months were more apt to get breast cancer than those who nursed for a longer time.

Breast feeding may not be the best method for all mothers, for example, in cases where it is extremely inconvenient for the mother or if she is ill, malnourished or has such temporary problems as inflammation of the breast or fissuring or cracking of the nipples. Mothers who smoke heavily may be advised not to breast feed.

For information about breast feeding, write to La Leche League International, 9616 Minneapolis Avenue, Franklin Park, Illinois, 60131 or get the La Leche book, *The Womanly Art of Breast Feeding,* available at libraries or bookstores. Expectant mothers should, of course, consult their physicians regarding breast feeding.

Breast milk can ordinarily be fed exclusively for the first four to six months of life. During the four to six month period the baby begins to teethe and develops an urge to chew. It is about this time that his natural supply of iron begins to give out and solid foods containing iron must be given. At this point the easy (and more expensive solution) is to feed prepared baby foods but those who want to avoid this dubious course will find some useful advice in several recently published books devoted to infant feeding. (See "For Further Reading," pages 354-359).

BAKING SODA AND BAKING POWDER

Prior to the general availability of sodium bicarbonate in the mid nineteenth-century, yeast was the principal leavener of bread and cakes. Yeast, however, takes several hours to do its work and hence impatient cooks tend to produce partially-leavened bread and cake which is generally less desirable than the fully-leavened product. Yeast works by releasing carbon dioxide gas which percolates through the dough leaving a network of holes and thus results in a light instead of heavy, solid loaf. When this principle was understood, chemists looked for other ways of producing carbon dioxide gas and found that soda bicarbonate, when mixed with an acid substance such as vinegar, fruit or buttermilk, produces the required carbon dioxide under oven heat.

Oddly enough, baking soda is not a good ingredient to use in cooking because it contains an alkali that destroys most of the B vitamins in the milk, flour and shortening. Such losses can be offset by adding extra milk solids, yeast or wheat germ to recipes. The common practice of adding a pinch of baking soda to retain the green color of cooked vegetable destroys vitamins that are sensative to alkali, particularly thiamine (B_1) and vitamin C.

Baking powder is a combination of baking soda plus an acid ingredient; no additional vinegar or other acid need be added to get the desired leavening action.

The type of acid in baking powder determines the rapidity of leavening. Those with tartaric acid or tartaric acid and cream of tartar are the quickest acting, those with calcium acid phosphate or sodium acid phosphate are somewhat slower acting while the slowest acting are the so called combination or double acting powders which contain sodium aluminum sulphate (S.A.S.) and calcium acid phosphate.

A potentially serious hazard is the aluminum salt (sodium aluminum sulfate) used in the double acting powders. On the basis of work done prior to World War II, it was believed that aluminum sulphate was poorly absorbed and hence was not a health hazard. Nevertheless, doubts about its safety persisted and were reinforced in 1972 with the publication of a study by Israeli researchers who found severe damage to laboratory rats given modest amounts of the aluminum salt in their drinking water. The authors of the study concluded that patients with renal failure should not use aluminum salts and that their use should be restricted by others at least until the issue is clarified.

EGGS

Eggs are an uncommonly nutritious food, low in calories and high in protein, vitamins, and minerals. Indeed, egg protein is so high in quality that it is commonly used as the standard by which the protein of other foods is judged. Eggs, of course, are an extremely rich source of cholesterol, a substance in the diet that may (or may not) be a causative factor in heart disease. (See "Cholesterol," page 196.)

Fertile Eggs and Free-Ranging Hens

There is considerable controversy regarding the nutritive value of eggs produced by modern mass production technology as compared to fertile eggs, that is, eggs from hens with free access to the rooster. Chickens will continue to lay eggs whether or not there is a rooster present to fertilize them. Because hens tend to lay more eggs on a regular basis when separated from the rooster, virtually all eggs sold are nonfertile. The only scientifically detectable difference between factory produced and fertile eggs appears to be slight differences in naturally occurring hormone levels. As there is no known need for chicken hormones in the human diet, this difference is of no importance. One authoritative text on egg science notes that fertile eggs are equivalent to nonfertile eggs nutritionally but deteriorate more rapidly.

Many nutrients can vary markedly from egg to egg depending on the chicken's diet. For example, vitamin A, which normally averages over 500 I.U. per egg, has been reduced to as low as 58 I.U. by poor diet while losses of manganese may be as high as 87 per cent.

Because the vitamins and certain minerals in eggs are directly dependent upon the hen's diet, some have speculated that hens given commercial feeds will be deficient in the nutrients available to the free-ranging hen in the barnyard which has access to natural food such as seeds and insects. Theoretically this could happen, but only if commercial feeds were little more than synthetic nutrients. Actually, commercial poultry feeds are composed of a number of nutritionally valuable natural foods, most of which are likely to provide a wide variety of nutrients. For example, one commercial ration designed for laying hens contains 63.5 per cent ground yellow corn, 18.75 per cent soybean meal, 5.25 per cent alfalfa meal, 2.5 per cent dried brewery residues, 1.75 per cent fat, 1.5 per cent dicalcium phosphate, and 0.25 per cent iodized salt. Vitamin supplements are also added to the feed. A British study published in 1974 showed eggs produced by free-ranging hens had about the same nutrient content as eggs produced by battery hens confined to cages except that the former had somewhat more vitamin B_{12} and folic acid.

Healthy chickens produce more eggs over their lifetime than those which are ill-fed, therefore egg producers are likely to provide nutritionally-balanced diets. Other things being equal, you can assume that the nutrient content of commercially produced eggs is not significantly different from fertile eggs or eggs from free-ranging hens.

However, other things may not be equal, for modern commercial production methods call for the addition of a variety of chemical additives to the feed, including hormones, systemic pesticides, and antibiotics, residues of which may persist in the eggs. Whether such residues in eggs constitute a health hazard is not clear. Many health food stores claim to carry "fertile" or "organic" eggs, implying freedom from pesticide residues but the claim must be taken on faith as there is just no way for the consumer to distinguish them from factory produced eggs.

For some, an alternative to buying eggs at the supermarket or health food store is to buy directly from a local farmer who raises his hens the old way. Eggs purchased this way may taste better because they are fresh. They will probably be free of hormone and antibiotic residues, but whether their nutritional values will be different is problematic, and depends on what the free-ranging hens have managed to pick up and eat.

Egg Substitutes

Recently, Standard Brands introduced Fleischmann's Egg Beaters, a virtually cholesterol-free egg substitute. This product, which comes in frozen liquid form, contains less than one milligram of cholesterol as compared to 240 or 280 for natural eggs. The nutritional value of Egg Beaters is roughly the same as natural eggs with respect to the better known nutrients. Information on values for other nutrients is not available.

The major ingredients, in order of importance, are egg whites, corn oil, nonfat dry milk and vegetable lecithin (an emulsifier), all nutritious substances. Egg Beaters also contain artificial flavor and color. The yolk, which contains all of the cholesterol and far more nutrients than the white, is not included.

This product is suitable as an ingredient in other foods or for making scrambled eggs, but not poached, soft boiled or fried eggs. Because the need to lower dietary cholesterol is one of the most controversial subjects in nutrition, it is not clear whether normally healthy people will benefit by replacing eggs with Egg Beaters. Those whose doctors have ordered a low-cholesterol diet may, however, find the product useful.

Buying and Storage of Eggs

Most eggs are not dated and therefore offer no assurance of quality and freshness. Grade AA or eggs labelled "Fresh Fancy Quality" are dated and may not, under federal regulations, be sold after the tenth day following inspection. Such eggs are, unfortunately, difficult to find in most areas.

As with virtually all other foods, the warmer the temperature the more rapid the destruction of nutrients. Eggs may be kept unrefrigerated for several days without significant effects, but for longer storage they should be refrigerated.

GELATIN

The value of gelatin lies in its ability to soak up fluids and to gel. Its nutritive value is scant. Pure, dry gelatin is about 85.5 per cent protein, but because the protein is lacking in the essential amino acids tryptophan and tyrosine, it is not adequate for sustaining life.

Knox Gelatin, Inc., has claimed that its flavored gelatin is a high quality protein that makes a substantial contribution to good health and to nutritional needs. In 1973, the FTC obtained a consent order to prohibit these claims. However, there is evidence that gelatin (about two teaspoons a day) corrects cracking and splitting fingernails.

Pure gelatin like Knox's is preferable to flavored products like Jello which contain artificial flavors and colors.

HERBS AND SPICES

Herbs come from the leaves and stems of soft, succulent plants and are usually grown in temperate climates. Among the most common are bay leaf, mint, basil, tarragon, oregano, marjoram and thyme. Spices are made from the seeds, fruit, bark, roots, stems or leaves of aromatic plants and are usually grown only in the tropics. Unlike herbs, spices are never used fresh, but are dried and come in whole or ground form. Allspice, cinnamon, cloves, ginger, mace, nutmeg, and turmeric are among the most commonly used spices.

There is probably more folklore concerning herbs and spices than any other type of food. Claims have been made that rosemary improves the memory, that sassafras "purifies the blood," that nettles cure tuberculosis, that the rock rose alleviates "terror and panic," that mistletoe is useful in cancer treatment and that dandelions cure diabetes. On the other hand, little of an adverse nature is said about spices that may have deleterious effects.

Safrole (from sassafras), which was used to flavor root beer, was banned by the FDA in 1960 because it produced cancer of the liver in test animals. Nutmeg and mace contain safrole and also a substance called myristicin, which has a pronounced narcotic effect. Very heavy doses of nutmeg or mace—an ounce in grated form—can cause liver damage and even death. Doses sufficiently strong to cause an immediate toxic effect are fortunately well above the level called for by recipes, but the possible carcinogenic threat from the safrole content remains. The possible dangers in other herbs and spices generally seem to be in over-use during an extended period and do not apply to normal use as called for in standard recipes. To the extent that herbs and spices are substituted for salt, they are probably beneficial.

Herbs and spices are highly concentrated sources of trace minerals but in the amount normally ingested do not supply nutritionally significant amounts of these nutrients, except possibly of chromium and manganese.

A continuing problem with herbs and spices is con-tamination with mold, insect fragments and excreta. These may originate during growing where such insects as ants, beetles, and grasshoppers are prevalent or in warehouses where the product may be attacked by roaches, weevils and rats. Spices stored under damp conditions may mold.

The FDA standards for controlling these conditions are surprisingly lenient. Nutmeg, for example, may have up to 10 per cent moldly pieces or have up to 10 per cent infested pieces and still pass inspection; curry powder is accepted if it has up to one hundred insect fragments or up to eight rodent hairs per 25 grams (slightly less than an ounce). The spice industry claims that such foreign matter is impossible to elimi-nate at reasonable cost while the FDA correctly points out that most of this matter is not a health hazard.

Spices should be protected against the air. Ground spices are particularly vulnerable to air because the grinding fractures the cell walls, thus expediting loss of the essential oils, which are the source of the flavor and aroma. Retail packages containing ground or flaked spices ordinarily provide sufficient protection against the air for twelve months or more after manufacture. Bulk spices such as those available from co-op stores are cheaper but may deteriorate more rapidly. Whole spices have a longer life and hence are preferable if buying from a bulk container. In the home, spices bought in bulk are best stored in small glass containers with tight fitting caps.

Herbs can be grown almost anywhere including city apartments. Those who are interested in growing their own will find useful information in several books listed in "For Further Reading," page 354.

INSTANT BREAKFAST

Instant breakfast is based on nonfat dry milk, sugar, and corn syrup solids fortified with vitamins and minerals. The product, which comes in powder form, is added to 8 ounces of while milk or skim milk. Pillsbury and Carnation, which are the leading brands, come in a variety of flavors, including chocolate, vanilla, chocolate malt, chocolate fudge, eggnog, imitation chocolate marshmallow, and imitation strawberry. In addition to its regular instant breakfast, Carnation puts out Special Morning, which has extra protein and vitamin/mineral fortification.

A typical formula for chocolate flavored instant breakfast might include 45 per cent nonfat dry milk, 30 per cent sugar, 10 per cent corn syrup solids, 8 per cent cocoa, 0.3 per cent salt and 1 per cent stabilizers and emulsifiers. Some flavors of these products contain more sugar than nonfat dry milk. In addition to sugar, all of the products contain one or more questionable additives such as carrageenan, unspecified artificial flavor or unspecified artificial color.

In terms of the protein, vitamins and minerals these products list on their packages they would seem to be valuable, but they do not supply fiber or as many trace minerals as, for example, an egg, sausage, toast, fruit and milk breakfast.

The inferior quality of these products was emphasized in December 1970, when the Federal Trade Commission obtained a consent order in which the Carnation Company agreed not to claim "that the regular use of Carnation Instant Breakfast as a 'balanced breakfast' or 'meal' is a good nutritional practice," as such claims are "false" and "misleading."

Instant breakfast has become such a popular item that the development of a solid version was perhaps inevitable. General Mills produces it in the form of Breakfast Squares, a fortified cake type food which looks and tastes like a brownie. This product, which is available in chocolate and other flavors including artificial butter pecan and artificial cinnamon, is based on sugar, shortening, dried milk protein, soy protein and enriched flour. Sugar is the leading ingredient in all flavors. In addition to unspecified artificial flavors, this product also contains unspecified artificial color. In the pantheon of nutritional devils, Breakfast Squares may yet occupy a more prominent place than Coca Cola or Kool Aid, for these products at least do not pretend to replace regular meals.

LOW-CALORIE FOODS

It is not surprising that "low in calories" is one of the major advertising themes of the food processors; after all weight reduction is a national obsession and could be called the leading food fad of the century.

Weight reduction may well be motivated principally

by aesthetic reasons but it is also fueled by fears of
the health consequences of obesity, fears which are
reinforced by food advertising. Physicians generally
favor weight reduction but they are by no means unan-
imous. For example, Dr. George Mann of Vanderbilt
University says:

"... obesity has been wrongly indicted as a major
public health problem ... Only extreme degrees
of obesity carry health hazards. The rest of us are
not impaired by the 15-35 per cent of our body
content which is fat. ... Unhappily the western
world is plagued by nutrition experts, professional
and otherwise, who view obesity—'in someone
else'—as a moral issue ... Nearly every form of
cancer has a higher cure rate than does adiposity.
We weep and sympathize over cancer and its in-
evitability, and yet we scold and accuse over
obesity. This fussing drives many fat people into
the hands of quacks and frauds. ..."

Dr. Mann goes on to say, "Our only effective treatment,
whether preventative or curative, is physical activity."
Exercise is necessary for keeping caloric intake in line
with energy needs. Harvard's Dr. Jean Mayer, one of
the leading experts in control of obesity, has demonstrated that above a certain level of activity, caloric
intake tends to follow precisely the body's needs while
below this activity level, more calories are taken in
than are needed, with consequent gain in weight. In
other words, the appetite does not function as a regu-
lator of calorie intake below a certain level of physical
activity. Mayer suggests moderate exercise (e.g., walk-
ing) for at least three-quarters of an hour per day and
vigorous exercise for no less than fifteen minutes at
least three times a week. Other practitioners may rec-

ommend different amounts of exercise depending on individual needs.

If the most important role in weight control and reduction is given to exercise, the importance of special low-calorie diet foods is downgraded. Indeed, most physicians recommend moderate portions of wholesome foods rather than the special low-calorie foods.

Some of the special foods such as the Weight Watchers low-calorie frozen dinners are useful in helping to achieve permanent weight loss because they acclimatize the dieter to the type of food that should be eaten to maintain ideal weight. Weight Watchers dinners provide convenience, but are expensive compared to the same type of food prepared at home. Pregnant women should read the labels carefully for some of the dinners contain MSG. (Those in pregnancy should, of course, not attempt to lose weight except under a doctor's supervision.) Other low-calorie foods, such as canned fruit packed in water rather than sugar syrup, may also be useful in weight reduction.

Metered calorie products such as Slender or Sego provide a measured amount of calories per serving, usually 225, thus making it easy to restrict a dieter, for example, to 900 or 1800 calories per day. The most popular form is the ready-to-drink liquid but powders to which milk is added are also available. Taken as recommended, these products result in substantial weight loss, but because they do not condition the dieter to everyday foods on which he must depend for maintenance of normal weight, they are not by themselves likely to result in permanent weight loss. The all-liquid diets tend to cause diarrhea in some individuals and constipation in others. Since these products contain little fiber their use over an extended period is questionable.

Ayds, a candy widely advertised for weight reduction, will, according to claims, "automatically" help you to "eat less at . . . mealtime . . . without any conscious effort." The idea is to take it fifteen to twenty minutes before meals with a cup of hot water, tea, or coffee. There is no widely accepted evidence that sugar (the leading ingredients in Ayds are corn syrup and sugar) has any therapeutic value in weight reduction. It is true that sugar or sugar with a beverage will temporarily depress hunger pangs, but few experts recommend this as the basis of a sound, long-range plan of weight reduction. If you want to try this technique, you can save money by drinking your tea or coffee with sugar (49¢ a pound) rather than using Ayds ($3.18 a pound).

There are a variety of diet jams and candy on the market. These foods are of marginal use in weight reduction programs because they do not help to reduce total caloric intake by a substantial amount and they do not promote good eating habits. Diet soft drinks are also marginal aids in weight reduction for the same reason and are not more useful in satisfying hunger pangs than plain water. Most low-calorie soft drinks contain saccharin, diet colas contain caffeine, while Fresca contains unspecified artificial color, artificial flavor and bromated vegetable oils, a questionable ingredient.

Maraschino Cherries

The beautiful bright red of the maraschino cherry is, unfortunately, based on a highly suspect dye called FD&C Red No. 4. The FAO has classified Red No. 4

(Ponceau SX) under "Colors found to be harmful and which should not be used in food." Tests conducted on dogs indicated damage to urinary bladder and adrenal glands. Red No. 4 was banned from hot dogs and a variety of other foods in 1966, but continued use was permitted in maraschino cherries on the theory that people don't eat them in great quantities.

Meat Tenderizers

The essential element in meat tenderizers, such as those marketed by McCormick and Adolph, is the enzyme papain. Papain is apparently harmless if cooked, but if taken uncooked (e.g., on steak tartar) may destroy gastrointestinal tissues. Under most circumstances normal saliva and mucous are adequate protection against small amounts of uncooked papain. An alternative for those who don't want to use meat tenderizers is, of course, to marinate the meat, e.g., in vinegar.

MSG (Monosodium Glutamate)

MSG is a flavor-enhancing chemical used in many processed foods. As a seasoning for home use it is available under the brand name Accent and is also combined with other seasonings in McCormick Season All.

"Chinese Restaurant Syndrome" is a reaction apparently caused by MSG. The symptoms, which begin fifteen to twenty minutes after ingestion of MSG, can be alarming: a numbness of the back of the neck that gradually spreads to arms and the back, a general weakness and palpitation, tightness in the chest, and severe headaches. Such dramatic reactions are experienced only by people who, for reasons unknown, are sensitive to the chemical and then only when it is taken in substantial amounts on an empty stomach.

In 1969 an experiment by Dr. John W. Olney, a professor of psychiatry at Washington University School of Medicine in St. Louis, showed that the chemical produced brain lesions in newborn mice, thus raising the possibility of danger to the human fetus. The publicity following Dr. Olney's disclosures was a factor in the decision of leading baby food manufacturers to voluntarily drop the chemical from their products, although industry spokesmen contend there was no danger. To be on the safe side, pregnant women and infants should avoid MSG flavoring and processed foods containing this additive. MSG must be noted on the label of all foods except mayonnaise, mayonnaise-type salad dressing, and French dressing. Commercially made soups generally have more of this additive than other foods.

It may seem odd that back in the 1940's there was much discussion about the possibility that glutamic acid might be used to improve intelligence. (MSG breaks down into sodium and glutamic acid in the body.) In one study, mentally deficient patients given glutamic acid enjoyed an apparent increase in intelligence, memory skill and personality. Subsequent studies cast doubt on the beneficial effects of glutamic acid but none of the studies noted any ailment more severe than gastric distress as a result of taking glutamic acid.

Few studies of MSG have been designed to detect possible long range adverse effects. One such study conducted among several thousand Hawaiians of Japanese descent disclosed no significant difference among heavy, light and non-users in terms of myocardial infarction, serum cholesterol level or obesity. Possible differences with respect to other diseases were not measured.

NUTS AND SEEDS

The most popular nuts and seeds are peanuts, cashews, English walnuts, almonds, pecans, filberts, Brazil nuts, chestnuts, sunflower seeds and sesame seeds. Others, such as hickory, pistachio, macadamia, black walnuts, butternuts, beechnuts and pignolia are consumed in far smaller quantities. Peanuts, which are by far the most popular, are not true nuts, but are members of the legume family which includes soy beans and peas.

Depending on type, nuts and seeds are 45 to 70 per cent fat, most of which is either polyunsaturated or monounsaturated.

Protein content of most nuts is high, ranging up to 29 per cent in pumpkin seeds, as compared to 20 per cent for porterhouse steak. Nuts, however, are relatively low in lysine and thus much of the protein is not available to the system. The protein value of nuts is enhanced if taken with a food having virtually complete protein, like milk, or with foods having a complementary amino acid pattern, like beans.

Nuts are rich in minerals but calorie-for-calorie, they have less mineral content than other foods such as vegetables. Like grains, most nuts are high in phytic acid, a substance which can bind minerals, thus making them unavailable to the system. (See "The Phytic Acid Problem," page 100.)

Processing of Nuts

The processing of nuts results in substantial losses of thiamine and reduces the protein value by destroying some of the lysine. This should not be a cause of concern for those who eat peanuts (and other roasted nuts) as an occasional snack, but vegetarians who may depend upon roasted nuts for meeting their minimum requirements should consider supplementing them with lysine rich foods such as dairy products and beans.

Roasting in oil, which probably is the most popular method of cooking, usually involves the addition of antioxidants such as BHA, BHT and propyl gallate to retard rancidity. Dry roasting, which has become an increasingly popular alternative to oil roasting, is done with radiant heat and does not ordinarily involve use of antioxidants. Nutrient content of dry roasted nuts is about the same as oil roasted nuts except that calories and, of course, fat content are slightly lower. Dry roasting appears to be a superior process and furthermore some brands, such as Planters, are available both with and without salt and MSG.

As any peanut lover knows, some peanuts in the shell contain salt. The salt is able to penetrate into the shell with the aid of a detergentlike wetting agent.

Nuts in the shell or in a vacuum container are

usually well-protected against deterioration which occurs primarily because of rancidity and moisture. Rancidity is promoted by ultraviolet light, oxygen, heat, certain enzymes, and moisture. At home, rancidity can be delayed by storing in the refrigerator. For shelled nuts an opaque jar is desirable.

Toxic Substances in Nuts

The most serious health threat in nuts is *Aspergillus flavus,* an aflatoxin-producing mold. Aflatoxin is the most potent carcinogen affecting several species of animals and is suspected of being a cause of liver cancer in humans. Liver cancer and aflatoxins are more prevalent in areas such as Kenya where the food supply is not as well controlled as in the U.S., but even in the U.S. there is concern that unnecessary risks are taken because of lax regulation. A 1969 study showed that 71 per cent of pecans used in bakery products were potential bearers of the toxin. Although inspection may have been improved since, the FDA has been severely criticized for setting a tolerance of twenty parts per billion when it is technically possible to detect 5 ppb or even less. The importance of lowering the tolerance is underscored by tests which showed that all rats fed 15 ppb of aflatoxin B_1, the most potent form of the toxin, developed liver cancer.

The danger of exposure to aflatoxin is reduced considerably by roasting. This does not eliminate the toxin, but does kill the molds which produce it. If roasting is done soon after harvesting, there is much less chance that toxins will have been produced. Anyone who eats a considerable amount of raw nuts should, therefore, consider switching to roasted nuts at least until the FDA enforces considerably lower tolerances.

Peanut Butter

The peanut butter manufacturers are obligated by law to use at least 90 per cent peanuts. The remainder of the product can be emulsifiers, sweeteners, salt and hydrogenated oil. The oil from the crushed peanuts is partially hydrogenated or partially hydrogenated vegetable oils are added.

The monoglycerides and diglycerides used in most peanut butter are not only harmless but wholesome, being natural constituents of food readily metabolized by the system. The smoothness and creaminess of supermarket peanut butter is not only due to the added oil but also to ultrasonic (very high frequency vibration) homogenization. The more intimate mix of ingredients possible with ultrasonic homogenization extends the shelf life by six months or more.

About 0.6 per cent salt is added together with about 5 per cent sweetening agent, usually sucrose, dextrose or corn syrup. No artificial flavors, artificial sweeteners, artificial or natural color or preservatives are pemitted according to federal regulations.

Peanut butter is a semiperishable product. It is not subject to bacterial spoilage but can go rancid. The addition of hydrogenated oil retards rancidity as does vacuum packing, refrigeration and protection against the ultraviolet rays in light.

Those who demand an unadulterated product can find it in health food stores and health-food sections of the supermarket but at a premium price. Those who want the freshest product available can get it simply by grinding shelled nuts in a blender and adding a small amount of oil. (Two cups of nuts with up to one-quarter cup of peanut oil provides a crunchy but satisfactory product.) Old fashioned peanut butter, whether bought in the store or made at home, should be refrigerated to retard rancidity. Peanut butter made without hydrogenated fat will separate at room temperature with an oil layer forming on top. This must be thoroughly stirred in before refrigeration to retard further separation. Unhydrogenated peanut butter stays fairly soft in the refrigerator while the hydrogenated type becomes hard and less easy to spread.

Aflatoxins, which are a matter of concern in the whole nut, may also be present in peanut butter. Consumers Union, in a 1972 report, found that eight out of twenty samples checked had detectable aflatoxin up to 3 ppb. Consumers Union has called for a zero tolerance but some experts believe that this would be impractical. These experts instead call for research to define more precisely the level below which no harmful effect is shown.

One of the most debased products to appear in many years is Koogle, an artificially flavored peanut butter product with large amounts of sugar. The product is available in several flavors, including chocolate, vanilla and banana, the last being artificially colored. Like many other junk foods, Koogle costs more than its more natural counterpart.

PIZZA

Pizza is often included in references made to "junk foods" in the American diet. This association is unfortunate since pizza is actually quite a nourishing product. Two slices of an average size sausage pizza (about 7 to 8 ounces or one-third of the pie) provide 28 per cent of the day's protein requirement but only 17 per cent of the calorie requirement. This amount supplies 24 per cent of the iron, 6 per cent of the thiamine (vitamin B_1), 15 per cent of the riboflavin, 10 per cent of the niacin, 40 per cent of the vitamin C and 27 per cent of the vitamin A requirement. It not only satisfies all the requirements for a main dinner dish but is a superior snack as it contains no sugar.

Consumers Union and others have attacked the makers of frozen pizza for having unacceptably high levels of bacteria. Cheese products, however, naturally have very high bacteria counts and are ordinarily harmless. In order to evaluate frozen pizza thoroughly, a check would have to be made specifically for pathogenic bacteria such as coliforms but unfortunately this has not been done.

Many pizza lovers may, of course, prefer freshly baked over frozen pizza because of taste or texture, but on strictly nutritional grounds the frozen products are highly acceptable. Some, however, contain sodium nitrite and sodium nitrate.

SALT

Common table salt is 39 per cent sodium and 61 per cent chloride. Both sodium and chloride are essential nutrients but no official dietary allowance has been established.

Many common foods contain substantial levels of sodium. For example, 3½ ounces of steak contain 52 mg., a cup of milk, 127 mg., an egg, 59 mg., a pat of butter, 69 mg., and a slice of bread, 117 mg. Many processed foods contain quite large amounts; most canned soups contain over 750 mg. per cup; most types of canned spaghetti contain over 1000 mg. per cup; a cup of canned pork and beans has about 1100 mg.; rice has over 500 mg., while flavorings such as Shake 'n Bake have up to 5000 m.g. per envelope. A dash of salt may have 10 to 15 mg. of sodium. Water that is artificially softened may also contain high levels of sodium for in the softening process, the sodium replaces the "hard" minerals, calcium and magnesium. In view of these possible sources of sodium it is not surprising that most Americans consume five to twenty-five times their probable minimum need of 500 mg.

Table salt usually contains about 2 per cent silicates or silicon dioxide which coats the salt grains and keeps them from becoming damp and clumping together.

These substances are biologically inert and are excreted from the kidneys harmlessly except for magnesium silicates and sodium silicates which have caused kidney damage to one type of test animal. The Joint FAO/WHO Expert Committee on Food Additives gives silicon dioxide and other silicates, except magnesium silicate (talc), full clearance but require more investigation of the latter while sanctioning its unrestricted use. Most salt sold in the U.S. contains forms of silicate such as sodium silico aluminate which have been found to be safe.

Yellow prussiate of soda is added to salt to make the crystals jagged and more bulky and thus less anti-caking agent is required. This chemical has no known toxic effect.

Does Salt Cause Hypertension?

People who use a lot of salt (for example, those who habitually salt food even before they taste it) have a high incidence of hypertension, while those who use little or no salt have a low incidence of the disease. People with hypertension can achieve dramatically lowered blood pressure by reducing the salt intake. In addition, epidemiological studies show a correlation between salt intake and the incidence of hypertension. For example, Eskimos in Alaska have both a low incidence of hypertension and a low salt intake, while Northern Japanese have a very high salt intake and 40 per cent of that group has hypertension.

Despite all this evidence, most authorities are not yet willing to agree that salt causes hypertension. Other factors such as heredity or race (blacks are particularly susceptible) appear to be important. It is possible that salt may exacerbate or promote a tendency among certain people to develop hypertension.

There are many groups which have thrived eating only the salt contained naturally in foods, for the body's true need is actually extremely low. Because adding salt to the diet serves no real biological need, and in the light of the circumstantial evidence linking salt with hypertension, there are many who will want to restrict salt intake and perhaps even to completely eliminate added salt from the diet. Complete elimination of all but the salt naturally present in food may be all but impossible for virtually all processed foods are heavily salted. Even those who attempt to follow a "low sodium diet" will still have a high salt intake because of the "hidden" salt in most food products.

The late Dr. Louis K. Dahl, who was probably the leading expert on sodium in the diet, gives this advice to those who want to cut intake drastically: 1. Never add salt to food during preparation or at the table; 2. Avoid all processed foods except fruits and juices (and even here examine labels); and 3. Avoid all milk and milk products.

Salt Substitutes

Salt substitutes based on potassium chloride are available under several labels, including McCormick and Adolph's. Potassium chloride has no adverse effect except for those with severe kidney disturbances. In order to mask the bitter taste, tartaric acid, glutamic acid, and monopotassium glutamate are added. Tartaric acid has no known adverse effect, but the other two ingredients are related to monosodium glutamate and hence are suspect. Monosodium glutamate and monopotassium glutamate are salts of glutamic acid and become glutamic acid in the body.

Despite the doctoring up with these chemicals, the potassium chloride salt substitutes are really not very tasty. For this reason, the Morton Salt Company brought out Morton Lite Salt, a mixture of potassium chloride and sodium chloride. This product is acceptable to most people who want to restrict sodium, but those on sodium-restricted diets must still use it with caution. There is at least one case on record of an elderly woman with a history of heart disease who used the product copiously apparently under the impression that it was a salt substitute. After using it for six weeks she was hospitalized with congestive heart failure.

Sea Salt

Sea salt is widely used by health conscious people primarily because of its reputed value in supplying trace elements. The package of sea salt sold in stores provide little information on mineral content nor is such information available from the standard sources.

Dr. Dahl, the specialist on hypertension and sodium, found nutritionally significant amounts of copper, manganese, nickel, fluorine, and tin in one sample of sea salt. Iodine was present, but not in nutritionally significant amounts. Whether Dahl's sample is representative is not clear for mineral content of sea salt can vary by location, time of year, and method of processing. Furthermore, several of the minerals in Dr. Dahl's sample—nickel and tin—although essential in trace amounts, can have adverse effects at high levels.

The sea salt that Dr. Dahl analyzed was used in a laboratory experiment in which its effect on hypertension was evaluated. One group of rats was given the sea salt while a second group was given regular table salt. The rats which were given sea salt were much more apt to develop hypertension than rats in the other group. This, of course, does not necessarily mean that humans will react in the same way, but it does raise questions about its toxicity.

The evidence indicates that sea salt, at two to four times the price of ordinary table salt is not a good bargain, particularly if it does not contain sufficient iodine to protect against goiter. All of the useful trace elements supplied by sea salt occur in substantial quantity in other foods such as whole grains, meat, fish, and nuts.

Iodized Salt

Supermarkets sell salt both with and without iodine. Iodine at a concentration of 76 micrograms per gram of salt is added as a public health measure to prevent goiter, an ailment that occurs when the diet is deficient in the nutrient.

Historically, the incidence of goiter has been highest in the so-called "goiter belt," an area where the soil is deficient in the mineral. The idea of a goiter belt is somewhat out of date because most people now eat foods from many parts of the country. The incidence of goiter fell sharply when iodized salt was introduced some years ago but in recent years there has been an increase coincident with a decrease in consumption of iodized salt. Whether the decline in use of iodized salt is actually a cause of increased goiter is not clear for there is recent evidence showing that people with the ailment are not always deficient in dietary iodine.

Despite some evidence suggesting its lack of effect on goiter prevention, most authorities support the value of supplementary iodine in goiter prevention. According to the Food and Nutrition Board, adults can safely take up to 1000 micrograms per day, an amount found in two to three teaspoons of iodized salt.

Iodized salt, of course, is not the only good source of iodine, for seafood and kelp both supply large amounts. Powdered kelp is a particularly convenient source. Plant foods, dairy products, and the local water supply are poor or unreliable sources. Processed foods are usually made with noniodized salt. Thus, a significant portion of the salt intake of the average American is noniodized.

SEAWEED

Seaweed products, which can be found in any health food store, are rich sources of minerals, particularly trace minerals. The most widely used type in North America is kelp, a brown seaweed which grows off the California coast. Granulated kelp is suitable for adding to baked goods, soups, stews, casseroles, salads and a variety of other dishes where salt is ordinarily used. Dried leaf kelp is suitable for adding to soups and stews. Kelp is also available in tablet form. Other seaweeds, such as dulse, agar, and carrageenan (Irish moss), are less widely used.

Nutrients in Seaweed

Seaweed is particularly rich in iodine and also generally contains moderate amounts of calcium, magnesium, phosphorus, iron, zinc, manganese, vanadium, nickel, molybdenum, selenium, copper, cobalt and chromium. Iodine content is usually shown on the package but content of other minerals is not. Mineral content depends on time of harvest: a Norwegian study showed that content may vary seasonally by a factor of two or more. Content may also vary because of location; seaweeds exposed to a greater proportion of fresh water from rivers will ordinarily have less mineral nourishment.

The amount of iodine in a teaspoon of a typical granulated seaweed is about fifteen times the Recommended Dietary Allowance for an adult male. Extremely large amounts over a prolonged period may actually cause goiter, the disease which normally occurs with iodine deficiency but cases of iodine induced goiter are extremely rare. The Food and Nutrition Board considers intakes of 100 to 300 micrograms (mcg.) to be desirable for adults and considers 50 to 1000 mcg. to be safe yet consistent use of a teaspoon of kelp a day would supply 2000 mcg., well above the FNB's upper limit.

Because intake of iodine should be limited, seaweed cannot be considered a major source of other trace minerals in the diet although as compared to multi-vitamin/mineral capsules, seaweeds have the advantage of supplying a wider range of trace minerals including some which future research may prove to be nutritionally valuable.

Carrageenan

Carrageenan, which is used commercially in a variety of food products, has acquired a bad name because of studies done in the late sixties by two British researchers, Dr. James Watt of the University of Liverpool and Dr. R. Marcus of Clatterbridge Hospital, Bebington, who showed that it caused changes in rabbits and guinea pigs resembling ulcerative colitis in man. These and other studies led the Food and Drug Administration in 1972 to remove carrageenan from the Generally Recognized as Safe list, but its use is still permitted pending additional evidence. Although the FDA action may not inspire confidence, there is no evidence that carrageenan causes ulcers in humans. In countries where seaweed is normally included in the diet such as Ireland, Japan and the South Pacific Islands, the incidence of ulcerative colitis is about the same as in other areas.

There is no evidence that dried carrageenan or other seaweeds of the type sold in health stores should not be consumed in moderate quantities, at least by adults.

Use of carrageenan in infant formulas is another matter. Dr. Michael F. Jacobson, Co-Director of the Center for Science in the Public Interest, has questioned the wisdom of allowing the substance in these foods in view of the apparent lack of studies of the effect on infants. He notes that carrageenan is not necessary as British formulas do not contain it.

SNACK FOODS

Custom dictates three meals a day but appetites rebel and so we have snacking. Nutritionists approve this practice, for good quality snacks aid some people in weight control by reducing the tendency to overeat at mealtime. Frequent small meals appear to be more healthful than a few large meals of equal caloric value. Nutrients from small meals are more thoroughly absorbed and utilized while other benefits—such as lowered serum cholesterol levels—are suggested by studies on both animals and humans.

In order to provide a convenient guide to snack selection, an index of nutritive quality has been calculated for thirty-two popular snacks as shown in Table I. As might be expected, snacks which rate low are highly processed and generally contain questionable additives. The better snacks are natural or lightly processed.

Table I

SNACK FOODS
INDEX OF NUTRITIVE VALUE *

Orange	+80	Potato Chips	+10
Banana	+70	Triscuit Whole Wheat	
Peanuts	+50	Cracker	+10
Yogurt, Plain	+40	Pringle Potato Chips	0
Rye Krisp	+40	Popcorn, Oil & Salt	0
Ice Cream, 10% Fat	+40	Doritos Tortilla Chips	0
Hunt's Snack Pack		Orange Sherbet	—10
Fruit Cup	+40	Fritos Corn Chips	—10
Apple, incl. skin	+40	Hostess Twinkies	—10
Pizza, Sausage &		Chocolate Chip Cookies,	
Cheese	+40	Homemade	—20
Cheddar Cheese	+30	Pretzels, Dutch Twisted	—20
Clam Dip, Cream		Hunt's Snack Pack	
Cheese, Homemade	+30	Pudding, Chocolate	—20
Onion Dip, Sour		Graham Crackers,	
Cream, Homemade	+20	Plain	—20
Yogurt, Swiss Style		Soda Crackers, Salted	—20
Strawberry	+20	Doughnut	—30
Borden's Cheese Kisses	+20	Cola	—50
Raisins	+10	Popsicle	—50
Milk Chocolate	+10		

* The Index of Nutritive Quality is calculated by assigning 10 points for each vitamin or mineral supplied in greater quantity than calories in relation to the Recommended Dietary Allowance. Ten points are also given if the snack contains 0.5 or more grams of crude fiber per 100 calories or the equivalent of 13.5 grams in a 2700 calorie diet. Ten points were subtracted if the snack food was not generally available without the addition of questionable additives such as artificial color or flavor. Ten points were also subtracted if sodium content was above 37 milligrams per 100 calories. The criterion for sodium was chosen because it is equivalent, in a 2700 calorie diet, to 1000 milligrams. Sodium in excess of 500 to 1000 milligrams has no physiological function and may possibly be harmful. Twenty points were subtracted if the product was based on refined grain. Refining of grain eliminates a wide variety of nutrients including trace minerals. A score of —50 was arbitrarily assigned to snacks such as cola which have no significant nutritive value other than calories. The maximum possible score is +100.

SOUP

As a convenience food, condensed soup is a relatively good nutritional buy. For example, gram-for-gram the protein in condensed beef soup and chicken soup costs only 15 to 25 per cent more than that in hamburger or chicken. Full strength ("ready-to-serve") soups generally cost two to three times as much as condensed soup.

The nutrient values in canned soup, as in home cooked soup, are affected by cooking but in most cases the losses are moderate because the water soluble vitamins are retained and not discarded as they might be, for example, in home cooking of vegetables. The vitamin losses in commercially processed soup are somewhat higher than those in home-processed soup because of the need to use higher temperatures that will sterilize the product in the can.

Canned soups contain several ingredients which some will find questionable, such as MSG and liberal amounts of sodium. A few varieties, such as Campbell's tomato soups do not contain MSG. Most soups contain sugar but the amounts are too small to markedly detract from the flavor. Among the soups that are not made with any sugar are New England clam chowder, oyster stew and scotch broth. Campbell sells a line of low-salt soups, but unfortunately, these are not stocked in most stores.

Dehydrated (Freeze Dried) Soup

Freeze drying is based on the principle of "sublimation" in which moisture in the form of ice crystals is transformed directly to water vapor in a vacuum without first going through the liquid phase. Because the temperature at which this is done is generally about −4° F, the process results in little loss of nutrients. The product can be stored up to twelve months at 100° F and still be acceptable and, moreover, does not suffer microbial deterioration. Soup made from mixes is about as nutritious or only slightly less so than those made from condensed soup.

The most widely used flavorings in dehydrated soups are hydrolyzed vegetable protein, disodium guanylate (GMP) and disodium inosinate (IMP). Hydrolyzed vegetable protein is vegetable protein that has been broken down to its constituent amino acids, and is considered entirely safe. GMP and IMP are similar to MSG but are considerably more potent in their flavor-enhancing ability and are considered safe except for those suffering from gout and other diseases in which purines must be avoided. Both are converted to uric acid which is excreted with no adverse effect by the healthy person but not by gout sufferers. Most of the dry soup mixes contain other additives which may not be so benign in their effect such as MSG, artificial flavor and, in some cases, even artificial color.

The Lipton mixes are the most widely distributed and, unfortunately, must be classified with the less desirable supermarket foods. Every one of the Lipton mixes contains a questionable additive such as MSG or unspecified artificial flavor. The ingredients in Lipton Cup-A-Soup New England Chowder, for example are, in order of importance, spray dried fat, modified food starch, whey solids, dehydrated potatoes, nonfat dry milk, dehydrated onions, salt, monosodium glutamate and, in ninth place, something called clam powder. Some dehydrated soups such as the Herb-Ox products contain none of the additives which make the Lipton products so objectionable.

The cost of dehydrated soups is about the same as condensed soups. Lipton's Cup-A-Soup, however, costs twice as much per serving as the regular Lipton soup mixes. Other instant mixes such as Herb-Ox cost less than a third as much per serving as Cup-A-Soup.

VANILLA AND ARTIFICIAL VANILLA

Aside from salt, vanilla is the world's most widely used flavoring. The extract comes from the pod of the vanilla plant, which is fermented in a solution of alcohol and water and concentrated through evaporation. The limited supply of vanilla and the lengthy processing have spurred chemists to synthesize vanillin, an artificial flavor. Vanillin lacks many of the flavor components of vanilla but is harmless. The human body actually produces a small amount of vanillin every day. In order to improve the flavor, ethyl vanillin, a chemical which is not produced by the body, is usually added to the vanillin. Ethyl vanillin, unlike vanillin, has not been adequately tested, but is used in artificial vanilla extract.

CHAPTER X

Nutritional Supplements

Are vitamin and mineral supplements the answer to good health?

Advocates of supplements—they are mostly non-experts—claim that it is good "nutritional insurance" to take them daily. Others claim that supplements can cure almost every disease from schizophrenia to the common cold. Experts on nutrition are skeptical, claiming that supplements are unnecessary, a waste of money, and can be dangerous.

As a general rule, most healthy people who satisfy their caloric needs by eating a large variety of lightly processed and properly prepared foods will get the Recommended Dietary Allowance (RDA) for all nutrients. Opponents of supplements point out that good natural diets supply adequate fiber and trace elements, deficiencies of which cannot be made up by any supplements now on the market.

The real possibility exists, however, that individual needs for certain nutrients are so high that they are not covered by the RDA. The National Research Council, which sets the Allowances, notes that they are designed to exceed the requirements of most individuals in order to take into account differences in genetic makeup. It emphasizes that the Allowances are designed to "meet the needs of healthy people and do not take into account special needs arising from infections, metabolic disorders, chronic diseases, or other abnormalities that require special dietary treatment." It also notes that "continued use of certain pharmaceutical preparations, such as oral contraceptives, may also influence specific nutritional needs" but that "RDA are not formulated to cover these effects."

In order to meet their needs, certain individuals may find it advisable to take supplements: women of childbearing age often need supplemental iron; women on oral contraceptives may need extra vitamin B_6, riboflavin, folic acid, and vitamin C; those who take aspirin more than once a week or who smoke or who are under great physiological or psychological stress may require more vitamin C; strict vegetarians (no dairy products) ordinarily need a vitamin B_{12} supplement. Marginal zinc deficiency may be widespread and could have serious adverse effects during pregnancy and early postnatal development.

To avoid possible adverse consequences, consult a physician about taking a supplement for those or any other conditions. Seven per cent of people who take self-prescribed iron supplements develop adverse symptoms, such as distress in the esophagus, nausea, or pain in the rectum.

Natural vs. Synthetic Supplements

Most authorities feel that synthetic forms of vitamins are as effective as the natural forms. Nevertheless, many supplement users are convinced of the superiority of natural vitamins and are willing to pay considerably more for them. In many cases, however, natural vitamins are not as "natural" as is generally believed. For example, "natural" vitamin C is in most cases partly synthetic. Most "natural" B complex supplements are synthetically produced and added to natural bases such as yeast or liver. "Natural" vitamin E is derived mainly from vegetable oils, which are treated intensively with several chemical solvents in order to concentrate the vitamin in a capsule small enough to swallow. Many vitamin preparations, both natural and synthetic, contain unnatural dyes, preservatives, and other chemicals, none of which need be specified on the label.

There is a case for natural vitamins. As one authoritative medical textbook puts it, "Since there are almost certainly some unidentified factors in the B complex, the use of artificially prepared mixtures of the pure B vitamins may promote a deficiency of these unknown factors by increasing their requirement. This contingency can be avoided by the inclusion in these mixtures of a concentrate of yeast or liver extract, either of which is likely to be the best source of any unknown factors."

Multivitamin/Mineral Supplements

Those who espouse multivitamin/mineral supplements point out that it makes sense to take all the nutrients in one capsule because they work together synergistically. Effective synergism implies that the vitamins be present in sufficient quantities to make interactions possible, but the amounts supplied in many formulations may indeed not be sufficient. One widely available supplement, for example, supplies 200 per cent of the RDA for riboflavin (vitamin B_6) but only 3 per cent of the RDA for niacin.

Geritol, like some other "multi" supplements, contains no minerals other than iron. Most supplements that are billed as containing both vitamins and minerals lack one or more important nutrients or supply them in negligible quantities.

Preparations that provide substantial quantities of all the nutrients may be difficult to find. In examining more than eighty products in health food and drug stores, we found only six of those fairly well-balanced in relation to the Recommended Dietary Allowances. In approximate order of increasing cost, these are G-154 Nutrins (General Nutrition Corp.), Formula TM (Nature Food Centers), Supertron (Nutrition Square), Plus Formula 7 (Plus Products), Theragran (E.R. Squibb), and One Plan (American Dietary Laboratories). However, none of these can be recommended without reservation either because of failure to meet the RDA for some nutrients or because of excessively high levels of other nutrients.

Adverse Effects of Supplements

Of the commonly available supplements, most have no toxic effect in healthy individuals, even when taken in very large amounts. The chief exceptions to this rule are vitamins A and D. Large amounts of niacin and vitamin C may cause adverse effects in some individuals. As a general rule, it is unwise to take large doses of individual vitamins or minerals except under a physician's guidance, as imbalances may result. For example, there is a possible danger that large amounts of one individual B vitamin may create an unsatisfied need for some of the other vitamins.

Megadoses of Vitamins

Many claims have been made that megadoses of vitamins—25 or more times the RDA—are effective in preventing disease. So far none of these claims are accepted by the majority of experts.

Dr. Linus Pauling, the Nobel Prize-winning biochemist, has made claims for the efficacy of vitamin C in doses of a gram or more per day. According to Pauling, large doses taken regularly help to prevent the common cold. Several large-scale tests have been conducted to evaluate his theory, but these have produced conflicting results. Critics of Pauling's thesis have suggested that patients who are especially susceptible to such conditions as cystinuria, gout, and those who have a tendency to form urate stones should not take large doses of vitamin C.

Many American blacks, Sephardic Jews, orientals, and certain other ethnic groups have a congenital deficiency of an enzyme in red blood cells called glucose 6-phosphate dehydogenase (G-6-PD). Large doses of vitamin C can cause severe anemia in individuals with a G-6-PD deficiency. Megadoses of this vitamin may also result in misdiagnoses of both diabetes and cancer of the colon through interference with standard test procedures.

Large doses of vitamin E—up to fifty times the RDA—have been advocated in the prevention of cardiovascular disease and a host of other ailments. None of the claims for such large doses have been substantiated by adequate testing. Although most studies show no toxic effects of vitamin E, there are a few reports of undesirable side effects of Vitamin E megadoses including headaches, nausea, fatigue, dizziness, blurred vision, inflammation of the mouth, chapped lips, muscle weakness, low blood sugar, and gastrointestinal disturbances. Vitamin E has been highly touted as an aid to virility, but the only scientific report relating to this shows that megadoses *decrease* functioning of the gonads (ovaries and testes).

Vitamin B_6 in megadoses produced liver disease in rats. A study of the effect on humans is now under way.

Claims for megadoses of these and other nutrients are met with skepticism by medical authorities. This is not to question the sincerity of advocates of nutritional supplements, and future research may well prove them right, but unlike the makers and sellers of supplements we do not recommend self-administration of megadoses of vitamins or minerals.

CHAPTER XI

Fiber and Health

Will fiber really save your life, or is it just another passing fad?

Denis Burkitt, Hugh Trowell and other British physicians claim the fiber is indeed a lifesaver. They claim it protects against cancer of the colon, heart disease, diverticular disease, and a host of others they call "diseases of civilization." Equally reputable physicians are very skeptical.

According to Burkitt and his colleagues, large amounts of fiber will speed the flow of food through the intestines, allowing less time for potentially harmful bacteria to thrive on the bowel's contents. Some of the bacteria which can thrive in the intestines are believed to produce cancer-causing chemicals, but a high fiber diet is claimed to help remove these carcinogens before they can do any harm.

Burkitt notes that the incidence of colon cancer is high in areas such as America and Europe where large amounts of refined, low-fiber foods are eaten but is extremely low in the underdeveloped countries of Africa and Asia where such foods are a rarity.

Trowell notes that American men get less than half the fiber of rural Bantus, a group virtually free of heart disease. He suggests that fiber lowers serum cholesterol by decreasing the absorption of bile salts, substances which carry cholesterol and fat into the blood-stream. Ancel Keys, the well-known proponent of saturated fat as a cause of heart disease, found that people with low cholesterol levels eat large quantities of fruits and vegetables while studies done with laboratory animals show that dietary fiber reduces serum cholesterol levels as well as the risk of heart disease. The beneficial effect of fiber on heart disease in humans is, however, a subject of controversy in medical circles.

Denis Burkitt joined with another noted British surgeon, Neil Painter, in claiming that diverticular disease is also caused by lack of fiber. This disease is characterized by inflamed pouches that form in the walls of intestines when (according to Burkitt and Painter) constipation produces a buildup of high pressures within the colon. They say that since diverticular disease is caused by a low-fiber diet, the worst possible treatment is a further continuance of such a diet. For over fifty years, a low-fiber diet has been the standard therapy for this disease (albeit with little success), but recently a number of researchers have experimented with high-fiber diets with such good results that this complete reversal of former therapy is receiving widespread acceptance. The diet prescribed by these researchers usually calls for special high-bran crispbreads or the addition of bran sprinkled on regular cereals, added to soups, etc. Substituting whole wheat bread for white bread and reducing the intake of sugar (white or brown) is also recommended as part of the therapy.

Burkitt and others have suggested, largely on the basis of epidemiological evidence, that lack of fiber is also associated with appendicitis, diabetes, gallstones, varicose veins, deep vein thrombosis, hiatus hernia, hemorrhoids, and obesity, diseases that are rare among rural Africans on high-fiber diets and rampant among those on typical Western low-fiber diets.

Fiber may play a protective role against the toxic effect of food additives and drugs. In one study, rats on a low-fiber diet with sodium cyclamate added exhibited marked retardation in growth, extensive diarrhea, and sickly appearance. Other rats that were fed cyclamates with such fibrous foods as alfalfa meal, wheat bran, and dried kelp, enjoyed good growth. Even more dramatic effects were seen with animals given the dye FD&C Red No. 2, formerly used in a variety of supermarket foods. Rats that were fed the dye in a low-fiber diet died within two weeks, but other rats given the dye in a high-fiber diet managed to thrive.

Several studies indicate that a high fiber diet can lower diabetics' blood glucose level, thus reducing their need for insulin.

Is Fiber Really That Good?

Some critics of the fiber theory claim that, historically, the increase in sugar consumption correlates better with the rise in coronary disease than the decline of fiber consumption. Other critics point out that on a worldwide scale the correlation between high-fiber diets and a low incidence of cancer of the colon does not always hold true. For example, American Indians have a high-fiber diet but suffer from cancer of the colon to the same extent as American Caucasians. One study based on analysis of data from thirty-seven countries shows that a more consistent correlation exists between intake of animal fat and cancer of the colon.

Some experts quite rightly point out that more experimental evidence on the effect of fiber on human physiology (including mineral metabolism) is needed before the medical profession can decide whether to recommend that people change their diets. Thus far, the beneficial effects of fiber have actually been proven in the treatment of only two conditions, constipation and diverticular disease. Fortunately, extra fiber in the diet from a variety of plant sources has no important adverse consequences for healthy people. Fiber, although it is sometimes called "roughage," actually becomes very soft inside the body because it absorbs water. For this reason, it does not irritate internal organs, although by its sheer bulk it may cause temporary discomfort from gas to those who shift from a low- to a high-fiber diet, especially if the food is not thoroughly chewed. Such distress should disappear in a few days and, moreover, can be minimized by working into the high-fiber diet gradually.

Which Foods Are Best for Fiber?

The growing awareness that fiber is not a simple unitary substance but a complex of substances that act in diverse ways may have an important bearing on the way in which we use fibrous foods. At least four components have thus far received attention:

1. *hemicellulose,* the principal component of bran, which may offer the greatest protection against developing disease of intestines and colon, especially diverticulitis, although this has yet to be definitely confirmed;

2. *pectin,* a fiber component that is found in fruit, particularly apples, the white inner rind of citrus fruits, and the type of fruits and berries used in making jellies, which apparently has the effect of reducing serum cholesterol and other blood lipids;

3. *cellulose,* which is sometimes used as a synonym for "fiber" but actually is only one component of the complex and in some foods, such as wheat bran, is a relatively minor component;

4. *lignin,* which is an apparently almost indigestible component of the fiber complex, may inhibit the action of other fiber components, and has antidiarrheal properties.

The standard tables give only the content of cellulose plus lignin, commonly described as "crude fiber." Total dietary fiber, which also includes hemicellulose, pectin, and other components, varies considerably in amount from one food to another and at least for some foods is grossly understated by the figures for crude fiber. There is also great variation in the type of fiber from one plant food to the next.

This wide variation in composition suggests the desirability of obtaining fiber from a wide variety of sources, including not only cereals but also fruits, vegetables, starchy roots, legumes, and nuts. Despite this, some popular writers have been promoting large amounts of unprocessed bran as an easy way to achieve a high-fiber diet without having to make fundamental changes in eating habits. For example, Dr. David Reuben, author of a best-selling book on fiber (*The Save-Your-Life Diet,* New York: Random House, 1975), suggests that some people may need up to three tablespoons of unprocessed bran a day to attain desirable stool volume. There is, however, a possible danger from continual use of large amounts of bran over an extended period because of its high phytic acid content. (See "The Phytic Acid Problem," page 100.) At least one condition, chronic renal disease, can be adversely affected by eating extra bran because of its high phosphorus content. It is significant that in the countries of Africa most often cited for their low levels of noninfectious intestinal disease and high-fiber intake, bran is practically unknown.

Peeling of fruits and vegetables reduces fiber content somewhat, but it is not entirely clear what effect cooking has on fiber. At least one researcher notes that boiling reduces the fiber content. In view of the possibility that cooking may be destructive, it would seem wise to include raw fruits and vegetables in the diet. Raw fruits and vegetables should be thoroughly chewed to break down the cell walls and thus make the maximum amount of nutrients available to the body.

Renunciation of a typical American diet for a high-fiber diet means giving up or drastically reducing the intake of meat, dairy products, fats and oils, and refined carbohydrates such as white bread, pastry, sugar, candy, and soft drinks. At least to the extent that intake of fat and refined carbohydrates are reduced,

Table I

FOODS GROUPED BY FIBER CONTENT

Foods with good to excellent fiber content

Wheat bran	Fresh vegetables (particularly raw)
Wheat germ	
Whole grain cereal products	Frozen vegetables**
Nuts and seeds, nut butters*	Frozen fruit
Legumes	Dried fruit*

Foods which have lost fiber in processing

Refined cereal products (macaroni, white rice, white bread)	Potato chips and other fried snacks*
	Fruit juices
Dehydrated potatoes	Canned fruits
French fried potatoes	Canned vegetables

Foods with no fiber

Meat	Eggs
Fish	Dairy products
Poultry	Fats and oils
Sugar and sweet syrups	Candy

* Substantial fiber but also high in calories, thus making it an inefficient source of fiber.
** Substantial fiber may be lost in trimming by processor.

switching to such a high-fiber diet would probably be beneficial.

Most people may not want to make such a drastic change in their diet, particularly as many of the claims are still not substantiated. However, those who take the easier course of going part-way toward the high-fiber diet may well get substantial benefits.

Those who do not enjoy complete good health should, of course, consult their physician before going on any radically different diet.

Food Colors, Food Flavors

Synthetic Colors

About three dozen substances are permitted as color additives in food, and 95 per cent of the 4,000,000 pounds of these colors used each year are synthetics derived from coal tar. Synthetic coloring is usually listed on retail packages as "artificial color" or "U.S. Certified Color." The latter term merely means that the batch of color is "certified" against containing more than a minimum amount of impurities and does not indicate that toxicological studies have been made.

Synthetic colorings serve no useful purpose in food other than to change their appearance. They do not add to the nutritional value nor do they protect against spoilage. It therefore seems reasonable that the standards for judging whether colors are to be permitted in foods should be even more rigorous than those pertaining to additives which provide a consumer advantage—for example, preservatives.

Since the beginning of food additive regulation a total of twenty-four different synthetic colors have been in use of which thirteen have been banned outright, most only after many years of "approved" use. Red No. 1, for example, was legally permitted in foods for fifty-four years before it was banned for causing liver cancer in test animals. FD&C Red No. 2, the most widely used color of all, was banned in 1976 when linked to cancer in test animals. Red No. 40, which replaced No. 2, is also under suspicion as a carcinogen.

Tests have thus far not indicated that any of the eleven artificial colors presently permitted in American foods are carcinogenic, but based on the historical record, this is no guarantee that they are indeed safe. As the editors of the *British Medical Journal* have said, "no system of safeguards merits absolute confidence, and if we mind our bellies very studiously and very carefully we will eschew all unnecessary adulteration of food. We can make a start by eliminating synthetic food colours."

Natural Colors

Despite the absence of scientific testing, the FDA has given permanent approval of food colors with natural origins. Colors such as annatto, carotene, and caramel, were judged safe based on their long-term usage in foods without apparent harm. The FAO-WHO

Joint Expert Committee on Food Additives has ques-
itoned this uncritical view of natural colors and has
called for toxicity testing of these additives along with
the artificial colors.

Artificial Flavors

While only eleven artificial colors are allowed in
food, 1,610 synthetic flavors are permitted. When the
502 flavor additives derived from natural sources are
included, the number of chemical compounds allowed
as flavor additives total 2,112 chemicals or almost 80
per cent of the 2,700 additives used in food as listed
by the National Academy of Sciences. Federal regulations place *no* restrictions on flavors other than the
admonishment that the quantity used be "in accordance
with all the principals of good manufacturing practice."

Very few artificial flavors have been adequately
studied for their potential to cause mutations, birth
defects or cancer, and indeed the limited testing that
has been done does not inspire confidence in the safety
of these compounds. Of forty-eight food flavorings
evaluated by the FDA in 1967, seventeen had adverse
effects. The U.N. Joint FAO/WHO Expert Committee
on Food Additives, in a report on thirty-three artificial
flavors, found only eleven to be acceptable without
reservation.

Even in the unlikely event that each of the two

thousand-plus flavor additives permitted in the U.S. were all thoroughly tested, such tests would be relatively useless for judging the safety of flavors in food products, for rarely are any of the chemicals used alone. Natural food flavors are extraordinarily complex and to create an acceptable man-made substitute many chemical compounds must be used. For example, to create an acceptable raspberry flavor for soft drinks, the food chemist must use twenty-eight separate compounds including such tongue-twisters as methoxyacetoxyacetophene, acetylmethylcarbinol and ethyl methyphenylglycidate. The effects of such elaborate combinations of chemicals are completely unknown and experimental techniques needed to test all likely combinations do not exist.

Naturally Derived Flavors

A natural origin is no guarantee of flavor safety. Safrole, for example, which is derived from the root of the sassafras tree, and widely used as a flavoring for root beer, was banned in 1960. Safrole not only causes cancer, but a host of other toxic effects as well, including liver, kidney, stomach and testicle damage. Courmarin and calamus oil, which have also been banned, are other naturally-derived flavorings shown to cause extensive organ damage in test animals. Most natural flavorings have not been adequately tested.

Allergic Reactions to Synthetic Colors

Many allergists have reported that certain individuals are extremely sensitive to artificial colors. These persons have allergic reactions ranging from urticaria (skin eruptions commonly called hives), to severe asthma and even to life-threatening anaphylactic shock.

The dye most frequently implicated is FD&C Yellow No. 5 (also called tartrazine) which is found in gelatin desserts, ice cream, sherbets, carbonated beverages, dry drink powders, candy, bakery products, cereals, spaghetti, puddings, and a number of drugs and vitamins with yellow-colored coatings.

In 1979 the Food and Drug Administration concluded that "the evidence of a causal relationship between FD&C Yellow No. 5 and serious allergic-type responses in certain susceptible individuals is sufficient to warrent label declaration." The FDA estimates that between 47,000 and 94,000 Americans are intolerant of the color, and that the sensitivity occurs primarily in individuals who are also intolerant of aspirin.

The FDA thus declared that all foods containing the color additive must list it on the label as FD&C Yellow No. 5 (instead of just "artificial color"). While not mandatory for food products until July 1, 1981, the FDA encouraged manufacturers to comply voluntarily "as soon as possible."

Hyperkinetic Reactions to Synthetic Colors and Flavors

One of the most intriguing theories of recent years has been advanced by Dr. Ben F. Feingold, Chief Emeritus of San Francisco's Kaiser-Permanente Medical Center Allergy Department. He believes that hyperkinesis in children is caused, at least in part, by artificial colors and flavors. He estimates that in the U.S. about five million children suffer from hyperkinesis-learning disability, a condition characterized by hyperactivity, impulsive, sometimes violent behavior, and inability to concentrate. Dr. Feingold has treated hundreds of hyperactive children on a special diet devoid of artificial flavors and colors and claims that about 50 per cent of them return to normal or near-normal behavior within a month, eliminating the need for the drugs normally used in the treatment of the condition.

Many parents of hyperactive children who have adopted the "Feingold Diet" remain enthusiastic despite the results of several independent research studies that failed to confirm Dr. Feingold's claims. Studies done at the universities of Wisconsin, Pittsburgh, and Maryland indicate virtually no effect of additive-free diets on the hyperactivity of school-age children. Thus, most authorities remain skeptical of the theory that food colors and flavors cause hyperactivity.

Nutrients in 100-Calorie Portions of Common Foods

This table compares the nutrients in 29 representative foods from each of the eight major food categories—cereals, fruits & vegetables, beverages, dairy, meat, poultry & fish, fats & oils, sweets, and other foods (in this case, eggs and nuts).

The values are based on food samples with equal calories. This is a useful way to compare foods. For example, 439 grams (about 2½ cups) of cooked spinach has 100 calories, while only 17 grams (about 1¼ tablespoons) of peanuts provides 100 calories. Comparing these two foods in the table shows that the nutrients in 100 calories-worth of spinach far exceed those in peanuts. Thus, except for calories, spinach is a far more concentrated course of nutrients than peanuts.

Pages 330 and 331 show the levels of protein and minerals in the 29 foods, while pages 332 and 333 list the vitamins, fat and fiber in the same foods.

A number in bold-face type indicates that a 100-calorie portion of the food provides more than 10 per cent of the Recommended Dietary Allowances (RDA). A dash (-) indicates information was not available, a small "t" means only a trace of the nutrient is present, and the symbol < means "less than" the number following it. Other explanations and footnotes appear at the end of the table on page 334.

	Weight of 100-Calorie Portion[2] (g)	Protein (g)	Protein Quality NPU[3] (mg)	Calcium (mg)	Phos- phorus (mg)	Mag- nesium[4] (mg)
RDA[1]		56	-	800	800	350
Bread, whole wheat	41	4.3	45	41	93	32
Bread, white	37	3.2	37	32	36	8
Carrots, raw	270	2.6	low	90	87	62
Lettuce, iceberg	786	7.1	low	157	171	86
Potatoes, baked in skin	107	2.8	60	10	70	47
Spinach, cooked	439	13.2	50	407	165	386
Tomato, raw	500	5.0	low	60	123	70
Peas, sweet, cooked	140	7.5	47	32	139	49
Soybeans, mature, cooked	77	8.5	61	56	138	39
Apple	187	.3	med.	13	18	15
Banana	173	1.3	low	10	31	39
Orange	281	2.0	low	84	41	22
Apple juice, bottled	214	.2	-	13	20	9
Orange juice, fresh	233	1.4	low	24	38	26
Milk, whole	153	5.3	82	181	143	20
Milk, skim	278	10.0	82	336	265	39
Cheese, cheddar	25	6.3	70	190	121	11
Beef, lean, cooked	46	13.6	67	6	67	8
Pork, lean, cooked	42	11.7	67	5	124	8
Chicken, roasted	40	10.9	65	4	96	-
Shrimp, raw	110	19.9	80	69	182	46
Tuna, canned in oil	50	14.6	80	4	119	-
Butter	14	.1	-	3	2	<1
Margarine, corn oil, stick	14	.8	low	3	2	-
Corn oil	11.4	0	0	0	0	-
Sugar, white	26	0	0	0	0	t
Egg, hard boiled	61	7.9	94	33	126	7
Peanuts	17	4.5	43	12	70	35
Pecans	15	1.3	42	10	42	21

Iron (mg)	Zinc[4] (mg)	Potassium (mg)	Copper[4] (mg)	Manganese[4] (mg)	Chromium[4] (mcg)	Selenium[4] (mcg)	Molybdenum[4] (mcg)
10	15	[5]	[5]	[5]	[5]	[5]	[5]
.9	.8	111	-	.06	-	27	-
.9	.3	38	.08	.07	1	10	-
1.7	1.1	820	.27	.03	4	3	22
4.3	2.9	1,371	.71	-	55	6	24
.8	.4	539	.11	.16	0	.3	4
9.7	3.9	1,422	.48	3.41	12	-	114
2.3	1.0	1,100	.55	-	5	1	-
2.5	1.5	275	-	.09	-	-	488
2.1	-	415	.90	-	-	-	-
.5	.1	190	.17	.06	4	.3	-
.8	.4	436	.30	-	-	1	5
.8	.3	411	.17	.10	-	4	-
1.3	-	216	.47	-	-	-	-
.5	< .1	481	.19	-	-	-	184
.1	.6	222	.06	.03	2	2	15
.1	-	403	.06	-	-	14	-
.3	1.0	21	.03	-	-	-	-
1.7	2.7	169	.40	< .01	4	14	0
1.5	1.6	165	.03	.01	4	10	156
.7	.4	-	.07	.08	10	5	0
1.8	1.9	242	.66	< .01	1	65	3
.9	.6	-	.06	-	-	-	-
0	< .1	3	-	.01	2	20	1
0	< .1	3	.01	-	5	-	-
0	< .1	0	-	.01	5	-	-
t	< .1	t	< .01	-	2	0	2
1.5	.6	79	.06	.03	< 1	7	30
.4	.6	120	.11	.12	-	9	-
.3	.7	87	.17	.51	-	< 1	-

	Vitamin A (IU)	Thiamin (mg)	Ribo-flavin (mg)	Niacin (mg)	Vitamin B6[4] (mg)	Vitamin B12[4] (mcg)
RDA[1]	5,000	1.4	1.6	18	2.0	2.0
Bread, whole wheat	t	.10	.05	1.1	.07	0
Bread, white	5	.09	0.8	.9	.01	0
Carrots, raw	26,430	.13	.13	1.3	.40	0
Lettuce, iceberg	2,570	.43	.43	2.8	.43	0
Potatoes, baked in skin	5	.10	.05	1.9	.35	0
Spinach, cooked	35,560	.32	.61	2.2	1.23	0
Tomato, raw	4,100	.28	.18	3.3	.50	0
Peas, sweet, cooked	754	.39	.16	3.2	-	0
Soybeans, mature, cooked	21	.16	.07	.5	.20	0
Apple	156	.05	.03	.2	.06	0
Banana	230	.06	.07	.8	.45	0
Orange	400	.20	.08	.8	.08	0
Apple juice, bottled	-	.02	.05	.2	.06	0
Orange juice, fresh	450	.21	.07	.9	.09	0
Milk, whole	220	.04	.26	.1	.06	.61
Milk, skim	11	.10	.50	.2	.12	1.11
Cheese, cheddar	340	.01	.11	t	.02	.25
Beef, lean, cooked	9	.02	.11	2.1	.20	.60
Pork, lean, cooked	0	.26	.11	2.3	.15	.23
Chicken, roasted	326	.03	.06	3.3	.34	.17
Shrimp, raw	-	.02	.03	3.5	.11	.99
Tuna, canned in oil	41	.03	.06	6.0	.22	1.10
Butter	460	-	-	-	t	t
Margarine, corn oil, stick	500	-	-	-	-	-
Corn oil	-	0	0	0	-	0
Sugar, white	0	0	0	0	-	0
Egg, hard boiled	720	.05	.17	t	.07	1.20
Peanuts	-	.06	.02	2.9	.05	0
Pecans	21	.12	.02	.1	.03	0

Folacin (mcg)	Pantothenic Acid[4] (mg)	Vitamin C (mg)	Vitamin E[6] (mg)	Total Fat (g)	Saturated Fat (g)	Linoleic Acid (g)	Crude Fiber (g)
400	[5]	45	15[7]	-	-	5	-
12	.31	t	.2	1.3	-	-	.7
6	.16	t	.1	1.2	.4	t	.1
22	.76	20	.2	.3	-	-	2.7
55	1.60	43	.46	.8	-	-	3.9
12	.53	21	< .1	.1	-	-	.8
329	1.32	122	10.8	1.2	-	-	2.6
44	1.65	105	1.6	1.0	-	-	2.0
27	-	28	.8	.5	-	-	2.8
56	.42	0	-	4.4	.8	2.3	1.2
4	.20	7	.6	1.0	-	-	1.9
17	.31	12	.4	.2	-	-	9
6	.70	103	.6	.5	-	-	1.4
< 1	-	2	-	.1	-	-	.1
11	.44	104	< .1	.5	-	-	.1
1	.52	1	< .1	5.3	3.4	.1	0
-	1.03	2	-	.2	-	-	0
4	.13	0	-	8.2	5.1	.1	0
4	.19	-	< .1	4.7	2.0	.2	0
3	.25	-	< .1	5.5	2.0	.4	0
1	.36	-	.2	5.9	1.6	1.2	0
2	.31	-	.7	.9	-	-	0
1	.16	-	-	4.2	1.5	1.0	0
-	-	-	.1	11.4	7.0	.3	0
-	-	0	-	11.3	2.2	4.1	0
-	-	0	4.0	11.4	1.4	6.4	0
-	-	0	-	0	0	0	0
3	1.00	0	.3	7.0	2.1	.7	0
10	.36	0	1.3	8.5	1.6	2.5	.5
4	.25	t	.2	10.4	.9	2.5	.3

[1] Recommended Dietary Allowance for 154 lb. male 23-50 years old.

[2] One ounce = 28.4 grams.

[3] Net Protein Utilization, a measure of protein quality.

[4] Values for magnesium, zinc, copper, manganese, chromium, selenium, molybdenum, folacin, vitamin B_6, and vitamin B_{12} are not available for most listed cooked foods and hence values for raw foods are shown. Of these nutrients, folacin and vitamin B_6 are substantially affected by the heat of cooking while most nutrients can be leached into cooking water or drippings.

[5] Nutrient essential but no RDA established.

[6] Alpha tocopherol only. Other components of vitamin E, not included in the figures, also have significant activity.

[7] The RDA for vitamin E is expressed as International Units, but the data on vitamin E content are commonly given in milligrams.

Note 1: Boldface type indicates that 100-calorie portion of food supplies more than 10 per cent of Recommended Dietary Allowance.

Note 2: The nutrients shown are the amounts present in the food but amounts available to the body may be less for several reasons, including presence of oxalic acid (which interferes with the use of certain foods, notably spinach) and phytic acid (which interferes with the absorption of calcium, phosphorus, magnesium, iron, and zinc in grains, nuts, and legumes).

Note 3: Niacin values do not include activity contributed by tryptophan, an amino acid that is a precursor of niacin. The niacin value of dairy products in particular would be improved if tryptophan activity was included.

t indicates trace

dash (-) indicates information not available.

$<$ = less than

Source: Principal sources are: Watt, B. K., and Merrill, A. L., *Composition of Foods, Agriculture Handbook No. 8* (Washington: 1963); Orr, M. L. *Pantothenic Acid, Vitamin B_6 and Vitamin B_{12} in Foods,* Home Economics Research Report No. 36 (Washington, USDA, 1969).

APPENDIX III

THE 100 MOST HEAVILY ADVERTISED FOOD BRANDS IN 1976

Brand (Company)	1976 Advertising Expenditures	Nutritive Rating*	Questionable Ingredients**
1 Wrigley Gum (William Wrigley, Co.)	$37,817,600	F	Sugar (1), artificial flavor-
2 Coca-Cola Soft Drink (Coca-Cola Co.)	24,625,000	F	Sugar (2), caffeine
3 Pepsi Cola Soft Drink (Pepsico, Inc.)	20,627,500	F	Sugar (2), caffeine
4 Campbell Canned Soups (Campbell Soup Co.)	20,115,700	B	MSG, salt
5 Maxwell House Coffee (General Foods)	17,849,400	F	Caffeine
6 Duncan Hines Baking Mixes (Procter & Gamble Co.)	16,280,200	C	Sugar (1), artificial flavor, artificial color, refined flour, salt
7 Betty Crocker Baking Mixes (General Mills)	16,196,900	C	Sugar (1), refined flour, artificial flavor, artificial color

* Grade of A = substantial value with little or no questionable ingredients; grade of B = substantial nutritive value but contains significant amount of questionable ingredients; grade of C = minimal nutritive value or nutritive value due chiefly to addition of synthetic vitamins and minerals; grade of F = no nutritive value or no nutritive value other than calories; NG = not graded.

** Where numbers in parentheses appear after the name of an ingredient, they indicate the rank of that ingredient in the ingredient listing. In the cases where the rank of an ingredient may vary by variety of brand, the range of variation is indicated.

Brand (Company)	1976 Advertising Expenditures	Nutritive Rating*	Questionable Ingredients**
8 Kool Aid Powdered Drink Mix (General Foods)	13,278,100	F	Artificial flavor, artificial color, sugar (1), (or directions call for adding large amounts of sugar)
9 7 Up Soft Drink (Seven Up Co.)	12,848,900	F	Sugar (2)
10 Kraft Cheese Products (Kraftco)	12,466,900	A	Artificial color (in some varieties), salt
11 Hunt Sauces (Norton Simon)	11,516,600	B	Hydrogenated oil, salt (5-6), sugar (5-7)
12 Nabisco Crackers (Nabisco Inc.)	11,348,900	C	Sugar (1-3), artificial flavor, artificial color, salt
13 Sanka Coffee (General Foods)	10,965,600	F	
14 Folgers Coffee (Procter & Gamble Co.)	10,924,800	F	Caffeine
15 Cheerios Cereal (General Mills)	10,255,600	C	Sugar (3), artificial color, salt (4)
16 Shake 'n Bake Coating Mixes (General Foods)	10,238,400	NG	Sugar (1-7), hydrogenated oil, artificial color, MSG, artificial flavor
17 Hawaiian Punch (R. J. Reynolds Ind. Inc.)	10,225,000	C	Sugar (2), artificial color
18 Jell-O Gelatin Dessert (General Foods)	10,208,600	C	Sugar (1), artificial color, artificial flavor
19 Fritos Snack Chips (Pepsico Inc.)	9,845,500	C	Hydrogenated oil, salt
20 Florida Citrus Juices (Fla. Citrus Commission)	9,432,300	A	
21 Nabisco Cookies (Nabisco Inc.)	9,320,600	C	Sugar (1-3, artificial flavor, artificial color, salt

Brand (Company)	1976 Advertising Expenditures	Nutritive Rating*	Questionable Ingredients**
22 Jell-O Pudding & Pie Filling (General Foods)	9,082,200	C	Sugar (1), hydrogenated oil, salt, artificial color, carrageenan, artificial flavor
23 Hostess Baked Goods (ITT)	8,900,000	C	Refined flour, artificial flavor, artificial color, many products high in sugar
24 American Dairy Association Products	8,884,100	A	
25 Royal Crown Beverages (Royal Crown Cola Co.)	8,723,300	F	Sugar (2), caffeine
26 Tasters Choice Coffee (Nestle Enterprises, Inc.)	8,392,200	F	Caffeine
27 Chef Boy-Ar-Dee Canned Meals (American Home Products Corp.)	8,230,700	C	Refined flour, salt, sugar, MSG
28 Lipton Soup Mixes (Lever Bros.)	8,020,100	B	Salt (2), hydrogenated oil, MSG, artificial colors
29 Crisco Oil (Procter & Gamble)	7,950,400	B	Hydrogenated oil
30 Tang Instant Breakfast Drink (General Foods)	7,936,700	C	Sugar (1), hydrogenated coconut oil, artificial flavor, artificial color
31 Trident Sugarless Gum (Warner-Lambert)	7,934,000	F	Artificial flavor, artificial color
32 Pringles Newfangled Potato Chips (Procter & Gamble)	7,786,500	B	Salt (5)
33 Doritos Tortilla Chips (Pepsico)	7,749,400	C	Salt (4)
34 Nescafe Instant Coffee (Nestle)	7,683,800	F	Caffeine
35 Post Raisin Bran (General Foods)	7,593,300	C	Sugar (3), salt (6)

Brand (Company)	1976 Advertising Expenditures	Nutritive Rating*	Questionable Ingredients**
36 Ragu Sauces (Chesebrough-Ponds Inc.)	7,564,800	B	Hydrogenated oil, salt (5-6), sugar (5-7)
37 Pillsbury Baking & Frosting Mixes (Pillsbury Co.)	7,407,400	C	Sugar, salt, refined flour, artificial flavor, artificial color
38 Kraft Margarines (Kraftco)	7,383,400	B	Hydrogenated oil, artificial flavor, artificial color, salt
39 Lipton Tea (Lever Bros.)	7,316,400	F	Caffeine
40 Brim Coffee (General Foods)	7,280,500	F	
41 Wylers Drink Mixes (Borden)	7,085,200	F	Artificial flavor, artificial color, sugar (1)
42 Pillsbury Refrigerated Dough Products (Pillsbury)	6,968,600	C	Sugar, salt, refined flour, artificial flavor, artificial color
43 TAB Low Calorie Beverage (Coca-Cola Co.)	6,947,200	F	Caffeine, saccharin
44 Minute Maid Frozen Juice (Coca-Cola Co.)	6,859,700	A	
45 Wesson Oil (Norton Simon)	6,655,400	B	Partially hydrogenated oil
46 Life Savers Candy (Squibb Corp.)	6,591,200	F	Sugar (1), artificial flavor, artificial color
47 Dentyne Gum (Warner-Lambert Co.)	6,573,400	F	Sugar (1), artificial flavor, artificial color
48 Mazola Oil (CPC International)	6,457,900	A	
49 General Foods International Instant Coffees (General Foods)	6,388,000	F	Sugar (1), hydrogenated coconut oil, artificial flavor
50 Keebler Cookies & Crackers (Keebler Co.)	6,364,000	C	Sugar (1-3), refined flour, artificial color, salt

Brand (Company)	1976 Questionable Expenditures	Nutritive Rating*	Advertising Ingredients**
51 Betty Crocker Frosting (General Mills)	6,342,000	F	Sugar (1), artificial flavor, artificial color
52 Skippy Peanut Butter (CPC International)	6,301,900	B	Sugar (3), hydrogenated oil, salt
53 Birds Eye Cool Whip Frozen Whipped Topping (General Foods)	6,291,000	F	Sugar (2), hydrogenated oil, artificial color, artificial flavor, carrageenan
54 Pepsi Light Diet Cola (Pepsico)	6,168,200	F	Caffeine, saccharin, artificial color, artificial flavor
55 Imperial Margarines (Lever Bros.)	6,157,400	B	Artificial flavor, salt, artificial color, hydrogenated oil
56 Hills Bros. Coffee (Hills Bros.)	6,120,400	F	Caffeine
57 Canada Dry Beverages (Norton Simon)	6,071,000	F	Sugar (2), some products have saccharin
58 Swifts Meats (Esmark Inc.)	6,041,900	B	Salt, sodium nitrate, sodium nitrite, in some varieties
59 Stove Top Stuffing Mix (General Foods)	5,976,100	B	MSG, artificial flavor
60 Post Grape Nuts (General Foods)	5,942,300	C	Salt (3)
61 Pam Dry Fry (American Home Products)	5,885,800	NG	Hydrogenated oil
62 Total Cereal (General Mills)	5,809,800	C	Sugar (2), salt (3)
63 Crisco Vegetable Shortening (Procter & Gamble)	5,664,600	C	Hydrogenated oil
64 California Milk Producers Advisory Board Products	5,645,300	A	
65 Blue Bonnet Margarines (Standard Brands)	5,631,000	B	Hydrogenated oil, artificial flavor, artificial color, salt

Brand (Company)	1976 Advertising Expenditures	Nutritive Rating*	Questionable Ingredients**
66 Kraft Salad Dressings (Kraftco)	5,621,700	B	Sugar (2-6), salt (4-7)
67 Kellogg's Rice Krispies (Kellogg Co.)	5,590,100	C	Sugar (2), salt (3), refined grains
68 Nestea Instant Tea (Nestle)	5,487,800	F	Caffeine
69 Good Seasons Salad Dressing Mixes (General Foods)	5,456,000	NG	Sugar (1-4), MSG, hydrogenated oil, artificial color, artificial flavor
70 Swanson Frozen Foods (Campbell Soup Co.)	5,246,400	B	Salt, MSG, artificial flavor
71 Diet Rite Cola (Royal Crown Cola Co.)	5,192,400	F	Caffeine, saccharin
72 Nestle's Candy (Nestle)	5,130,800	F	Sugar (1), artificial flavor
73 Dr. Pepper softdrink (Dr. Pepper Co.)	5,081,700	F	Sugar (2), artificial flavor, caffeine
74 Nestle's Morsels (Nestle)	5,055,800	F	Sugar, artificial flavor
75 Hormel Meat Products (George A. Hormel & Co.)	5,033,600	B	Salt, sodium nitrate, sodium nitrite, in some varieties
76 Country Time Drink Mixes (General Foods)	5,019,600	F	Artificial flavor, artificial color, sugar
77 Diet Pepsi Cola (Pepsico)	4,964,300	F	Caffeine, saccharin
78 Armour Meats (Greyhound Corp.)	4,954,800	B	Salt, sodium nitrate, sodium nitrite, in some varieties
79 Kellogg's Frosted Rice (Kellogg Co.)	4,928,100	C	Sugar (2)
80 JIF Peanut Butter (Procter & Gamble)	4,866,000	B	Sugar (2), hydrogenated oil, salt
81 Mazola Soft and Regular Margarine (CPC International)	4,838,400	B	Hydrogenated oil, artificial flavor, artificial color, salt

Brand (Company)	1976 Advertising Expenditures	Nutritive Rating*	Questionable Ingredients**
82 Kellogg's Sugar Frosted Flakes (Kellogg Co.)	4,762,100	C	Sugar (2), salt (3)
83 Kellogg's Special K Cereal (Kellogg Co.)	4,733,000	C	Sugar (3), refined grains, salt (5)
84 Life Cereal (Quaker Oats Co.)	4,619,200	C	Sugar (2), salt (5), artificial color
85 M & M's Candy (Mars Inc.)	4,568,800	F	Sugar (1), artificial flavor, artificial color
86 Wonder Bread & Rolls (ITT)	4,566,100	C	Refined flour
87 Fleischmann's Margarines (Standard Brands)	4,541,400	B	Hydrogenated oil, artificial flavor, artificial color, salt
88 Freshen-Up Gum (Warner-Lambert Co.)	4,457,200	F	Sugar (1) (2) (4), artificial flavor, artificial color
89 Hellman's Mayonnaise (CPC International)	4,247,000	A	Sugar (7), salt (6)
90 Coffee-Mate Coffee Creamer (Carnation)	4,243,600	F	Sugar (1), artificial flavor, artificial color, hydrogenated oil
91 Kraft Dinners (Kraftco)	4,223,800	C	Refined flour, salt (6), artificial color
92 Minute Rice (General Foods)	4,192,500	C	
93 Fresca Sugar-Free Beverage (Coca-Cola Co.)	4,182,400	F	Saccharin, artificial flavor, artificial color, salt, BVO
94 Thomas' English Muffins (CPC International)	4,161,900	C	Refined flour
95 Post Honey Combs (General Foods)	4,157,400	C	Sugar (2), salt (4), hydrogenated oil (5)
96 Heinz Tomato Ketchup (H. J. Heinz Co.)	4,127,700	NG	Sugar (3)
97 Care-Free Sugarless Gum (Squibb Corp.)	4,098,300	F	

Brand (Company)	1976 Advertising Expenditures	Nutritive Rating*	Questionable Ingredients**
98 Golden Grahams (General Mills)	4,044,800	C	Sugar (2) (4) (7), artificial flavor
99 Log Cabin Syrup (General Foods)	3,988,400	F	Sugar (1), artificial flavor
100 Wheaties Cereal (General Mills)	3,986,500	C	Sugar (2), salt (3), artificial color

Source: Figures are derived from *Competitive Brand Cumulative*, published by Leading National Advertisers, Inc., Box 525, Norwalk, Conn. 06856 including magazine and newspaper supplement data as compiled by LNA, Leading National Advertisers, Inc. for PIB, Publishers Information Bureau; network television, spot television and network radio data as prepared by BAR, Broadcast Advertisers Reports, Inc.; and outdoor data as prepared by LNA, Leading National Advertisers, Inc. in cooperation with IOA, Institute of Outdoor Advertising for markets over 100,000 population.

Note: The 1976 expenditure data in this table are believed to be indicative of those for later years and would show more or less the same brands among the top hundred and approximately the same proportion of foods with low nutritive value.

Dietary Goals for the United States

In February 1977, the Senate Select Committee on Nutrition and Human Needs issued a staff report entitled "Dietary Goals for the United States." The report summarized the Senate Committee's findings based on several years of receiving testimony from dozens of experts on the subject of the American diet. The Dietary Goals call for a dramatic change in American eating patterns by reducing the intake of sugars, fats, salt, meat, and eggs, and urge Americans instead to increase their consumption of fruits, vegetables, whole grains, low-fat dairy products, poultry, and fish.

Publication of the Dietary Goals aroused a storm of controversy. Although many nutritionists and dieticians hailed them as a positive step toward improving the health and well-being of Americans, many others criticized the goals as simplistic, misleading, and inappropriate. Especially critical were representatives of the meat and egg industries, and they were later granted special hearings to present their views. As a result of the controversy, the Senate Select Committee decided to release a Second Edition of the Dietary Goals in December 1977. The Second Edition takes into consideration testimony from the later hearings and includes numerous revisions of the original text.

The Dietary Goals for the United States, Second Edition, are:

1. To avoid overweight, consume only as much energy (calories) as is expended; if overweight, decrease energy intake and increase energy expenditure.

2. Increase the consumption of complex carbohydrates and "naturally occurring" sugars from about 28% of energy intake to about 48% of energy intake.

3. Reduce the consumption of refined and processed sugars by about 45% to account for about 10% of total energy intake.

4. Reduce overall fat consumption from approximately 40% to about 30% of energy intake.

5. Reduce saturated fat consumption to account for about 10% of total energy intake; and balance that with polyunsaturated and monounsaturated fats, which should account for about 10% of energy intake each.

6. Reduce cholesterol consumption to about 300 mg a day.

7. Limit the intake of sodium by reducing the intake of salt to about 5 gm a day.

To achieve these goals, the report suggests the following changes in food selection and preparation:

1. Increase consumption of fruits and vegetables and whole grains.

2. Decrease consumption of refined and other processed sugars and foods high in such sugars.

3. Decrease consumption of foods high in total fat, and partially replace saturated fats, whether obtained from animal or vegetable sources, with polyunsaturated fats.

4. Decrease consumption of animal fat, and choose meats, poultry, and fish which will reduce saturated fat intake.

5. Except for young children, substitute low-fat and

nonfat milk for whole milk, and low-fat dairy products for high-fat dairy products.

6. Decrease consumption of butterfat, eggs, and other high cholesterol sources. Some consideration should be given to easing the cholesterol goal for premenopausal women, young children, and the elderly in order to obtain the nutritional benefits of eggs in the diet.

7. Decrease consumption of salt and foods high in salt content.

The differences between the current American diet and the Dietary Goals are illustrated in the following table.

To meet the Dietary Goals, most Americans would have to significantly alter their eating habits. During 1965 and 1966, the USDA's Household Food Consumption Survey collected data on the food eaten by thousands of individuals. After the release of the Senate Committee's Dietary Goals, USDA experts compared the actual diets of over 6,000 persons from the 1965-66 survey with the diet proposed by the Dietary Goals. *Fewer than three per cent* of the people met the Goals for fat and carbohydrates. This variance between the Goals and actual diets means that Americans are being asked to radically change their dietary habits even though the reasons for doing so are still highly controversial.

Perhaps the most controversial aspect is the tacit assumption by the Select Committee that heart disease can be prevented by dietary changes such as reducing consumption of eggs and animal fat. Many experts question the usefulness of such advice, especially for women and children. Dr. Robert Olson, Chairman of the Department of Biochemistry at the St. Louis University Medical School and a leading nutritionist, says that "the proposal is disastrous. . . . These dietary goals might be considered guidelines for . . . overnourished middle-aged men [but] they are certainly inappropriate . . . for infants, children, adolescents, pregnant women, and the aged." Professor A. E. Harper of the University of Wisconsin declared that "for the general population, there is little basis for a guideline other than to stress the importance of avoiding obesity." Dr. George Mann of Vanderbilt University, an outspoken gadfly of the medical and nutritional establishment, alleges that "the goals reflect the biased interests of selfish scientists and segments of the food industry which hoodwinked [the Committee] staff."

On the other hand, the Dietary Goals were defended by Michael C. Latham, Professor of International Nutrition at Cornell University. He declared that "it is the responsibility of a government to provide guidelines and to have a well-reasoned and consistent food and nutrition policy. It is the duty of nutritionists to help the public consume a diet that provides the balance and amount of nutrients they now need and also one that will help them maintain optimum health in the future. These goals are a first step in providing that help. . . ."

Glossary

ACID/ALKALI: The degree of acidity/alkalinity is expressed by pH value which ranges from 0 (very acid) to 14 (very alkaline) with a ten-fold difference between each level. Thus, a pH of 4 is ten times more acidic than a pH of 5 and one hundred times more acidic than pH 6. Soft drinks and fruit juices have a pH in the range of 2 to 4, milk is about 6.5, pure water 7.0 (neutral) and milk of magnesia is 10.5.

ATHEROSCLEROSIS: A degeneration of the circulatory system characterized by deposits of cholesterol and other fatty material on the inside walls of the blood vessels. Atherosclerosis is a chief cause of heart attacks because it reduces the flow of blood to the heart.

CARBOHYDRATES: An important source of energy for metabolism. Consists of mono- or disaccharides (sugars) and polysaccharides (starches, cellulose, glycogen).

CARCINOGEN: Any cancer-producing substance.

CARDIOVASCULAR DISEASE: Pertaining to the heart and blood vessels. Includes diseases of the heart as well as hypertension (high blood pressure) and cerebrovascular diseases such as stroke.

CARIES: Erosion of tooth enamel from acids pro-

347

duced by bacteria which cling to the teeth. *Cariogenic:* Caries-producing.

CAROTENE: A yellow pigment found in plant and animal tissues and particularly abundant in yellow or orange vegetables such as carrots, and in dark green leafy vegetables such as spinach. Readily converted to vitamin A by the body.

COMPLEMENTARY PROTEINS: Proteins are said to complement each other when, taken together, they have more value than when taken separately. The value of protein increases as it approaches that of the more or less ideal amino acid pattern of egg protein. An example: wheat protein is deficient in lysine but fairly strong in the sulphur amino acids whereas the protein of beans has an abundance of the former and a deficiency of the latter. Put wheat and beans together in the same meal and the combined amino acid pattern is closer to that of the egg.

CHOLESTEROL: A fatty substance found in all body tissues and necessary as a precursor of certain hormones. *Serum* cholesterol is that which is found in the blood. The role played by cholesterol in foods in the causation of heart disease is controversial as large amounts are synthesized daily in the normal human liver.

CONTROLLED STUDY: In a controlled study some subjects receive the test substance while others (called the controls) receive no test substance or receive a similar appearing but inert material called a *placebo*.

ENZYME: Complex proteins produced by living cells. They act as catalysts, i.e., produce chemical changes in other substances without undergoing change themselves. Enzymes are very specific, acting only upon certain substances and not others. Enzymes are often identified by adding "-ase" to the name of the substances on which they act. Thus, proteases break down proteins, while lipases break down lipids.

EPIDEMIOLOGY: The study of causative factors explaining the incidence and distribution of diseases by geographic area and by demographic group.

ESSENTIAL AMINO ACIDS: Proteins are composed of amino acids of which there are approximately twenty, all necessary for metabolism or growth. Those termed "essential" cannot be synthesized by the body but must be obtained in food. They are leucine, isoleucine, lysine, methionine, phenylalanine, theronine, tryptophan and valine. Cystine and tyrosine are called semi-essential because they can partially substitute for, respectively, methionine and phenylanine. Methionine and cystine are called the sulphur-containing amino acids. Histidine is classified as essential for infants.

FATTY ACIDS: Organic compounds of carbon, hydrogen and oxygen which combine with glycerine to form a fat. Especially important are groups of carbon atoms linked together in long chains. There can be anywhere from two to over twenty of these carbon atoms in a row, with atoms of hydrogen and oxygen attached to certain parts of the chain. One such chain is called a *fatty acid* and several fatty acids linked to-together form a triglyceride such as those found in fats and oils.

HORMONE: A product of glands that is transported by the blood producing a specific effect remote from its point of origin. An example is estrogen which can originate in the ovaries and stimulates the development and maintenance of female sexual characteristics throughout the body.

LIPID: Any one of a group of fatty or oily substances insoluble in water but soluble in alcohol and ether. The term encompasses fatty acids, triglycerides, cholesterol, phospholipids, soaps, waxes and other substances.

MUTATION: Biological changes in the genes of an organism which initially occur suddenly but are then transferred to future generations. Rare but useful mutations are the basis of evolutionary change but most mutations are considered harmful. *Mutagenic:* causing mutations.

ORGANIC: In chemistry, the term denotes substances containing large amounts of carbon and synthesized by living cells such as petroleum or vitamins. In referring to foods the term commonly means "grown without the aid of synthetic pesticides and fertilizers."

OXIDATION OF FATS AND OILS: Under certain conditions, oxygen atoms will become attached at the double bond points of unsaturated fatty acids. When this occurs the fat is said to become *oxidized,* a chemical change which is destructive as it causes the fat to become rancid. Rancid fats and oils have an acrid smell and a bitter taste and may destroy certain nutrients in the body if ingested.

PATHOGENIC: Producing disease, e.g., a pathogenic microorganism.

PROTEIN: Large molecules found in every living cell and necessary for growth and maintenance. *Complete* proteins (e.g., as in milk or meats) are composed of essential amino acids in proportions similar to those found in the egg. *Incomplete* proteins (e.g., those found in grains and other plant foods) have an amino acid distribution differing markedly from that of the egg.

SALMONELLA: Bacteria commonly present on foods, especially meat and poultry. Pathogenic salmonella may produce mild intestinal upset but some forms cause acute and even fatal food poisoning.

SATURATION OF FATS AND OILS: The chains of carbon atoms in saturated fatty acids are connected to hydrogen atoms in this manner:

$$
\begin{array}{ccccc}
H & H & H & H & H \\
| & | & | & | & | \\
-C & -C & -C & -C & -C- \\
| & | & | & | & | \\
H & H & H & H & H
\end{array}
$$

This arrangement is called *saturated* because all four linkage points of each carbon atom are occupied. In an *unsaturated* fat or oil, carbon atoms are linked to only three other atoms, the fourth linkage being a *double bond* between two carbons:

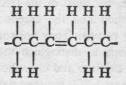

Monounsaturated fats have one such double bond while *polyunsaturated* fats have two or more.

The most important polyunsaturates with two, three, and four double bonds, respectively, are *linoleic* acid, *linolenic* acid, and *arachidonic* acid. *Oleic* acid is the most common form of monounsaturate. Virtually all naturally-occurring vegetable oils contains each of these fatty acids in varying proportions.

Among the saturated fats, the most widely present in foods are *stearic* and *palmitic*. Palmitic acid and two others, *myristic* and *lauric,* are apparently the only saturated fatty acids that raise blood cholesterol levels.

SUBCLINICAL: Initial stage of a disease or condition occuring before the appearance of typical overt symptoms detectable by the usual clinical tests.

TERATOGENIC: That which causes a severely deformed fetus. Unlike mutations, such change are not inherited.

TRACE ELEMENTS: Essential trace elements are those present in the body or required in very minute amounts, usually less than 15 mg. daily. They usually function at the cellular level as components of enzyme systems. The elements included in the group are cobalt, chromium, copper, iodine, fluorine, manganese, molybdenum, nickel, selenium, silicon, tin, vanadium, and zinc. Iron is also sometimes included. Recommended dietary allowances for most of the trace elements have not been established and the essentiality of some is suspected but not proven. They are sometimes referred to as *micronutrients* to distinguish them from *macronutrients* such as calcium and phosphorus with requirements ranging up to 1,200 mg. per day.

TRIGLYCERIDES: Lipids used by the body mainly to provide energy. Excess quantities in the blood may predict heart disease.

VITAMINS: Organic compounds essential for normal metabolism. Vitamins act principally as co-enzymes, which are required for many metabolic processes, such as energy transformation. Vitamins cannot be manufactured by the body in amounts normally required and must be obtained from food. Classified as fat-soluble (vitamins A, D, E, and K), and water-soluble (vitamin C and most of the B-complex).

For Further Reading

The following publications have been chosen either because they contain practical information or present stimulating, but not necessarily generally accepted, points of view. All should be available in well-stocked, central libraries.

Most books on nutrition are either appalling, dull, or larded with faddist fictions. One of the liveliest and best researched is James Trager's *Bellybook* (New York: Grossman Publishers, 1972). Those who want the official word on nutrients should look at *Recommended Dietary Allowances,* 8th Ed. (Washington: National Academy of Sciences, 1974) and for a dissident and extremely well-documented (and not at all dull) view of nutrition, see Roger J. Williams' *Nutrition Against Disease* (New York: Pitman Publishing, 1971). Those who might enjoy an analysis of nutrition from a sociological-biochemical point of view, should look into Ross Hume Hall's *Food for Nought* (New York: Harper & Row, 1974).

Nutritional Evaluation of Food Processing, edited by Robert S. Harris and Harry von Loesecke, is the most comprehensive work in its field. Although more than fifteen years old, most of the facts are still pertinent. (It was originally published in 1960 and reprinted in 1973 by Avi Publishing, Westport, Conn.) An updated 1976 edition containing new material is more a supplement to than a replacement of the original. Although these are technical texts, dedicated food buffs will find them rewarding. Probably the most comprehensive text on food technology is Georg Borgstrom's two-volume *Principles of Food Science* (New York: Macmillan Co., 1968).

Several recent books that expose the rascality of the food industry are *Food Pollution* by Gene Marine and Judith Van Allen (New York: Holt, Rinehart and Winston, 1972), *Health Foods, Facts and Fakes* by Sidney Margolius (New York: Walker and Co. 1973), *The Supermarket Trap* by Jennifer Cross (New York: Berkley Pub. Corp., 1970), *Eat Your Heart Out* ("How food profiteers victimize the consumer") by Jim Hightower (New York: Crown Publishers, 1975), and William Robbins' *The American Food Scandal* (New York: William Morrow, 1974). *Food for People, Not for Profit* (New York: Ballantine Books, 1975) is a collection of articles by over fifty experts on such topics as food production practices, food additives, the reasons for high food prices, malnutrition among the American rich and poor, and the world food problem.

Corruption and foot dragging at the FDA are extensively documented in James Turner's *The Chemical Feast* (New York: Grossman Publishers, 1970). A more up-to-date view on the same subject will be found in Jacqueline Verrett's excellent inside view, *Eating May be Hazardous to Your Health* (New York: Simon and Schuster, 1974). Dr. Verrett has been a research scientist with the FDA for fifteen years and was the first to alert the nation to the danger of cyclamates in 1969.

No home should be without a copy of Michael F. Jacobson's highly useful little book *Eater's Digest: The Consumer's Factbook of Food Additives* (Garden City: Doubleday & Co., 1972). We hope that it will soon be updated and expanded. Parents of little children may be interested in Dr. Ben Feingold's *Why Your Child Is Hyperactive* (New York: Random House, 1975). Dr. Feingold believes that food colors are among the responsible agents in hyperactivity. A useful antidote to those who believe that only synthetic additives cause harm is Alfred Werthheim's *Natural Poisons in Natural Foods* (Seaucus, N.J.: Lyle Stuart, 1974).

Philip Boffey has some important things to say about The National Academy of Sciences in *The Brain Bank of America* (New York: McGraw-Hill Book Co., 1975). The NAS sets the Recommended Dietary Allowances and has considerable influence on food additive decisions by the FDA.

Linus Pauling's *Vitamin C and The Common Cold* (New York: Bantam Books, 1971) and Irwin Stone's *The Healing Factor* (New York: Grosset & Dunlap, 1972), also on vitamin C, are quite readable. One of the best of the orthodox critiques of Pauling's vitamin C thesis is "Ascorbic acid and the common cold" by Dr. Michael Dykes and Paul Meier, Ph.D. in the March 10, 1975 issue of *The Journal of the American Medical Association* (231:1073).

The most readable and informative book on vitamin supplements is John J. Fried's *The Vitamin Conspiracy* (New York: Saturday Review Books, 1975). Although skeptical of the value of supplements, Fried carefully presents both sides of the issue.

As of 1978, no reliable popular book on fiber has been published. A technical work, much of which is comprehensible to laymen, is *Refined Carbohydrates and Disease* by Drs. Denis Burkitt and Hugh Trowell (New York: Academic Press, 1975). Two quite readable articles on fiber are "Dietary Fiber and Disease" by Dr. Burkitt and colleagues in August 19, 1974 issue of *The Journal of the American Medical Association*

(229:1068) and "Roughage in the Diet" (Anon.) in the September 6, 1974 issue of *Medical World News* (15:35).

Those who want to become better produce buyers will find much useful information in *The Greengrocer* (New York: Pyramid Books, 1972), by Joe Carcione and Bob Lucas.

Those interested in growing their own herbs will find practical help in *How to Grow Herbs for Gourmet Cooking* by Frederick O. Anderson (New York: Meredith Press, 1967) and in *Herbs to Grow Indoors* by Adelma G. Simmons (New York: Hawthorn Books, 1969). *The Rodale Herb Book* (Emmaus, Pa.: Rodale Press, 1974) is one of the most complete and useful guides to the subject (but read the chapter on "The Healing Herbs" as fiction, not fact). Max Alth's *Making Your Own Cheese and Yogurt* (New York: Funk and Wagnalls, 1973) is by far the best in its field.

Disquieting news for meat eaters will be found in Harrison Wellford's exposé of agribusiness and the meat industry, *Sowing The Wind* (New York: Grossman, 1972). If *it* doesn't push you into vegetarianism, try Jon A. McClure's *Meat Eaters are Threatened* (New York: Pyramid Books, 1973). McClure, a former butcher, details some of the nastier tricks of the trade.

Vegetarian cookbooks abound but many are not very substantial. Among the better bargains are Walter and Jenny Fliess's *Modern Vegetable Cookery* (Baltimore: Penguin Books, 1964), Ellen Buchman Ewald's *Recipes for a Small Planet* (New York: Ballantine, 1973) and Frances Moore Lappé's *Diet for a Small Planet,* revised edition (New York: Ballantine, 1975). Lappé's book has an excellent section on the ecological aspects of meat eating.

Among omnivore cookbooks, *The Joy of Cooking* by

Irma Rombauer and Marion Becker (Indianapolis: Bobbs-Merrill, 1974) is justly famous for its scope. Jean Hewitt's *The New York Times Natural Foods Cookbook* (New York: Quadrangle Books, 1971) is one of the best of the "natural" cookbooks. Adelle Davis's *Let's Cook It Right* (New York: Signet, 1970) has many useful recipes and sound advice on retaining nutrients in cooking, but you may want to disregard some of the philosophy. ("Milk cannot be overemphasized.")

The evils of sugar are discussed in *Sweet and Dangerous* (New York: Bantam, 1972) by Dr. John Yudkin, the foremost authority on the subject. *Diet, Coronary Thrombosis and The Saccharine Disease* second edition, (Bristol, U.K.: John Wright & Sons, 1969) by Dr. T. L. Cleave and associates is also interesting reading.

The evils of saturated fat and cholesterol are documented by the American Heart Association in a variety of free pamphlets. The best of these, written for physicians but available to laymen, is *Diet and Coronary Heart Disease* (New York: 1973). A dissident reappraisal of cholesterol and fat will be found in Dr. Edward R. Pinckney's *The Cholesterol Controversy* (Los Angeles: Sherbourne Press, 1973). Dr. Pinkney emphasizes the dangers of polyunsaturated fat. Both his views and those of the AHA are controversial.

Those who are obese will find information of value in Dr. Jean Mayer's *Overweight: Causes, Cost and Control* (Englewood Cliffs, N.J.: Prentice-Hall, 1968) which is considered the authoritative work on the subject. This is a technical book but easy to get into. The practical problems of cutting down fat in the kitchen are dealt with in many books; two of the best are *Low Fat Cookery, revised edition* (New York: McGraw

Hill, 1959) by Evelyn S. Stead and Gloria K. Warren and *The Fat and Sodium Control Cookbook,* third edition (Boston: Little, Brown & Co., 1966) by Almo Smith Payne and Dorothy Callahan. Those who wish to cut down on sodium should also look at *Fat-Controlled and Sodium Restricted Cookery* by Milton E. and Betty Jean Dupuy (New York: Doubleday, 1971).

Those interested in avoiding packaged baby foods will find help in a number of baby food cookbooks. Among the best of these is *The First Babyfood Cookbook* by Melinda Morris (New York: Grosset & Dunlap, 1972). Unlike most of the books of this kind, it does not specify salt or spices and very few of the recipes require sugar. *The Natural Babyfood Cookbook* by Margaret Kenda and Phyllis Williams (Los Angeles: Nash Publishing, 1972) is also useful if the injunction to add salt to recipes is disregarded.

If you have ever wondered why advertising has been so effective in selling toxic junk food read Carl Wrighter's *I Can Sell You Anything* (New York: Ballantine Books, 1972). Wrighter tells you how to spot all the subtle gimmicks used in television commercials.

Reference Notes

Chapter I: An Overview of the Food Industry

Page	Lines	
4	16-17	*New York Times*, March 24, 1975.
6	2-10	Agricultural Research Service, *Dietary Levels of Households in the U.S., Spring 1965, A Preliminary Report* (Washington: United States Department of Agriculture, 1968), p. 10.
8 9	7-13 1-3	Calculated from: National Commission on Food Marketing, *Cost Components of Farm-Retail Price Spreads for Foods, Technical Study No. 9* (Washington: 1966), p. 53.
11	20	Davis, Adelle, *Let's Get Well* (New York: Signet, 1972), p. 370.
11	22-28	Rynerson, E. A., *Nutr Rev Supp*, July 1974, p. 1.
12	1-9	Wertheim, Alfred, *The Natural Poisons in Natural Foods* (Secaucus, N.J.: Lyle Stuart, 1974), p. 138.
13	1-2	Jukes, T. H., *J Am Diet Assoc*, 59:203 (1971).
13	10-15	Gussow, J. D., *Nutr Today*, March/April 1974, p. 31.

Chapter II: Dairy Products

16	2-5	*Buffalo Evening News*, Apr. 10, 1974.
16	6-8	Carque, Otto, quoted in Hereward Carrington, *The Natural Food of Man* (Mokelumne Hill, Ca.: Health Research, 1963; reprint of work originally published at date unknown), p. 169.

Page *Lines*
18   6-8   Hardinge, M. G. and Stare, F. J., *J Clin Nutr*, 2:73 (1959).
25   31-35   Anon., "Ice Cream," *Consumer Reports*, Aug. 1972, p. 495.
30   19-22   Fomon, Samuel J., *Infant Nutrition*, 2nd ed. (Philadelphia: W. B. Saunders Co., 1974), p. 399.
31   7-9   Jacobson, Michael F., *Eater's Digest* (Garden City, N.Y.: Doubleday, 1972), p. 97.
34   6-10   Oster, K. A., *Am J Clin Res*, 2:30 (1971).
34   20-23   Shaw, J. C. L. *et al.*, *Br Med J*, 2:12 (1973).
38   22-29   Rubini, M. E., *Am J Clin Nutr*, 22:163 (1969).
38   33-36   Committee on Nutrition, American Academy
39   1-11   of Pediatrics, *Pediatrics*, 49:770 (1972).
40   20-21   Alth, Max, *Making Your Own Cheese and Yogurt* (New York: Funk and Wagnalls, 1973), p. 18.
40   24-26   Seneca, H. *et al.*, *Am Pract Digest Treat*, 1:1252 (1950).
40   27-29   Alth, p. 15.
41   1-3   *Ibid.*
41   13-18   Anon., "Bacid, lactinex and yogurt," *Med Let*, 14:59 (1972).
42   6-12   Mann, G. V., and Spoerry, A., "Studies of a surfactant and cholesteremia in the Maasai," *Am J Clin Nutr*, 27:464 (1974).
42   24-25   Richter, C. P. and Duke, J. R., "Cataracts produced in rats by yogurt," *Science*, 168: 1273 (1970).

Chapter III: Fruits and Vegetables

51   9-11   Heinze, P. H. *Nutritional Qualities of Fresh Fruits and Vegetables*, P. L. White and N. Selvery, eds. (Mount Kisco, N.Y.: Futura Pub. Co., 1972), p. 133.
52   5-8   Heinze, p. 143.
52   11-17   Anon., *Consumer Reports*, Jan., 1973, p. 68.
53   1-5   Epstein, S., *Environ*, 12:16 (1970).
54   8-11   Borgstrom, Georg, *Principles of Food Science*, Vol. I (New York: Macmillan, 1968), pp. 375-376.

Page *Lines*
54   13-17   Hueper, W. C., *Arch Pathol*, 71:355 (1961).
56   22-28   Turner, James S., *The Chemical Feast* (New York: Grossman, 1970), p. 145-146.
57   1-3   Kroger, M., *J Pediatr*, 80:401 (1972).
57   31-35   Harris, R. S., in *Nutritional Evaluation of Food*
58   1-12   Processing, R. S. Harris and H. W. Von Loesecke, eds. (Westport, Ct.: Avi Publishing Co., 1973). [Reprint of work originally published in 1960 by John Wiley & Sons, N.Y., pp. 10-14, 23-24.]
58   15-20   Harris, pp. 22-23.
59   13-17   Hopkins, H. T. *et al.*, *Am. J Clin Nutr*, 18:390 (1969).
65   23-24   *FAO Nutrition Meetings Report Series*, 53A:
66   1-3   104 (1974).
66   19-27   Phillips, W. E. J., *Food Cosmet Toxicol*, 9:219 (1971).
69   7-13   Winter, Ruth, *Beware of the Food That You Eat* (New York: Signet, 1972), pp. 213-214.
70   1-4   de Groot, A. P. and Van Stratum, P. G. C., "Biological Evaluation of Legume Proteins in Combination with Other Plant Protein Sources," *Qual. Plant Materiae Vegetabiles*, 10:174, (1963).
71   4-9   Kehr, A. E., in *Nutritional Qualities of Fresh Fruits and Vegetables*, op. cit., p. 163.
72   8-11   *FAO*, 53:130 (1974).
91   13-15   Schuphan, W., *Proteins as Human Food*, R. A. Laurie, ed. (Westport, Conn.: Avi Publishing Co., 1967), p. 270.
93   13-16   Rackis, J. J., *J Am Oil Chem Soc*, 51:161A (1974).
93   24-27   *FAO*, 48:21 (1971).
95   7-13   A typical example is Banerjee, S. *et al.*, *Food Res*, 20:545 (1955). Other reports in the series are *Indian Pharm*, 5:63 (1949); 5:121 (1950); 5:202 (1950); *Food Res*, 16:230 (1951); 17:402 (1952); 19:134 (1954); *Science*, 113:600 (1951); *Indian J Med Res*, 43:497 (1955).
96   8-14   Paigen, Beverly, personal communication.

Chapter IV: Cereals

Page Lines
97 1   Stare, Frederick, J., *Eating for Good Health* (New York, Cornerstone Library, 1957) pp. 122-123.

97 4-5   Margolius, Sidney, *Health Foods: Facts and Fakes* (New York: Walker and Co., 1973).

97 9-11   Burkitt, D. P. and Painter, N. S., *JAMA*, 229: 1068 (1974).

98 8-14   Schroeder, H. A., *Am J Clin Nutr*, 24:562 (1970).

99 18-19 Mellanby, M. & Mellanby, H., *Bri Med J*, 2:409 (1948); *Bri Med J*, 1:1341 (1950); *Bri Med J*, 1:51 (1951).

99 18-19 Toverud, G., *Proc R Soc Med*, 42:249-258 (1949).

99 18-19 Takeuchi, M., *Int Dent J*, 11:443-457. (1961).

99 21-22 Jenkin, G. N., *Adv Oral Biology*, 2:67 (1966).

100 5-10 McCance, R. A. and Widdowson, E. M., *Br J Nutr*, 2:401-403.

100 23-25 Harris, R. S. *Nutr Rev*, 13:257 (1955).

101 8-12 Kent-Jones, D. W. and Amos, A. J., *Modern Cereal Chemistry* (London: Food Trade Press, 1967), p. 418.

101 16-18 Haghshenass, M. *et al.*, *Am J. Clin Nutr*, 25:1143 (1972); Prasad, A. S. *et al.*, *Arch Internal Med*, 111:407 (1963).

101 22-24 Mickelsen, O. and Makdani, D. D., in *Nutritional Evaluation of Food Processing*, 2nd ed,. Robert S. Harris and Endel Karmas, eds. (Westport, Conn.: Avi Publishing Co., 1975), p. 630.

101 25-29 Harris, *op. cit.*

102 6-8   Rackis, J. J., *J Am Oil Chem Soc*, 51:161A (1974).

102 16-21 Mollgaard, H. *et al.*, *Biochem J*, 40:589 (1946).

102 24-32 Summers, J. D. *et al.*, *Cereal Chem*, 44:318 (1967).

102 32-34 Mollgaard, *op. cit.*

103 19-20 Jenkins, G. N., "Enamel protective factors in food," *J Dent Res*, Supp to No. 6:1318 (1970).

Page *Lines*
103 20-23   Kleavy, M. *et al.*, *Am J Clin Nutr*, 28:426
              (1975).
105 11-12   Jansen, G. R., in *Symposium: Seed Proteins*,
              G. E. Inglett, ed. (Westport, Conn.: Avi
              Pub. Co., 1972), p. 21.
107 26-28   Matz, Samuel A., *The Chemistry and Tech-
              nology of Cereals as Food and Feed* (West-
              port Conn.: Avi Pub. Co., 1959), p. 628.
108 11-13   Consumer Subcommittee of The Committee on
              Commerce, United States Senate, 92nd Con-
              gress, *Nutritional Content and Advertising
              for Dry Breakfast Cereals*, March 2, 1972,
              pp. 37-38.
105 14-17   *Consumer Reports*, Feb. 1975, p. 76.
109 21-25   Consumer Subcommittee of the Committee on
              Commerce, p. 38.
109 28-29   Butler, H. S., *Br Med J*, 4:363 (1972).
110 1-5
110 9-11   Bjorn-Rasmussen, E., *Nutr Metabol*, 16:101
              (1974).
118 14-16   de Groot, A. P. *et al.*, *Lancet*, 2:303-304 (1963).
122 4-7   Sure, B., *J Agri Food Chem*, 2:1108 (1954).
125 6-7   Moran, E. T. and Summers, J. D., *Cereal Chem*,
              45:304 (1968).
126 27-28   *FAO Nutrition Meetings Report Series*, 35:155,
              159 (1964).
127 12-14   *FAO*, 40A:109 (1967).
127 15-18   *FAO*, 40:15 (1966).
129 23-28   Williams, Roger J., *Nutrition Against Disease*
              (New York: Pittman Publishing, 1971), p. 204.

Chapter V: Meat, Poultry and Fish

131 4-8   *The World Food Problem*, a report of the
              President's Science Advisory Committee, Vol.
              II, (Washington: 1967) p. 338.
123 1-4   Borgstrom, Georg, *The Hungry Planet* (New
              York: Macmillan, 1965), pp. 8, 18, 20.
132 7-9   *Ibid.*
133 28-32   Hegstead, D. M. *et al.*, *J Nutr*, 56:555 (1955).
134 11-13–   *Buffalo Evening News*, March 20, 1972.
135 1-3

Page *Lines*

135 27-28– Duggan, R. E. and Lipscomb, G.O., *Pestici*
136 1-4 *Monitor J*, 2:162 (1969).

137 12-16 *Report of the Joint Committee on Antibiotics in in Animal Feeding* (London: Agricultural Research Council and Medical Research Council, 1962).

137 23-25 Jukes, T., *Ann NY Acad Sci*, 182:372 (1971).

137 26-27 Huber, W. G., *Adv Vet Sci Comp Med*, 15:101 (1971).

137 27-29 Algird, J. R., *Conn Med*, 30:878 (1966). Umberger, E. J., *Toxicol*, 3:3 (1975).

138 4-6 *Chemicals and The Future of Man*, Hearings, Subcommittee on Executive Reorganization and Government Research, Committee on Government Operations, U.S. Senate (1971).

139 13-17 *Regulation of Food Additives and Medicated Animal Feeds*, Hearings before a Subcommittee of the Committee on Government Operations, U.S. House of Representatives, March 1971, p. 446.

139 18-23 Caruna, L. B. a review, *Am J Med Technol*, 40:101 (1974).

139 25-26 Seah, S. K. K., *Can J. Public Health*, 64: (Supp) 93 (1973).

140 1-2 Caruna, *op. cit.*

140 17-24 *Ibid.*

140 27-29 Jacobs, L., *Adv Parasitol*, 11:631-669 (1973).

140 30-33 *Ibid.*

141 10-12 Anon., *Lancet*, 1:791 (1974).

141 13-15 Gregor, O. *et al.*, *Gut*, 10:1031 (1969); *Scand J. Gastroenterol*, 9:79 (1971).

141 15-19 Drassar, B. A. and Irving, D., *Br J. Cancer*, 27:167 (1973).

141 21-26 *New York Times*, October 21, 1971.

142 1-6 Jose, D. G. and Good, R. A., *Nature*, 231:323 (1971).

142 7-12 Hill, M. J. *et al.*, *Lancet*, 1:95 (1971).

142 13-20 Visek, W. J., *J Agric Food Chem*, 22:174 (1974).

143 5-9 Lijinsky, W. and Shubik, P., *Science*, 145:53 (1964).

143 12-16 Lijinsky, W. and Ross, A. E., *Food Cosmet Toxicol*, 5:343 (1967).

143 17-23 *Ibid.*

143 24-27 Elmenhorst, H. and Dontenwill, W., *Z Krebsfors*, 70:157 (1967).

Page *Lines*
144 14-19 Wellford, p. 46.
145 6-7 *New York Times*, March 28, 1972, p. 87.
148 24-24 Miller, G. E. *et al.*, *Science*, 175:1121 (1972).
149 1-4 Anon., *New Engl J Med*, 286:840 (1972).
151 15-18 Anon., *Consumer Reports*, March 1972, p. 185;
         Consumer Reports, Sept., 1970, p. 545; May,
         1965, p. 235; July, 1966, p. 332.
151 18-19 Tarr, R. L. A., *Nutritional Evaluation of Food
         Processing*, Robert S. Harris and Harry von
         Loesecke, eds. (Westport, Conn.: Avi Pub-
         lishing Co., 1970), pp. 287-300.
152 10-14 *Consumer Reports*, Oct., 1967, p. 529.
152 17-20 De Ritter, E. *et al.*, *J Am Diet Assoc*, 64:391
         (1974).
152 29-32 *Consumer Reports*, (1967) *op. cit.*
153 25-29 *Consumer Reports*, Aug., 1971, p. 478.
154 5-8 Anon., *Media and Consumer*, June, 1973, p. 12.
154 15-18 *Buffalo Evening News*, July 27, 1972.
155 19-25 Burger, I. H. and Walters, C. L., *Proc Nutr
         Soc*, 32:1 (1973).
158 16-19 *New York Times*, March 28, 1972.
160 15-22 Bailey, E. J. and Dungal, N., *Br J Cancer*, 12:
         348 (1958).
160 22-24 Rhee, K. S. and Bratzler, L. J., *J Food Sci*,
         35:146 (1970).
160 25-27 Howard, J. W. and Fazio, T., *J Agr Food Chem*,
         17:527 (1969).
161 6-9 Malanoski, A. J. *et al.*, *J Assoc Offic Anal
         Chemists*, 51:114 (1968).
161 20-24 Rhee, *op. cit.*
161 31-35 Lijinsky, W. and Shubik, P., *Toxicol Appl
162 1-3   Pharmacol*, 7:337 (1965).
162 20-22 Wasserman, A. E. and Wolf, I. A. (letter),
         Science, 180:1322 (1973).
162 22-25 Fiddler, J. W. *et al.*, *J Food Sci*, 38:1084.
164 24-27 Anon., "Frankfurters," *Consumer Reports*, Feb.,
         1972, p. 73.
165 33-35 Anon., "Canned hams," *Consumer Reports*, Oct.,
166 1-4   1970, p. 581.
167 14-21 Okun, "Meal in a box," *Buffalo Evening News*,
         Jan. 26, 1973, p. 71.
170 22-24 Koff, R. S. *et at.*, *N Engl J Med*, 276:737
         (1967).
170 24-27 Center for Disease Control, *Morbidity, Mortality
         Weekly Rep*, 21(2):20 (1972).

Page *Lines*
171 2-3   Koff, R. S. *et al.*, *N Eng J Med*, 276:703 (1967).
172 30-32   Yang, S. P. and Christian, J. H., *J Am Diet Assoc* 42:414 (1963).

Chapter VI: Fats and Oils

172 27-32   Food and Nutrition Board, National Research Council, *Recommended Dietary Allowances*, 8th ed. 1974, (Washington: National Academy of Sciences) p. 50.

176 31-33   *FAO Nutrition Meeting Report Series*, 48A:110 (1970).

177 7-12   Howard, J. W. *et al.*, *J. Assoc Off Anal Chem*, 49:1236 (1966).

177 12-15   Howard, J. W. and Fazio, T., *J Agr Food Chem*, 17:527 (1969).

178 8-11   Lange, W., *J. Am Oil Chem Soc*, 27:414 (1950).

179 33-35   Kummerow, F. A., *J Food Sci*, 40:12 (1975).

180 5-11   Egwin, P. O. and Kummerow, F. A., *J Nutr*, 102:783 (1972).

180 12-17   Kummerow, *op. cit.*

180 18-23   Kummerow, F. A., *J Am Oil Chem Soc*, 51:255 (1974).

180 26-29   Anderson, J. T. *et al.*, *J Nutr*, 75:388 (1961).

180 32-35   Alfin-Slater, R. B., *et al.*, *J Nutr*, 63:241 (1957).
181 1-11

182 1-4   Brown, W. D. *et. al.*, *Aust J Exp Biol*, 37:533 (1959).

182 5-7   Ulland, B. M. *et al.*, *Food Cosmet Toxicol*, 11:199 (1973); Cumming, R. B. and Walton, M. F., *Food Cosmet Toxicol*, 11:547 (1973).

182 7-9   Shamburger, R. J. *et al.*, *Proc Nat Acad Sci*, 70:1461 (1973); Wattenberg, L. W. *J Nat Cancer Inst*, 48:1425 (1972)

182 10-16   Shamberger, R. J. *et al.*, *Cleveland Clinic Quar*, 39:119 (1972).

182 19-22   Branen, A. L., *J Am Oil Chem Soc*, 52:59 (1975).

182 22-25   FAO, 53A:10 (1974).

182 26   *Ibid.*

182 27-28   Feuer, G. *et al.*, *Food Cosmet Toxicol*, 3:457 (1965).

Page *Lines*
183 6-11   Harris, P. L., *Vitamins and Hormones*, 20:603 (1962).

184 1-3   Food and Nutrition Board, p. 59.

184 8-12   Bieri, J. G. and Evarts, R. P., *J Am Diet Assoc*, 66:134 (1975).

185 13-17   Pearce, M. L. and Dayton, S., *Lancet*, 1:464 (1971).

185 27-31   Pinckney, E. R. *Med Counterpoint*, 5:53 (1973).

185 31-35   Gammal, E. B. *et al.*, *Cancer Res* 27 (Part I): 1737 (1967); Harman, D., *J Gerontol*, 26:451 (1971).

186 1-2   Anon., *Nutr Rev*, 15:345 (1957).

186 3-5   Poling, E. C. *et al.*, *J Nutr*, 72:109 (1960).

186 8-14   Sugai, M. *et al.*, *Cancer Res*, 22:510 (1962).

186 15-16   Dugan, *op. cit.*

187 1-4   Kritchevsky, D. *et al.*, *J Am Oil Chem Soc*, 38:74 (1961).

187 4-8   Kritchevsky, E., and Tepper, S. A., *J Atheroscler Res*, 7:647 (1967).

187 8-9   Anon., *Nutr Rev*, 26:244 (1968).

187 13-15   Kritchevsky and Tepper (1967) *op. cit.*

187 17-18   *Consumer Reports*, Sept., 1973, p. 553.

188 1-2

188 8-12   Fleischman, A. L. *et al.*, *J Am Diet Assoc*, 42:394 (1963).

188 26–   Reitz, C. A. and Wanderstock, J. J., *A Guide to*
182 1-2   *the Selection, Combination and Cooking of Foods, Vol. 2: Formulation and Cooking of Foods* (Westport, Conn.: Avi Pub. Co., 1965), p. 117.

190 1-2   FAO, 46A:151

190 3-6–   Reitz, C. A. and Wanderstock, J. J., *op. cit.*
190 7-11

191 10-11   American Heart Association, *Eat Well But Eat Wisely*, pamphlet (New York: 1969).

191 18-20   Altschule, M. D., *Med Clinics North Am*, 58:397 (1974).

191 21-23   Keys, A. *et al.*, *Am J Clin Nutr*, 27:188 (1974).

192 1-4   Reiser, R., *Am J Clin Nutr*, 26:524 (1973).

192 19-21   Conner, W. E. and Connor, S. L., *Prev Med*, 1:49 (1972).

193 14-16   FTC, Docket C-2377, *Federal Trade Commission Decisions*, 82:1176 (1973).

194 1-6   Pinckney, E. R., *Med Counterpoint*, Feb. 73, p. 53 (1973).

Page *Lines*
194 6-10   Pinckney, E.R., *Br Med J*, 4:1 (1973).
195 1-3   Brown, H. B. and Page, I. H., *Circulation*, 24: 1085 (1961).
195 8-14   Select Committee on Nutrition and Human Needs, U.S. Senate, *Dietary Goals for the United States*, second ed. (Washington, D.C.: 1977).
195 14-18   Conner, *op. cit.*
196 9-12   Reiser, *op. cit.*
196 13-16   Mayer, Jean, *New York Times Magazine*, Apr. 8, 1973, p. 72.
196 17-24   Kannel, W. B., *Med Clin North Am*, 58:363 (1974).
197 1-7   Kritchevsky, D. *et al.*, *J Food Sci*, 40:8 (1975).
197 26-30   Pinckney, Edward R. and Pinckney, Cathy, *The Cholesterol Controversy* (Los Angeles: Sherbourne Press, 1973), p. 25.
200 19-21   *FAO*, 38B:15 (1965).
200 22-23   *FAO*, 38B:16 (1965).
202 18-21   Fleischmann, *op. cit.*
204 2-4   Alfin-Slater, R. B., *J Am Oil Chem Soc,* 43:110 (1966).
204 22-23   *FAO*, 53A:179, 468 (1974).
206 7-8   *FAO*, 53A:171 (1974).
206 9-10   *FAO*, 53A:151 (1974).
206 10   *FAO*, 46A:155 (1969).
207 18-20   Gooding, C. M., *Chem Ind*, 8:344 (1966).
210 13-17   *FAO*, 53A:328 (1974).

Chapter VII: Beverages

216 16-29   Colton, Theodore *et al.*, *Clin Pharm Thera*, 9:31 (1968).
216 27-30   Ritchie, J. M., in *The Pharmacological Basis of Therapeutics*, L. S. Goodman and A. Gilman, eds. (New York: Macmillan, 1970), p. 358.
217 17-21   Klatsky, A. L. *et al.*, *JAMA*, 226:540 (1973).
217 21-25   Dawber, T. R. *et al.*, *N. Eng J Med*, 291:871 (1974).
217 26-29   Doll, R., *Nutrition and Cancer*, 1(3):35 (1979).
218 8-10   Shepard, Thomas H., *Catalog of Teratogenic Agents* (Baltimore: Johns Hopkins Univ. Press, 1973), p. 26.

Page *Lines*

218   10-16   Jacobson, Michael F., *op. cit.*, pp. 91-93.

218   24-25   Ritchie, *op. cit.*

219   18-21   Anon., *Food Cosmet Toxicol*, 9:456 (1971).

221   7-9   Bieri, J. G. *et al.*, *Arch Biochem*, 11:33 (1946).

221   16-19   Elsbury, W. B., *Br Dent J*, 93:177 (1952).

221   20-25   Hicks, H., *Oral Sur*, 4:858 (1951).

222   1-5   Miller, C. D., *J Nutr*, 41:63 (1950).

222   8-18   McCay, C. M. *et al.*, *Fed Proc*, 4:158 (1945); McCay, C. M. and Will, L., *J Nutr*, 39:313 (1949).

223   1-6   Council On Dental Health, American Dental Association, *J Am Dent Assoc*, 47:387 (1953).

226   6-7   *New York Times*, Feb. 13, 1975.

231   8-13   *New York Times*, July 17, 1975.

231   14-24   Anon., "The Politics of Cancer," CBS News Special, June 22, 1976.

233   27-29   Anon., "Orange juice," *Consumer Reports*, July 1967, p. 394.

234   24-27   Hickey, C. A. *et al.*, *Am J Digest Dis*, 17:383 (1972).

237   9-14   Segelman, A. B., *et al.*, *JAMA*, 236:477 (1976).

238   4-7   Siegel, R. K., *JAMA*, 236:473 (1976).

240   15-18   Yudkin, John, *Sweet and Dangerous* (New York: Peter W. Wyden, 1972), p. 178.

241   21-36   Groisser, D. S., *Am J Clin Nutr*, 31:1727 (1978).

241   28-32   Anon., "Editorial comment," *Lancet*, 1:314 (1973).

241   32-35   Anderson, J. B. (letter), *Lancet*, 1:314 (1973).

244   4-6   Anon., "Water quality, trace elements, and cardiovascular disease," *WHO Chronicle*, 27:534 (1973).

244   16-19   Anon., "Bird-dogging the bottlers," *Time*, Sept. 13, 1971.

244   19-21   Anon., "Bottled Water," *Saturday Review Science*, March, 1973, p. 12.

244   23-25   Anon., "Hitting the bottle," *Newsweek*, Aug. 2, 1971, p. 55.

245   5-7   *New York Times*, Nov. 8, 1974.

245   7-10   Anon., "Water quality, trace elements, and cardiovascular disease," *WHO Chronicle*, *op. cit.*

Chapter VIII: Sweets

Page *Lines*
248 16-18 *New York Times*, Mar. 13, 1973.
248 24-26 Shaw, J. H., and Sweeney, E. A., in *Modern*
249 1-11   *Nutrition in Health and Disease*, 5th ed., Robert S. Goodhart and Maurice G. Shils, eds. (Philadelphia: Lea & Febiger, 1973), p. 733.
249 20-25 Osborn, T. W. B. and Noriskin, J. N., *J Dent Res*, 16:431 (1937).
250 8-12   Jenkins, G. N. *et al.*, *Br Dent J*, 106:362 (1959).
250 13-15 Wakerman, E. J. *et al.*, *J Dent Res*, 27:489 (1948).
252 23-26 *Federal Trade Commission Decisions*, 81:711, Docket C-2308 (1972).
252 10-13 Sassoon, H. F., *Am J Clin Nutr*, 26:776 (1973).
253 14-15 Lepkovsky, S., *Am J Clin Nutr*, 26:272 (1973).
253 15-21 Yudkin, J., *Chem Ind*, Sept. 2, 1964 (1967).
255 3-6   McCracken, R. D., "The case against sugar," *Let's Live*, May, 1971, p. 40.
255 9-15   Rodale, J. I., *Natural Health, Sugar and the Criminal Mind* (New York: Pyramid Books, 1968).
255 15-17 Ibarra, J. D., "Hypoglycemia," *Postgrad Med*, February, 1972, p. 89; Anderson, J. W. and Herman, R. H., "Classification of reactive hypoglycemia," *Am J Clin Nutr*, 22:646 (1969).
256 4-5   Cleave, T. L.; Campbell, G. D. and Painter, N.S., *Diabetes, Coronary Thrombosis and The Saccharine Disease*, 2nd ed., (Bristol: John Wright & Sons, Ltd., 1969), pp. 15-59.
256 12-15 Yudkin, J., *Heart J*, 80:844 (1970).
256 20-22 Grande, F. *et al.*, *J Nutr*, 86:313 (1965).
256 22-28 Ahrens, *op. cit.*
257 10-13 *Ibid.*
258 3-6   *Ibid.*
258 6-9   Schroeder, H. R., *Am J Clin Nutr*, 21:230 (1968).
258 9-14   Bruckdorfer, K. R. *et al.*, *Nutr Metab*, 13:36 (1971).
261 19-20 Stephan, R. M., *J Dent Res*, 45:1551 (1966).

Page *Lines*

262 1-3 Allen, M. J. *et al.*, *Br J Cancer*, 11:212 (1957).
262 3-5 Anon., *Food Cosmet Toxicol*, 11:1126 (1973).
262 5-7 Hicks, R. M. *et al.*, *Nature*, (Lond) 243:347 (1973).
263 5-7 Mueller, W. S. *et al.*, *J Dairy Sci*, 26:951 (1943).
263 7-10 Lipman, L. D., *J Dairy Sci*, 24:399 (1941).
263 10-13 Mirone, L. *et al.*, *J Am Diet Assoc*, 5:87 (1943).
263 18-21 Kohn, L. A., *Am J Clin Nutr*, 23:2 (1970).
263 24-29 Keys, A. *et al.*, *Am J Clin Nutr*, 27:188 (1974).
263 34-35 Fulton, J. E. *et al.*, *JAMA*, 210:2071 (1969).
264 1-3
264 3-7 Hankin, L. *et al.*, *Clin Ped*, 13:1064 (1974).
264 11-13 West, E. S. and Judy, F. R., *J Dent Res*, 17:499 (1938).
264 20-22 *FAO*, 53A:19 (1974).
265 4-12 Slack, G. L. *et al.*, *Brit Dent J*, 133:371 (1972).
265 12-13 Stephan, *op. cit.*
266 2-4 Konig, K. G., *Ala J Med Sci*, 5:269 (1968).
266 4-6 Hartles, R. L., *Am J Clin Nutr*, 20:152 (1967).
266 27-28 Wakeman, E. J. *et al.*, *J Dent Res*, 27:489 (1948).
267 1-2
267 2-6 Konig, *op. cit.*
267 9-14 *Consumer Reports, Apr.,* 1972, p. 195.
268 11-13 Von Loesecke, H. W., *Outlines of Food Technology*, 2nd ed., (New York: Reinhold, 1949), p. 363.
268 29-32 Willits, C. O. and Tressler, C. J., *Food Res*, 3:449 (1938).
271 5-7 *Federal Trade Commission Decisions*, 81 Docket C-2284, 1972, p. 352.

Chapter IX: Other Foods

273 17-18 Foman, Samuel J., *Infant Nutrition*, 2nd ed. (Philadelphia: W. B. Saunders Co., 1974), p. 429.
273 18-22 Dahl, L. K., "Salt and Hypertension," *Am J Clin Nutr*, 25:231 (1972).
273 22-25 Dahl, L. K. *et al.*, *Proc Soc Exp Biol Med*, 133:1405 (1970).

Page *Lines*
273 25-27 Lowe, C. V., *Am J Clin Nutr,* 25:245 (1972).
274 3-7 Anon., *Modern Medicine,* Sept. 16, 1974, p. 24Y.
274 10-13 Shukla, A., *Br Med J,* 4:507 (1972).
274 23-27 Lowe, *op. cit.*
274 31-33 Reiser, R. and Sidelman, Z., *J Nutr,* 102:1009 (1972).
275 9-11 Jacobson, Michael F., *op. cit.,* p. 97.
275 24-28 *New York Times,* May 16, 1973.
275 31-33 *New York Times,* Feb. 25, 1975.
276 1-6 Nelson, Waldo E., ed., *Textbook of Pediatrics,* 9th ed. (Philadelphia: W. B. Saunders Co., 1969), pp. 144-145.
276 7-8 Anon., *Nutr Rev,* 31:116 (1973).
276 8-9 Graeber, T. M., *Orthodontics, Principles and Practices,* 2nd ed. (Philadelphia: W. B. Saunders Co., 1966), p. 316.
276 9 Bullen, C. and Willis, A. T., *Br Med J,* 3:342 (1971).
276 10-11 Anon., *Med World News,* June 16, 1975, p. 26.
276 11-14 Moore, F. D. *et al., New Engl J Med,* 277:293 (1967).
278 22-25 Berlyne, G. M., *Lancet,* i:564 (1972).
Cook, F. and Briggs, G. M., in *Egg Science and Technology,* W. J. Stadelman and O. J. Cotterill, eds., (Westport, Conn.: Avi Publishing Co., 1973), p. 107.
279 16-19 Everson, G. J. and Souders, H. J., *J A m Diet Assoc,* 33:1244 (1957).
280 9-14 Tolan, A. *et al., Br J Nutr,* 30:181 (1973).
282 16-20 *Federal Trade Commission Decisions,* 82:1495, Docket C-2408 (1973).
282 26-22 Michaelson, J. B. *et al., J Soc Cosmet Chem,* 14:443 (1963).
283 26-27 Hall, R. L., *Toxicants Occurring Naturally in Foods* (Washington: National Academy of Sciences/National Research Council, 1966), pp. 168-169.
286 4-10 *Federal Trade Commission Decisions,* 77:1547, Docket C-1833 (1970).
287 7-19 Mann, G. V., *Am J Public Health,* 61:1491 (1969).
287 31-34 Mayer, Jean, *Overweight* (Englewood Cliffs, N.J.; Prentice-Hall, 1968), pp. 201, 273.
290 1-2 Davis, K. J. *et al., Toxicol App Pharm,* 8:306 (1966).

Page *Lines*

291 13-17 Olney, J. W., *Science,* 164:719 (1969).

292 4-9 Go, G. *et al., Hawaiian Med J,* 32:13 (1964).

294 9-11 Lillard, H. S. *et al., Appl Microbiol,* 19:128 (1970).

294 12-18 Anon., *Med World News,* Sept. 22, 1972, p. 35.

294 19-21 Mann, E. G. *et al., J Agric Food Chem,* 15:1090 (1967).

296 13-16 Anon., "Peanut butter," *Consumer Reports,* May, 1972, p. 286.

296 16-20 Anon., "Cancer is Food," *Lancet,* 2:1133 (1973).

297 11-13 Anon., "Frozen Pizza," *Consumer Reports,* June, 1972, p. 364.

298 22-26 *FAO,* 53A:21 (1974).

298 29-32 *FAO,* 53:15 (1974).

299 2-6 Dahl, L. K. and Love, R. A., *JAMA,* 164:397 (1957).

299 9-12 Dahl, L. K., "Salt and hypertension," *Am J Clin Nutr,* 25:231 (1972).

299 19-21 Dahl, L. K., *New Engl J Med,* 258:1152 (1958).

300 1-5 Dahl, (1972).

300 8-11 Keith, N., *Ann Intern Med,* 16:879 (1942).

300 6-7 *FAO,* 53:512 (1974).

300 24-28 Synder, E. L. *et al., New Engl J Med,* 292:32 (1975).

301 12-14 Schroeder, H. A. *et al., J Chron Dis,* 15:51 (1962); *J Chron Dis,* 17:483 (1964).

301 14-21 Dahl, L. K. and Heine, M., *Am J Cardiol,* 8:726 (1961).

302 8-12 Anon., *Nutr Today,* Spring 1969, p. 22.

302 12-16 Trowbridge, F. L. *et al., Am J Clin Nutr,* 28:712 (1975).

303 17-20 Yamamoto, T. and Ishibashi, M., in *Proceedings of the 7th International Seaweed Symposium,* Sapporo, Japan (New York: John Wiley & Sons, 1972), p. 511.

304 3-6 Food and Nutrition Board, p. 97.

304 20-24 Marcus, R., and Watt, J., *Lancet,* 2:489 (1969).

304 28-31 Watt, J. and Marcus, R., *Gut,* 14:506 (1973).

305 6-11 Jacobson, *op. cit.,* p. 97.

305 18-21 Fabry, P. and Tepperman, J., *Am J Clin Nutr,* 23:1059 (1970).

308 15-22 Jacobson, *op. cit.,* 112-114.

309 13-14 Jacobson, *op. cit.,* pp. 188-190.

Chapter X: Nutritional Supplements

Page *Lines*
310 18-20   Food and Nutrition Board, National Research Council, *Recommended Dietary Allowances,* 8th ed. (Washington: National Academy of Sciences, 1974), p. 3.

311 9-11   Lumeng, L. *et al, Am J Clin Nutr* 27:326 (1974).

311 11-12   McLeroy, V. J. and Schendel, *Am J Clin Nutr* 26:191 (1973).

311 12-14   Loh, H. S. *et al, J. Clini Pharmacol,* 13:480 (1973).

311 14-15   Grant, F. W. *et al, Biopsychiatry,* 5:289 (1972).

311 23-27   Bryan II, J. A., *Am Fam Physician* 7:120 (1973).

Chapter XI: Fiber & Health

316 1-21   Burkitt, D. P., *Cancer,* 28:3 (1971).
         Burkitt, D. P., *Lancet,* 2:1408 (1972).

316 22-25   Trowell, H., *Am J Clin Nutr,* 25:926 (1967).

317 1-4   Keys, A. *et al, J Nutr,* 70:257 (1960).

317 12-14   Painter, N. S. and Burkitt, D. P., *Br Med J,* 2:450 (1971).

317 12-16   Plumley, P. F. and Francis, B., *JAMA,* 63:527 (1973).

317 17-21   Painter, N. S. *et al, Br Med J,* 2:137 (1972).

318 4-10   Ershoff, B. H., *Proc Soc Exp Biol Med,* 141:857 (1972).

318 10-15   Ershoff, B. H. and Thruston, E. W., *J Nutr,* 104:937 (1974).

320 3-7   Cummings, J. H., *Gut,* 14:69 (1973).

320 8-13   Ershoff, B. H., *Exp Med Surg,* 21:108 (1963).

320 14-21   Cummings, *op. cit.*

231 4-9   Reuben, D., *Woman's Day,* May 1975, p. 36.

321 13-15   Piepmeyer, J. L., *Am J Clin Nutr,* 27:106-107 (1974).

Appendix: Food Colors, Food Flavors

Page *Lines*

324 16-19   Anon, *Br Med J*, 1:417 (1975).

325 1-4   *World Health Organization Technical Report Series,* 309:10 (1965).

325 11-14   *Code Federal Regulations,* 121:1164.

325 21-24   Hagan, E. C. *et al., Food Cosmet Toxicol,* 5:141 (1967).

326 1-5   *FOA Nutrition Meeting Report Series,* 44:12-13 (1968).

326 20-21   Hagen, *op. cit.*

327 20-23   Michaelson, G., and Juhlin, L., *Br J Dermatol,* 88:525 (1973).

Index

Other Grove Press Paperbacks

☐ ALLEN, DONALD M., ed. *The New American Poetry.* E237/$3.95
☐ ARSAN, EMMANUELLE. *Emmanuelle.* B361/$1.95
☐ BECKETT, SAMUEL. *Three Novels. Molloy; Malone Dies; The Unnamable.* B78/$1.95
   —*Waiting for Godot.* E33/$1.95
☐ BERNE, ERIC, M.D. *Games People Play.* B186/$1.95
☐ BRAUTIGAN, RICHARD. *A Confederate General from Big Sur.* B283/$1.50
☐ BRECHT, BERTOLT. *Galileo.* B120/$1.95
   —*Mother Courage and Her Children.* B108/$1.50
☐ BURROUGHS, WILLIAM S. *Naked Lunch.* B115/$1.95
☐ CUMMINGS, E. E. *100 Selected Poems.* E190/$1.95
☐ FANON, FRANTZ. *The Wretched of the Earth.* B342/$1.95
☐ GENET, JEAN. *The Balcony.* E130/$2.95
☐ IONESCO, EUGENE. *Four Plays. The Bald Soprano; The Lesson; The Chairs; Jack, or The Submission.* E101/$1.95
☐ KEROUAC, JACK. *The Subterraneans.* B300/$1.50
☐ LAWRENCE, D. H. *Lady Chatterley's Lover.* B9/$1.95
☐ MALCOLM X. *Autobiography of Malcolm X.* B146/$1.95
☐ MILLER, HENRY. *Tropic of Cancer.* B10/$1.95
   —*Tropic of Capricorn.* B59/$1.95
☐ PINTER, HAROLD. *The Homecoming.* E411/$1.95
☐ REAGE, PAULINE. *Story of O* (film ed.). B396/$1.95
☐ SNOW, EDGAR. *Red Star Over China.* E618/$3.95
☐ STOPPARD, TOM. *Rosencrantz & Guildenstern Are Dead.* B319/$1.95
   —*Travesties.* E661/$1.95
☐ TRUFFAUT, FRANCOIS. *The Story of Adele H.* B395/$2.45

At your bookstore, or order below.

Grove Press, Inc., 196 West Houston St., New York, N.Y. 10014

Please mail me the books checked above. I am enclosing

$_____

(No COD. Add 35¢ per book for postage and handling.)

Name _____

Address _____

City _____ State _____ Zip _____